Workshop on the Impact of Machine Translation 2020

Held at AMTA 2020

Online
6 – 9 October 2020

ISBN: 978-1-7138-2377-3

The 14th Conference of The Association for Machine Translation in the Americas

www.amtaweb.org

WORKSHOP PROCEEDING

Workshop on the Impact of Machine Translation

Organizers:
Sharon O'Brien (ADAPT, CTTS Dublin City University)
Michel Simard (National Research Council Canada)

Contents

Proceedings of the 14th Conference of the Association for Machine Translation in the Americas
October 6 - 9, 2020, Workshop on the Impact of Machine Translation

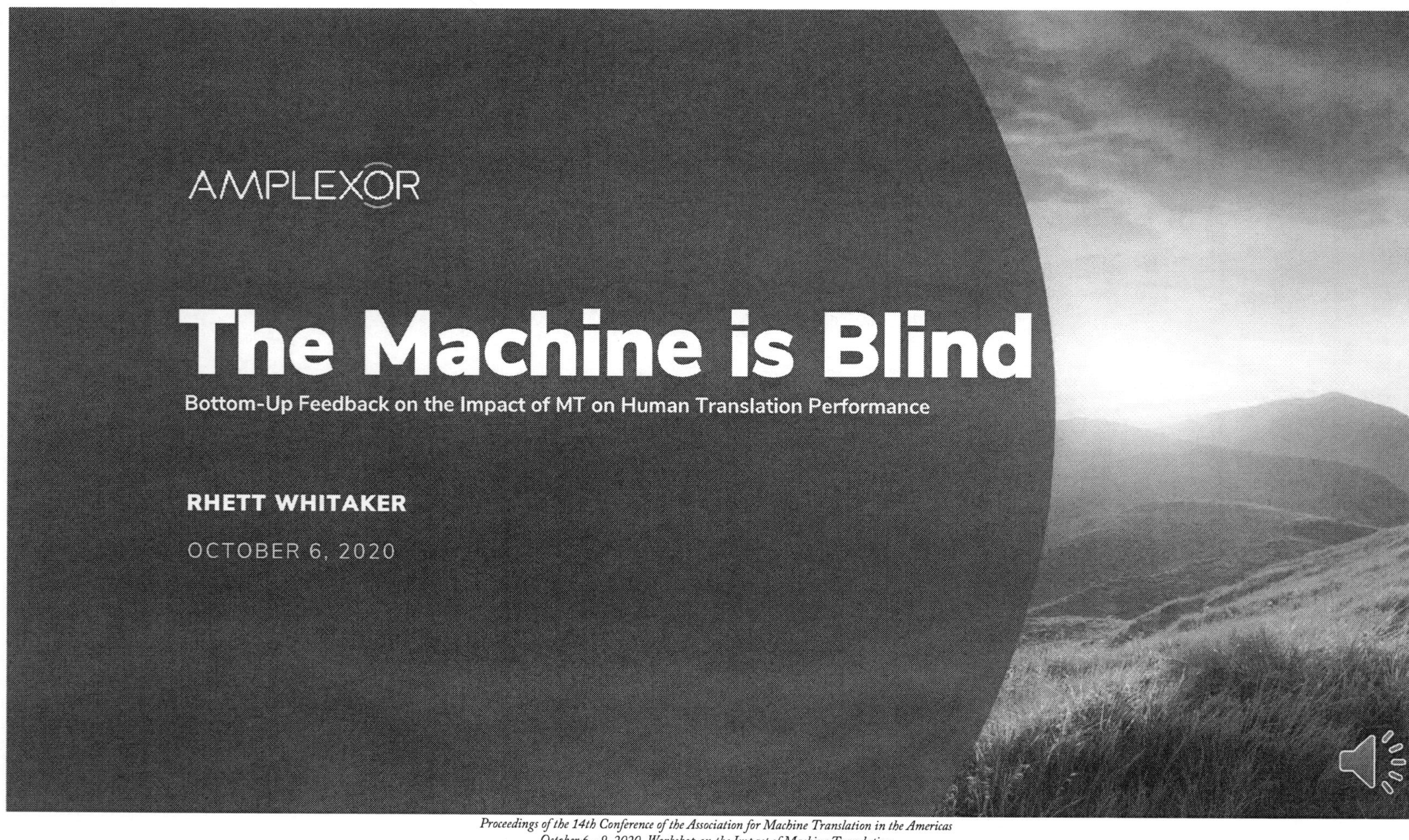

AMPLEXOR
The Machine is Blind
Bottom-Up Feedback on the Impact of MT on Human Translation Performance
RHETT WHITAKER
OCTOBER 6, 2020

A Brief Overview

- Blind spots and information flow
- What do translators really think of MT?
- The challenge facing translators
- Impacts in the short and long term
- Recommendations

Proceedings of the 14th Conference of the Association for Machine Translation in the Americas
October 6 - 9, 2020, Workshop on the Impact of Machine Translation

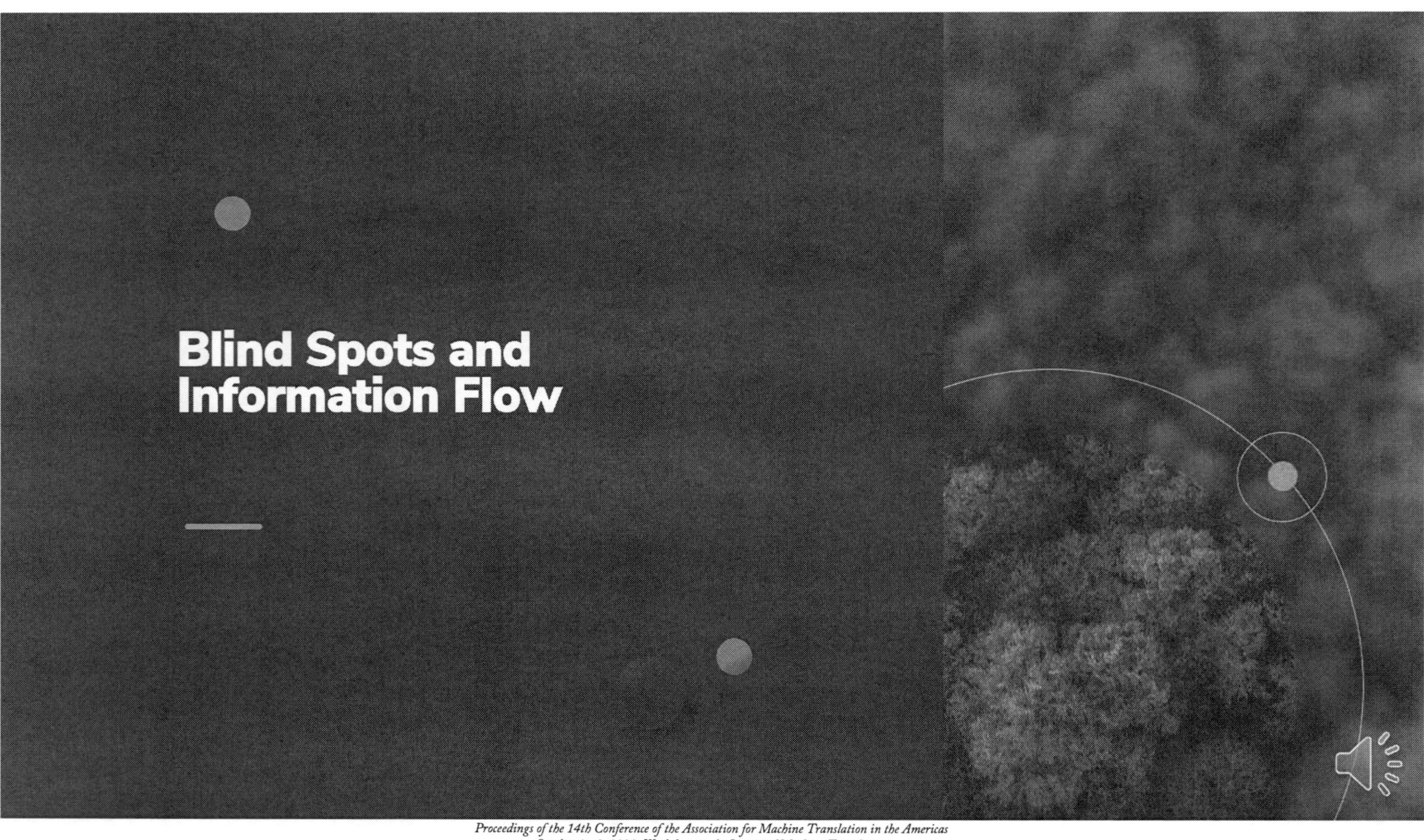

Blind Spots and
Information Flow

Know How Your Information Flows

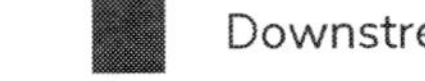

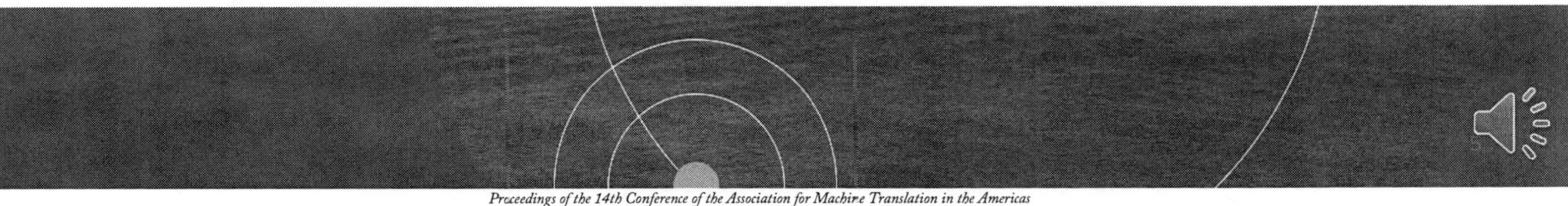

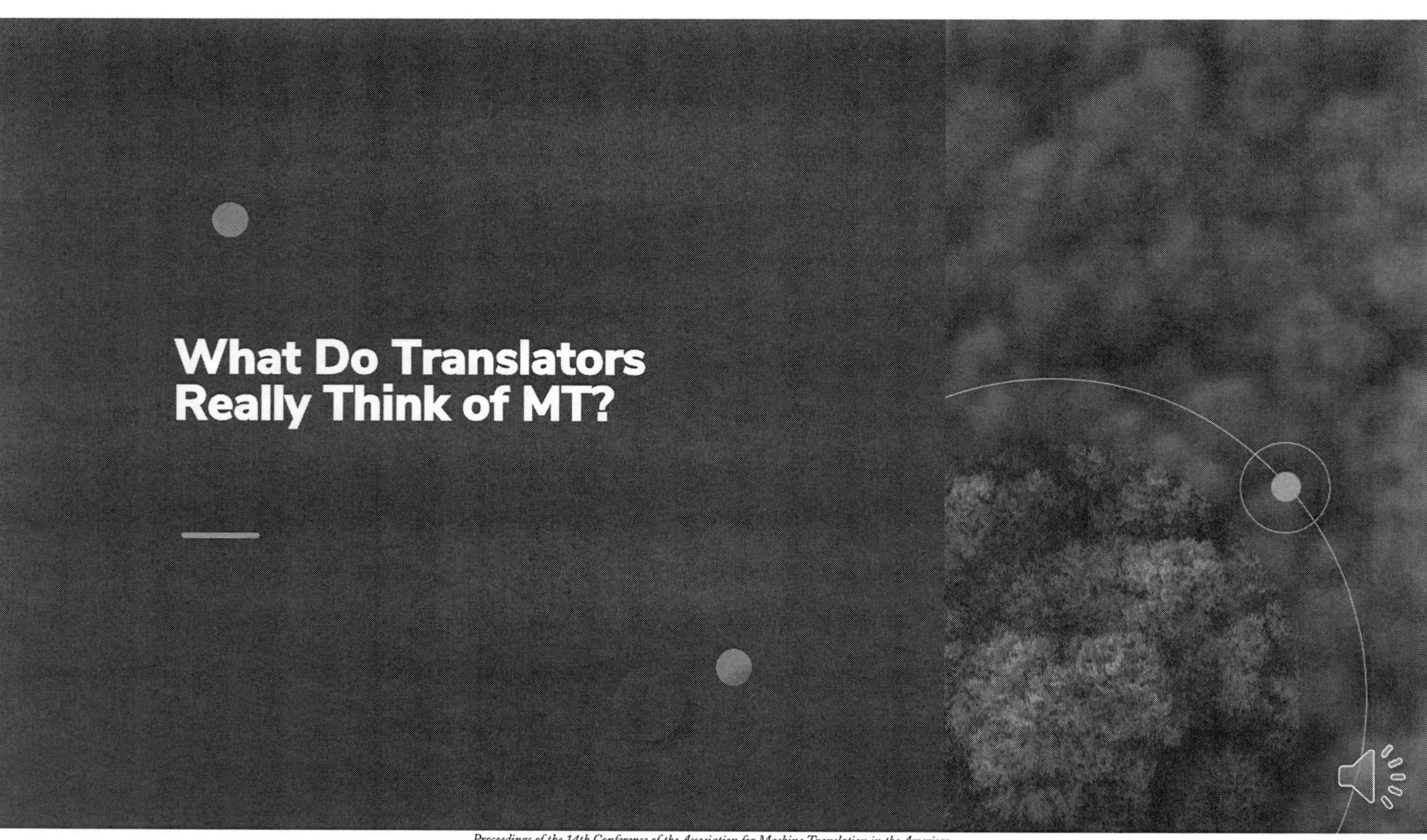

Proceedings of the 14th Conference of the Association for Machine Translation in the Americas
October 6 - 9, 2020, Workshop on the Impact of Machine Translation

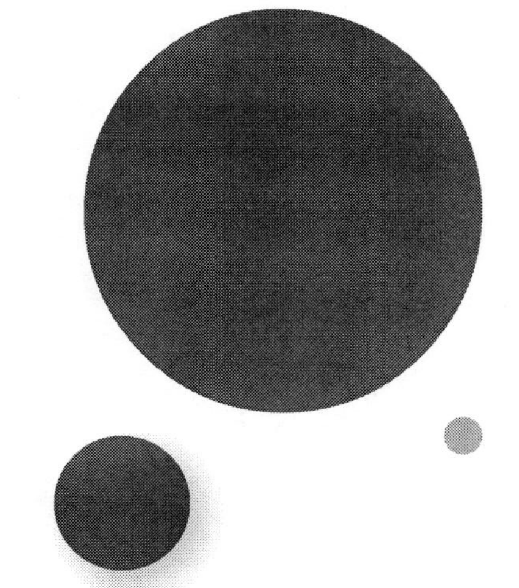

Positive feedback

"MT frees me up for other, more valuable tasks."

Proceedings of the 14th Conference of the Association for Machine Translation in the Americas
October 6 - 9, 2020, Workshop on the Impact of Machine Translation

Negative feedback

"This is more work than translating from scratch."

"I don't know why it's making these errors."

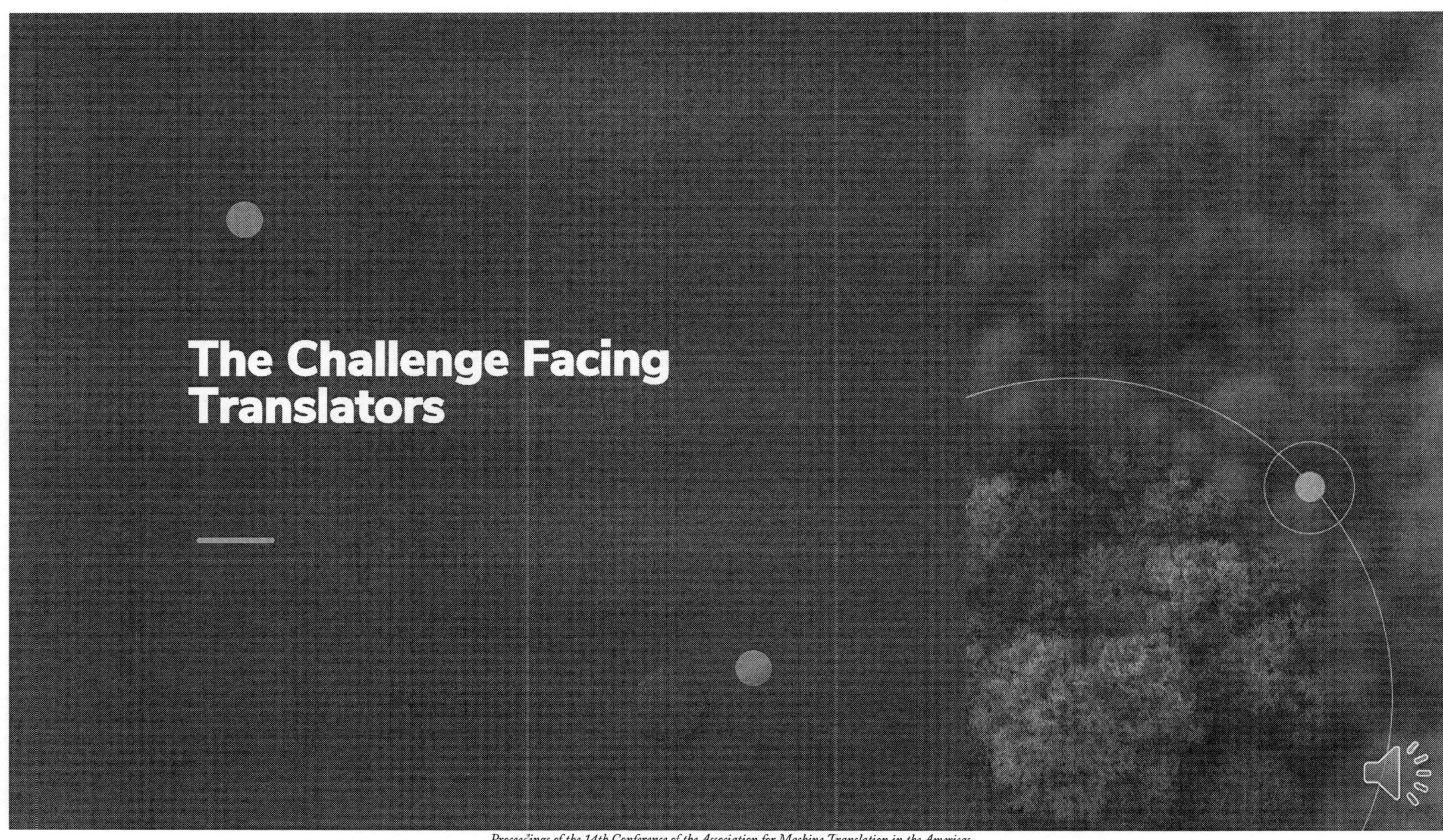

Proceedings of the 14th Conference of the Association for Machine Translation in the Americas
October 6 – 9, 2020, Workshop on the Impact of Machine Translation

A Challenging Situation

TRANSLATORS BETWEEN A ROCK AND A HARD PLACE

LESS PAY

LSPs tend to prorate what they pay for MT post-editing services, sometimes to a significant degree.

MORE WORK

In particular, high-quality translators view poorly implemented MT as a hindrance to their work.

MORE TEDIOUS

Long intervals between retraining MT engines can lead to frustration on the translator's part.

DEAF EARS

Bottom-up feedback that is ignored can act as a significant demotivating force.

"Is this kind of work still worth doing?"

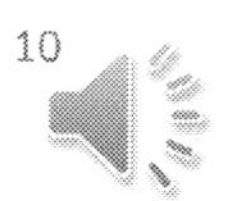

Proceedings of the 14th Conference of the Association for Machine Translation in the Americas
October 6 - 9, 2020, Workshop on the Impact of Machine Translation

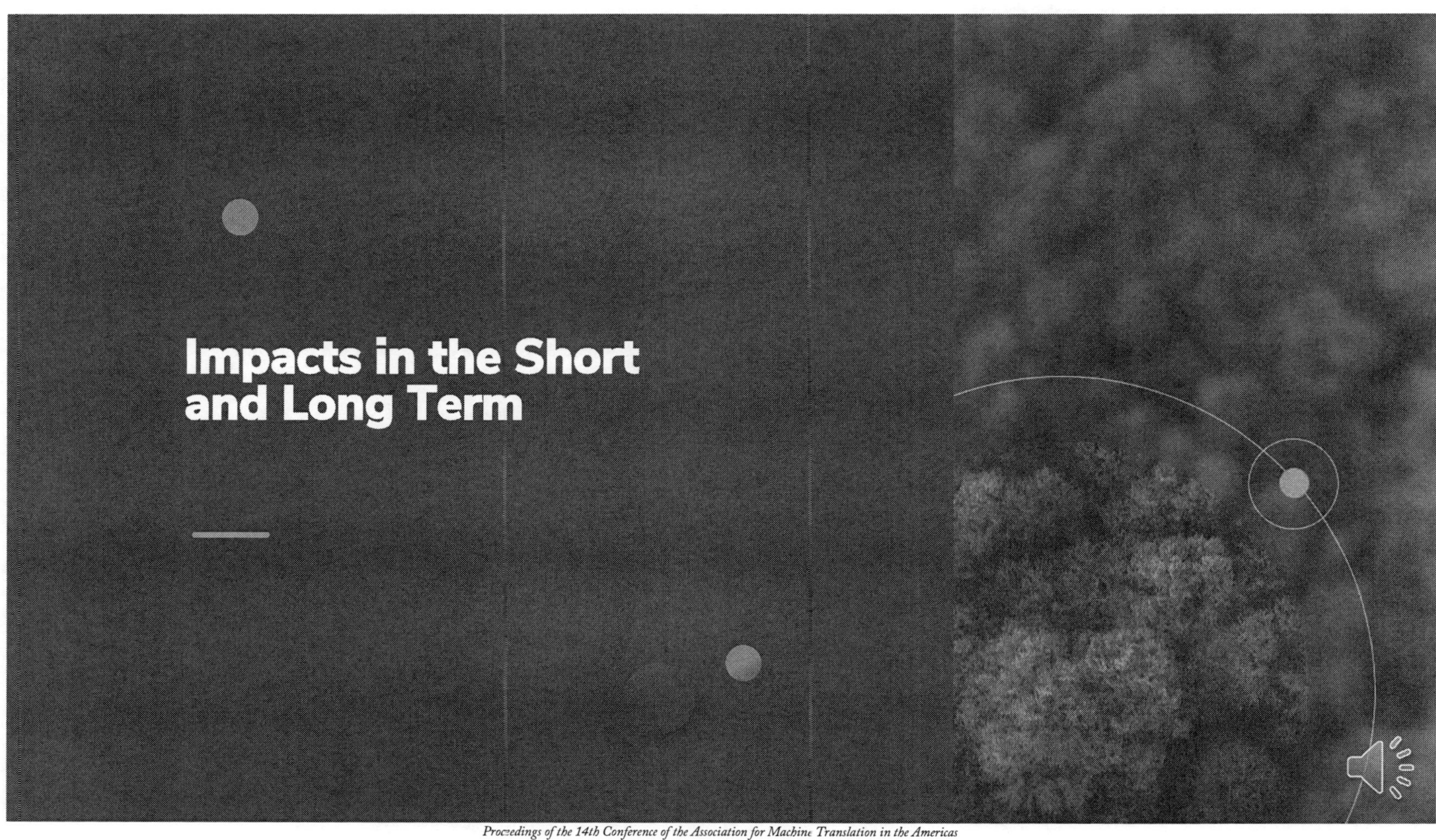

Proceedings of the 14th Conference of the Association for Machine Translation in the Americas
October 6 – 9, 2020, Workshop on the Impact of Machine Translation

Short term

Translators dealing with poorly implemented MT are often unfocused, unmotivated, and less effective. This could produce the following short term impacts:

- Translators increasingly reject MT post-editing jobs
- Translators raise rates to compensate for prorated pay
- Organizations see declining quality, similar overall costs, and diminished capacity

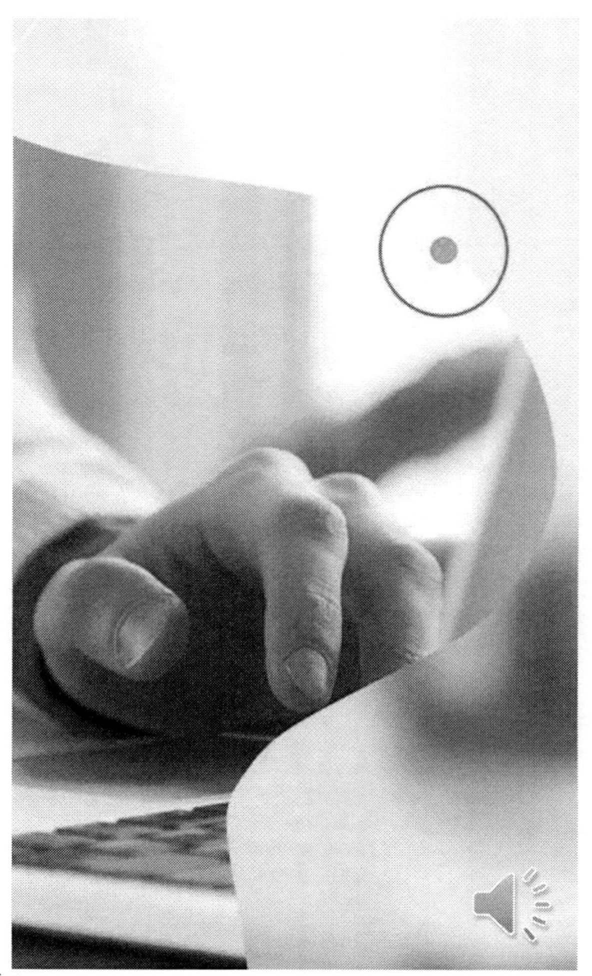

Long term

Sustained negative attitudes toward MT and frustration with the post-editing process can be a serious demotivating force for translators. This can produce the following long term impacts:

- Translators leave the talent pool permanently
- The availability of highly-skilled professionals drops below critical thresholds
- Organizations face serious challenges to profitability and ultimately an existential threat

Proceedings of the 14th Conference of the Association for Machine Translation in the Americas
October 6 – 9, 2020, Workshop on the Impact of Machine Translation

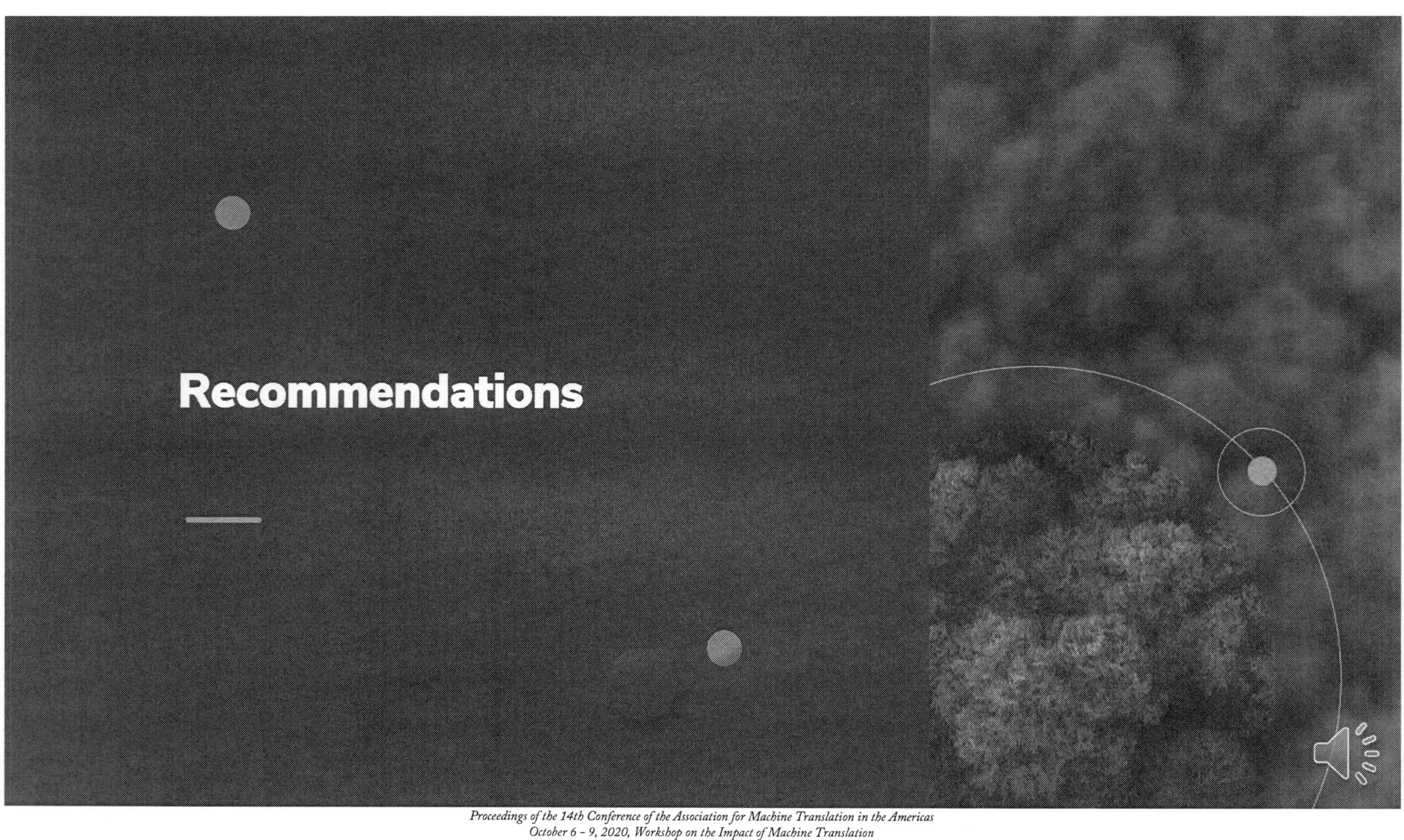

Proceedings of the 14th Conference of the Association for Machine Translation in the Americas
October 6 - 9, 2020, Workshop on the Impact of Machine Translation

Countermeasures

KEEPING YOUR EYES OPEN

Be diligent in implementing MT

Give yourself the best chance for successful MT integration and translator retention. Don't rush implementation.

Don't reduce rates prematurely

Make sure your translators are fully on board with the concept of MT before you think about adjusting their pay.

Establish upstream feedback channels

You can't react to outcomes you don't know about. Take measures to acquire reliable, actionable information.

Act on upstream feedback

Use feedback to improve your MT systems and processes. It can help keep translators at the top of their game and bolster profitability.

Proceedings of the 14th Conference of the Association for Machine Translation in the Americas
October 6 – 9, 2020, Workshop on the Impact of Machine Translation

Proceedings of the 14th Conference of the Association for Machine Translation in the Americas
October 6 - 9, 2020, Workshop on the Impact of Machine Translation

AMPLEXOR
EMBRACE THE FUTURE

Responsible
Gist MT Use in the Age of Neural MT

Marianna J. Martindale, iSchool PhD Candidate

University of Maryland, College Park

Also: Computational Linguist, Center for Applied Machine Translation, USG

OBLIGATORY DISCLAIMER: Opinions in this talk are my own and not necessarily those of any part of the U.S. Government

Proceedings of the 14th Conference of the Association for Machine Translation in the Americas
October 6 – 9, 2020, Workshop on the Impact of Machine Translation

What Makes Neural MT (NMT) Different?

- Scores well on automated metrics & human evaluations
- Improves many types of errors (especially fluency)
- More languages & platforms than ever

But…

Sometimes fails catastrophically

Humorous Catastrophic Failures

Facebook, 29 April 2020

Proceedings of the 14th Conference of the Association for Machine Translation in the Americas
October 6 - 9, 2020, Workshop on the Impact of Machine Translation

(Semi-)Humorous Catastrophic Failures

Facebook says technical error caused vulgar translation of Chinese leader's name

REUTERS

By Poppy McPherson

3 MIN READ

YANGON (Reuters) - Facebook Inc FB.O on Saturday blamed a technical error for Chinese leader Xi Jinping's name appearing as "Mr Shithole" in posts on its platform when translated into English from Burmese, apologizing for any offense caused.

Proceedings of the 14th Conference of the Association for Machine Translation in the Americas
October 6 – 9, 2020, Workshop on the Impact of Machine Translation

Dangerous Catastrophic Failures

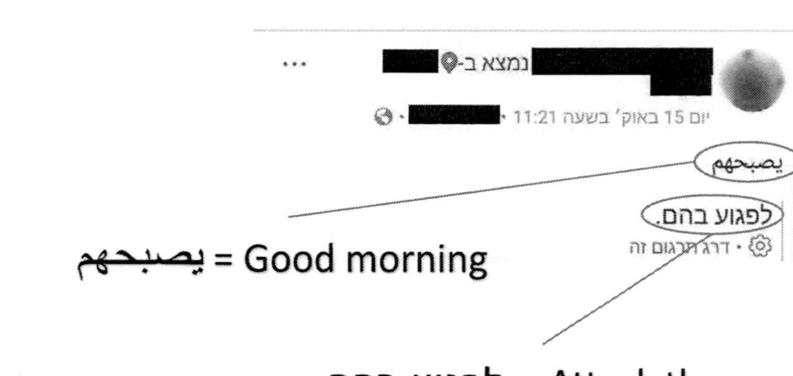

يَصبحهم = Good morning

לפגוע בהם ~ Attack them

Proceedings of the 14th Conference of the Association for Machine Translation in the Americas
October 6 – 9, 2020, Workshop on the Impact of Machine Translation

Dangerous Catastrophic Failures

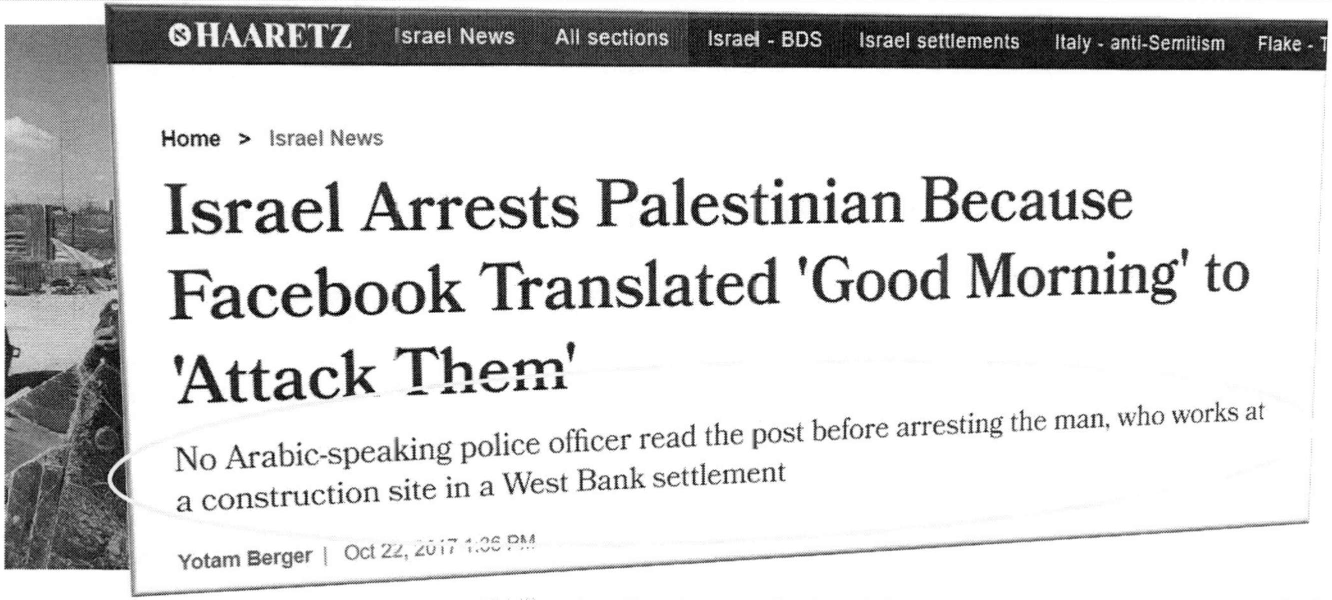
HAARETZ | Israel News | All sections | Israel - BDS | Israel settlements | Italy - anti-Semitism | Flake - T

Home > Israel News

Israel Arrests Palestinian Because Facebook Translated 'Good Morning' to 'Attack Them'

No Arabic-speaking police officer read the post before arresting the man, who works at a construction site in a West Bank settlement

Yotam Berger | Oct 22, 2017 1:36 PM

https://www.haaretz.com/israel-news/palestinian-arrested-over-mistranslated-good-morning-facebook-post-1.5459427

When are (N)MT Errors Dangerous?

- Output is believable (in context)
- Lack of means and/or motivation to verify
- Use case involves MT informing action

Proceedings of the 14th Conference of the Association for Machine Translation in the Americas
October 6 - 9, 2020, Workshop on the Impact of Machine Translation

Believable Output

Believability = Fluency + Plausibility + Human Judgment

- Fluency: Does it "feel" like the target language?
  - Users more likely to trust fluent output (Martindale & Carpuat 2018)
  - NMT more likely to produce fluent but not adequate output (Martindale et al 2019)

- Plausibility: Does it make sense?
  - MT output is more believable when it is plausible (Work in progress)

- Human: People use heuristics to judge credibility of information[1]

[1] Rieh, S. Y. (2010). "Credibility and cognitive authority of information." In M. Bates & M. N. Maack (Eds.), *Encyclopedia of Library and Information Sciences* (3rd ed., pp. 1337-1344).

Proceedings of the 14th Conference of the Association for Machine Translation in the Americas
October 6 - 9, 2020, Workshop on the Impact of Machine Translation

When are NMT Errors Dangerous?

✓ • Output is believable (in context)
- Lack of means and/or motivation to verify
- Use case involves MT informing action

Gist MT?

Proceedings of the 14th Conference of the Association for Machine Translation in the Americas
October 6 – 9, 2020, Workshop on the Impact of Machine Translation

When are Gist MT Errors Dangerous?

Lack of means and/or motivation to verify?

Gist MT use characteristics

- High volume of foreign language text and/or tasks

- Impractical to translate everything or hire only bilinguals
  - Especially bilinguals with domain expertise

- Monolingual domain experts use MT to triage text or glean information

- Ideally: Bilinguals translate/evaluate documents/info monolinguals find
  - In practice: people may cut corners…

Proceedings of the 14th Conference of the Association for Machine Translation in the Americas
October 6 – 9, 2020, Workshop on the Impact of Machine Translation

When are Gist MT Errors Dangerous?

Use case involves MT informing action?

Gist MT use examples

- Journalist looking for relevant, local Tweets after an event

- Business analyst monitoring press for info about foreign competitors

- Investigator checking social media as part of background check

Proceedings of the 14th Conference of the Association for Machine Translation in the Americas
October 6 - 9, 2020, Workshop on the Impact of Machine Translation

Example: USCIS Refugee Vetting

Appendix C: Translations

Internet Translation Services

The most efficient approach to translate foreign language contents is to utilize one of the many free online language translation services provided by Google, Yahoo, Bing, and other search engines.

if needed. Use the following steps to translate using Google:

In-Person Translation Services

Occasionally, officers will encounter foreign text written in a dialect or colloquial usage that does not necessarily translate easily using the available online tools mentioned above. Furthermore, there are currently no tools available to translate text written on images. Officers are responsible for determining

"Information collected from social media, by itself, will not be a basis to deny refugee resettlement"

Official statement, September 2019

Example: USCIS Refugee Vetting

"Information collected from social media, by itself, will not be a basis to deny refugee resettlement" --Official statement, September 2019

However...

- Incorrect MT could tip scales of suspicion (in either direction)

- Social media is out of domain from MT training

- Often low-resource languages

Proceedings of the 14th Conference of the Association for Machine Translation in the Americas
October 6 – 9, 2020, Workshop on the Impact of Machine Translation

Is NMT for Gisting Worth the Risk?

- IMHO: Yes!

Good news:

- Truly misleading output is rare

- Faster to read, easier to understand

- Users like it

Just need to mitigate risk

Proceedings of the 14th Conference of the Association for Machine Translation in the Americas
October 6 - 9, 2020, Workshop on the Impact of Machine Translation

How can we mitigate the dangers?

Dangers

- Output has errors
- Output is believable (in context)
- Lack of means and/or motivation to verify
- Use case involves MT informing action

Mitigation goals

- ~~Error-free MT~~
- Encourage *appropriate* skepticism
- Make it easier to recognize potential errors
- Verify before acting

Proceedings of the 14th Conference of the Association for Machine Translation in the Americas
October 6 – 9, 2020, Workshop on the Impact of Machine Translation

How can we mitigate the dangers?

Dangers

- Output has errors

- Output is believable (in context)

- Lack of means and/or motivation to verify

- Use case involves MT informing action

Mitigation goals

- ~~Error-free MT~~

- Encourage skepticism

- ~~Make it easier to recognize potential errors~~

- Verify before acting

Mitigation Strategies

Policy interventions
- Normative principles organizations with gist MT use cases should follow
- Changes to procedures and training

Technological interventions
- Changes to the technology environment or the technology itself
- Requires additional research and development

Policy Interventions

1. Independent, in-domain evaluation

2. Training for MT users

3. Workflows that require validation before action

Proceedings of the 14th Conference of the Association for Machine Translation in the Americas
October 6 – 9, 2020, Workshop on the Impact of Machine Translation

P1: Independent, In-Domain Evaluation

Principle: An organization should not deploy or encourage the use of MT without independent evaluation in the domain(s) and language pair(s) it is intended to be used on.

- If the intended use shifts/expands, additional testing should be conducted

Why? MT quality varies by language/domain

Independent – Not conducted by the MT company

Domain – Style and/or topic

Evaluation – Formal or informal

- Evaluators should know source language

Proceedings of the 14th Conference of the Association for Machine Translation in the Americas
October 6 - 9, 2020, Workshop on the Impact of Machine Translation

P2: Training for MT Users

Principle: Users should be trained to understand the technology well enough to expect variations in quality including dropped or hallucinated words and phrases.

Why? NMT is not intuitive! Hard to recognize what you don't expect.

Example hands-on exercises:

- Change context window, capitalization, punctuation, etc and observe output changes
- Compare output from high- and low- resource languages
- Try to get the system to hallucinate (e.g. fake Hawaiian)

Proceedings of the 14th Conference of the Association for Machine Translation in the Americas
October 6 – 9, 2020, Workshop on the Impact of Machine Translation

P3: Require Validation Before Action

Principle: Organizations with workflows that include critical decisions or actions informed by MT should require validation by someone who knows the source language before taking action.

Why? Establishing a consistent process deters corner-cutting.
- Even professional translation services rely on at least one level of quality control!

Considerations
- Level of validation proportionate to impact of action/decision
- E.g., Self-validation through other resources *may* be sufficient for minimal-impact actions/decision

Proceedings of the 14th Conference of the Association for Machine Translation in the Americas
October 6 – 9, 2020, Workshop on the Impact of Machine Translation

Technological Interventions

1. Provide access to multiple MT outputs

2. Provide access to additional language resources

3. Build in "nudges" to help the user recognize quality issues

T1: Multiple MT Outputs

What: Display outputs from two or more MT systems/models

LOE: Moderate
- Obtain licenses and/or build models
- Modify/create interface to display

Why? Users can observe differences to flag possible errors

Anecdote: Users actually prefer this anyway!

Proceedings of the 14th Conference of the Association for Machine Translation in the Americas
October 6 - 9, 2020, Workshop on the Impact of Machine Translation

T2: Additional Language Resources

What: Provide CAT-like tools to MT users

LOE: Low-Moderate
- Teach users features in existing services (e.g. Google Translate, Systran, Wiktionary, Linguee)
- Obtain access to resources (dictionaries/terminologies/TMs, etc)
- Integrate access alongside MT

Why?
- Individual word lookup can validate/clarify MT output
- Terminologies can resolve technical terms
- TM lookup can provide alternate contexts

Preceedings of the 14th Conference of the Association for Machine Translation in the Americas
October 6 – 9, 2020, Workshop on the Impact of Machine Translation

T3: Nudges

What: Automatically flag questionable output
- Quality estimation
- Diff on multiple outputs

LOE: High
- QE is an open research area

Why? Draw user's attention to problem areas

Proceedings of the 14th Conference of the Association for Machine Translation in the Americas
October 6 - 9, 2020, Workshop on the Impact of Machine Translation

Summary

Dangers	Mitigation goals	Recommended Interventions
• Output has errors	• ~~Error-free MT~~	• *(Continue improving)*
• Output is believable (in context)	• Encourage *appropriate* skepticism	• P1 (Evaluation), P2 (Training), T3 (Nudges)
• Lack of means and/or motivation to verify	• Make it easier to recognize potential errors	• T1 (Multi-outputs), T2 (Lang resources), T3 (Nudges)
• Use case involves MT informing action	• Verify before acting	• P3 (Verify)

Proceedings of the 14th Conference of the Association for Machine Translation in the Americas
October 6 – 9, 2020, Workshop on the Impact of Machine Translation

Conclusion

- There can be risks to gist MT use

- Steps can be taken to mitigate them

- These are just examples

- Stakeholders should be looking at these mitigations and others
  - Organizational leadership
  - MT integrators
  - MT researchers

- See also: AI Ethics

Proceedings of the 14th Conference of the Association for Machine Translation in the Americas
October 6 - 9, 2020, Workshop on the Impact of Machine Translation

For further information or questions contact:
Marianna J. Martindale
mmartind@umd.edu

Preceedings of the 14th Conference of the Association for Machine Translation in the Americas
October 6 - 9, 2020, Workshop on the Impact of Mechine Translation

A Different, Ethical MT is Possible:

English-Catalan Free/ Open-Source NMT

Vicent Briva-Iglesias

SFI Centre for Research Training in Digitally-Enhanced Reality (D-REAL), Dublin City University

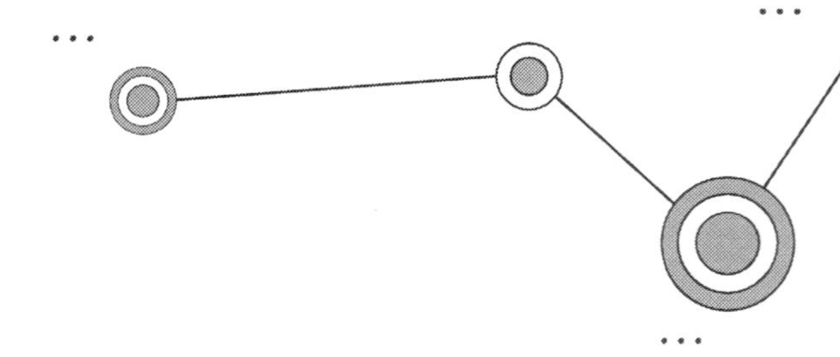

Proceedings of the 14th Conference of the Association for Machine Translation in the Americas

October 6 – 9, 2020, Workshop on the Impact of Machine Translation

Overview

01
Understanding the Problem
Current context of MT.

02
Variables
MT engines and methodology.

03
Results
Relative ranking, quality,
and post-editing evaluation.

04
iMpacT
Effects and use-cases.

Proceedings of the 14th Conference of the Association for Machine Translation in the Americas
October 6 – 9, 2020, Workshop on the Impact of Machine Translation

Understanding the Problem

01 Catalan context

Minoritized, stateless language. Low-resource.

02 NMT Requirements

Huge computational power (GPUs). Difficulty to find high-quality corpora for low-resource languages.

03 Literacy

You have the corpora. Now, how is an MT engine trained?

04 Data Privacy

Confidential information may be at stake.

Proceedings of the 14th Conference of the Association for Machine Translation in the Americas
October 6 – 9, 2020, Workshop on the Impact of Machine Translation

What is the iMpacT of open-source MT for low-resource languages?

1. Which MT engine evaluated [Apertium, Softcatalà, Google] offers a higher translation quality?

2. Which MT engine evaluated offers a bigger productivity increase when introducing it into a translation workflow?

3. Can a free/open-source MT engine for a low-resource language beat the flagship MT engine for the English-Catalan language combination?

Proceedings of the 14th Conference of the Association for Machine Translation in the Americas
October 6 – 9, 2020, Workshop on the Impact of Machine Translation

Variables – MT Engines

Apertium

- Free/Open-Source RBMT engine
- Originally developed for close languages (e.g. ES-CA)

Softcatalà Translator

- Free/Open-Source EN<>CA NMT engine (OpenNMT)
- Trained with TMs from the Softcatalà project («in-domain»)

Google Translate

- Flagship of commercial MT
- NMT from 2020
- Thousands of language combinations (including CA)

Proceedings of the 14th Conference of the Association for Machine Translation in the Americas
October 6 – 9, 2020, Workshop on the Impact of Machine Translation

Variables – Text

HomeAssistant.io

- Open-source smart home software (GitHub)

- Preparation of the text with Okapi Framework

- Segments chosen randomly for the creation of the samples to be evaluated

Proceedings of the 14th Conference of the Association for Machine Translation in the Americas
October 6 – 9, 2020, Workshop on the Impact of Machine Translation

Methodology – Human Evaluation 1

<u>Relative Ranking</u>
11 professional evaluators.
200 segments.

Rànquing de TA (Rank Comparison)

Source (English (United Kingdom))

Start

Current | This entity does not have a unique ID, therefore its settings cannot be managed from the UI.

Next | The {platform} integration is not loaded.

Target (Catalan)

0 | Aquesta entitat no té un ID únic, per tant la seva configuració no es pot gestionar des de la IU.

0 | Aquesta entitat no té un ID únic, per tant, la seva configuració no es pot gestionar des de la interfície d'interès.

0 | Aquesta entitat no té un únic ID, per tant no es poden abastar els seus paràmetres des del UI.

(Info)

Comments

Characters left: 500

Proceedings of the 14th Conference of the Association for Machine Translation in the Americas
October 6 – 9, 2020, Workshop on the Impact of Machine Translation

Methodology – Human Evaluation 2

<u>Adequacy & Fluency</u>
11 professional evaluators.
100 segments.

Precisió i fluïdesa S2, TA2

Source (English (United Kingdom))

Start

Current — This service is run by our partner, a company founded by the founders of Home Assistant and Hass.io.

Next — Go to the integrations page.

Target (Catalan)

Start

Current — Aquest servei el gestiona el nostre soci, una empresa fundada pels fundadors de Home Assistant i Hass.io.

Next — Vés a la pàgina d'integracions.

Fluency:
○ Incomprehensible   ○ Disfluent   ○ Good   ○ Flawless   (More Info)

Adequacy:
○ None   ○ Little   ○ Most   ○ Everything   (More Info)

Proceedings of the 14th Conference of the Association for Machine Translation in the Americas
October 6 – 9, 2020, Workshop on the Impact of Machine Translation

Methodology – Human Evaluation 3

<u>Post-Editing Evaluation</u>

6 evaluators (2 groups of study: professionals & volunteers).
2 texts of 100 segments.

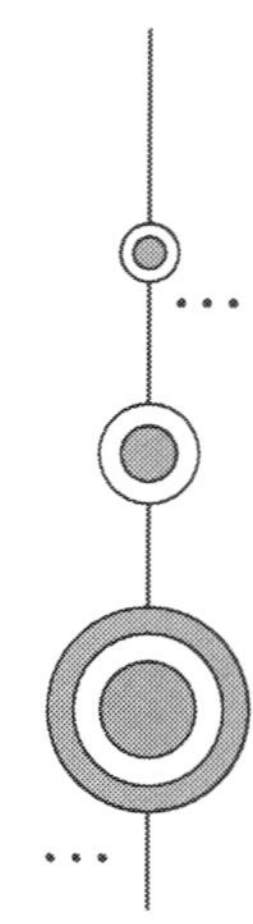

Post-Editing Evaluation (Explanation)

	Text 1, Engine 1	Text 1, Engine 2	Text 2, Engine 1	Text 2, Engine 2
Evaluator 1	✓	✗	✗	✓
Evaluator 2	✗	✓	✓	✗
Evaluator 3	✓	✗	✗	✓
Evaluator 4	✗	✓	✓	✗

Proceedings of the 14th Conference of the Association for Machine Translation in the Americas
October 6 - 9, 2020, Workshop on the Impact of Machine Translation

Results – MT Ranking

% of times an engine has received Ranking 1 evaluation

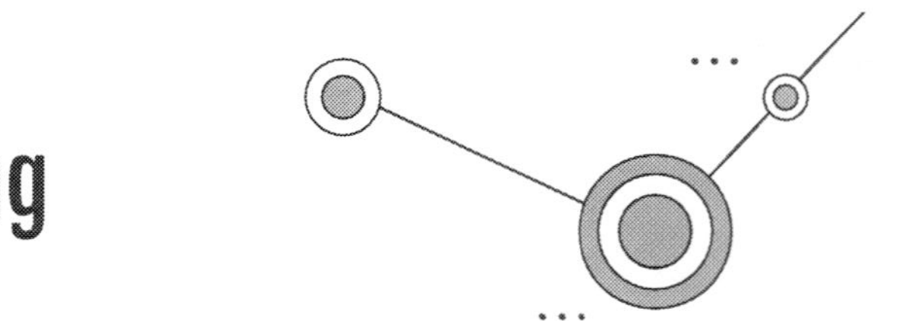

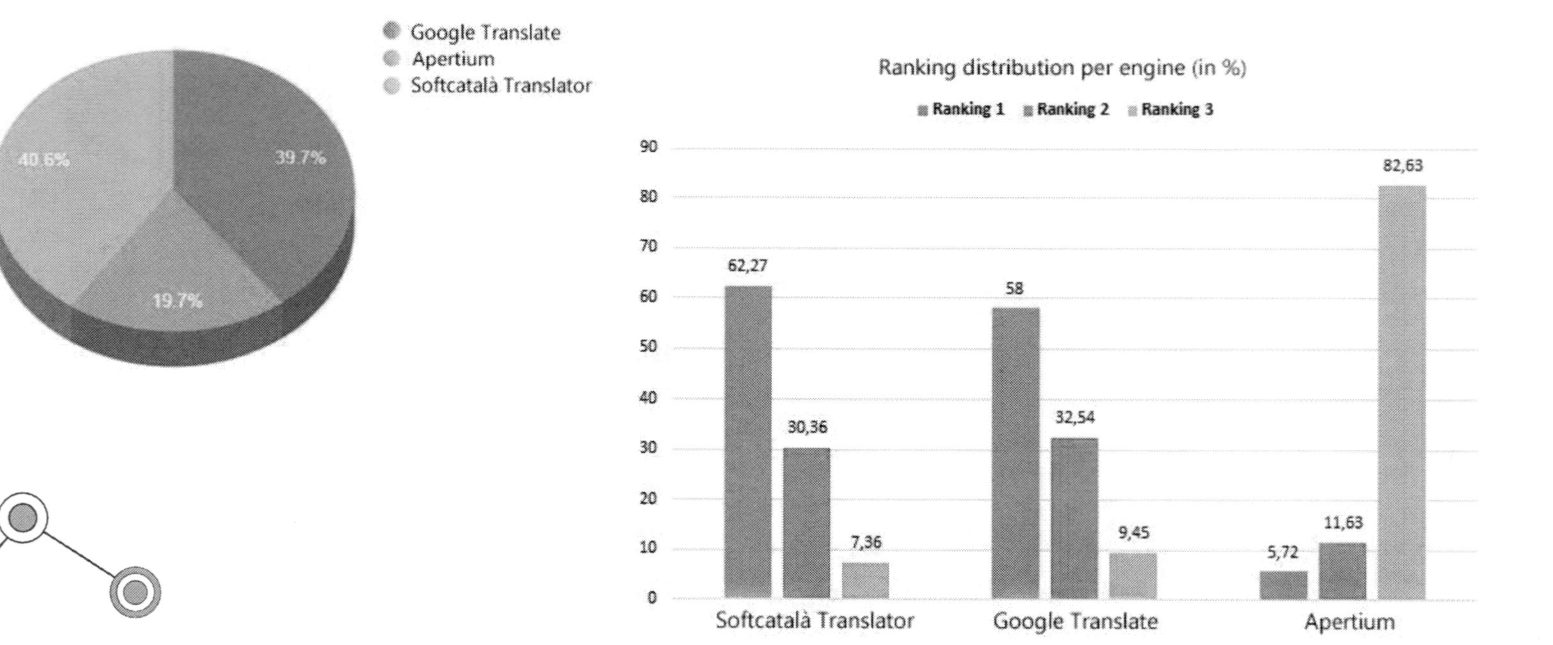

Proceedings of the 14th Conference of the Association for Machine Translation in the Americas
October 6 – 9, 2020, Workshop on the Impact of Machine Translation

Results – Fluency & Adequacy

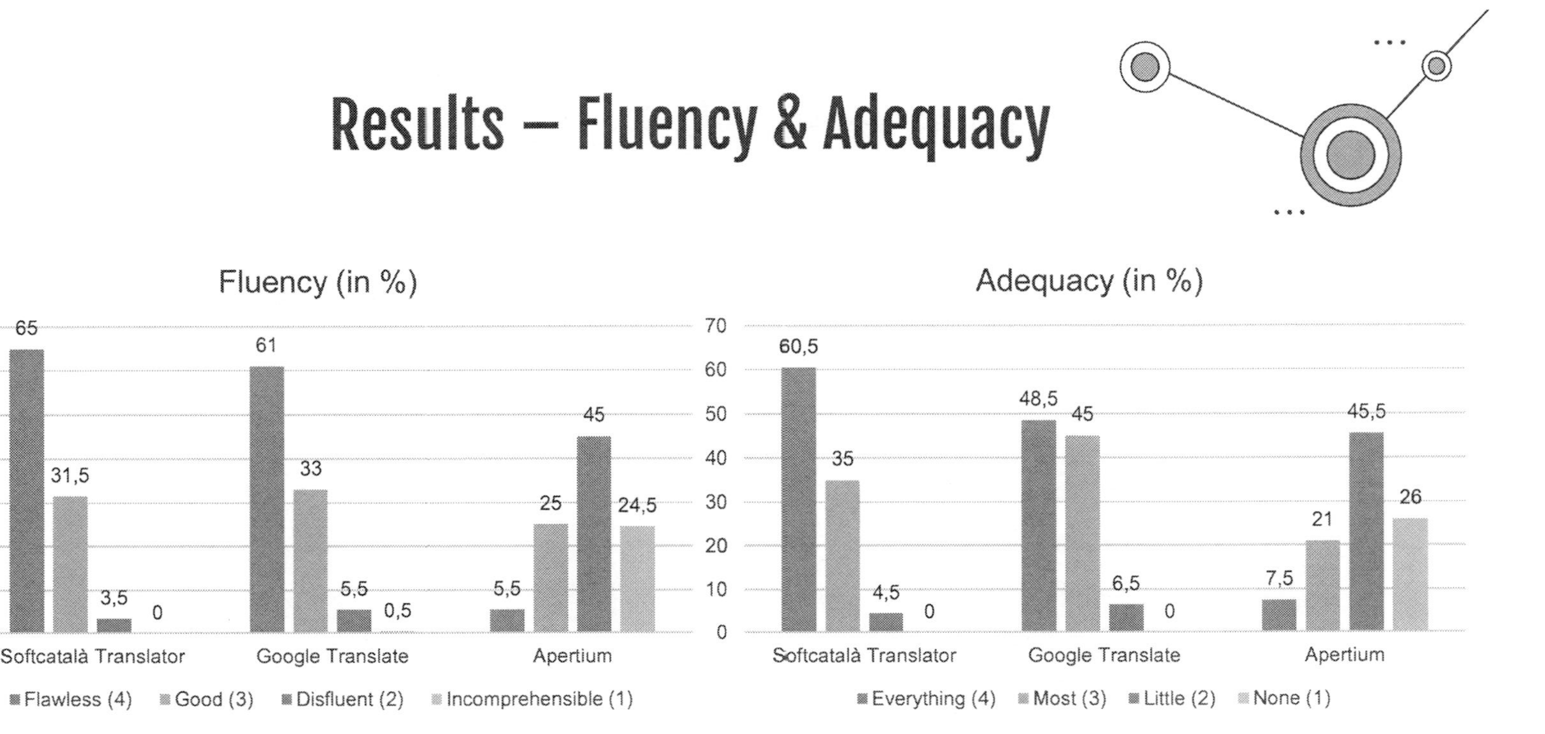

Proceedings of the 14th Conference of the Association for Machine Translation in the Americas
October 6 - 9, 2020, Workshop on the Impact of Machine Translation

Results – Post-Editing Productivity (group of study 1: Softcatalà-Google)

	Softcatalà Translator	Google Translate
	Median	Median
PE Time (s)	3909.07	4131.64
Edit Distance* (segment)	9.79	10.35

222.563 seconds of difference; 5.69% productivity increase

		1-5 words	6-15 words	16 or >16 words
		Median	Median	Median
PE Time (s)	Softcatalà	8.15	18.44	34.08
	Google	9.41	20.08	33.67
Edit distance* (seg.)	Softcatalà	5.34	11.53	9.79
	Google	12.22	9.31	11.20

Proceedings of the 14th Conference of the Association for Machine Translation in the Americas
October 6 - 9, 2020, Workshop on the Impact of Machine Translation

Results – Post-Editing Productivity (group of study 2: Softcatalà-Apertium)

	Softcatalà Translator	Apertium
	Median	Median
PE Time* (s)	1859.51	3743.41
Edit Distance* (segment)	6.81	24.85

1883.89 seconds of difference; 101.31 % productivity increase

		1-5 words	6-15 words	16 or >16 words
		Median	Median	Median
PE Time* (s)	Softcatalà	5.95	14.18	25.83
	Apertium	14.11	28.64	55.70
Edit distance* (seg.)	Softcatalà	6.21	10.73	10.11
	Apertium	40.65	37.76	36.15

Proceedings of the 14th Conference of the Association for Machine Translation in the Americas
October 6 – 9, 2020, Workshop on the Impact of Machine Translation

iMpacT and Effects

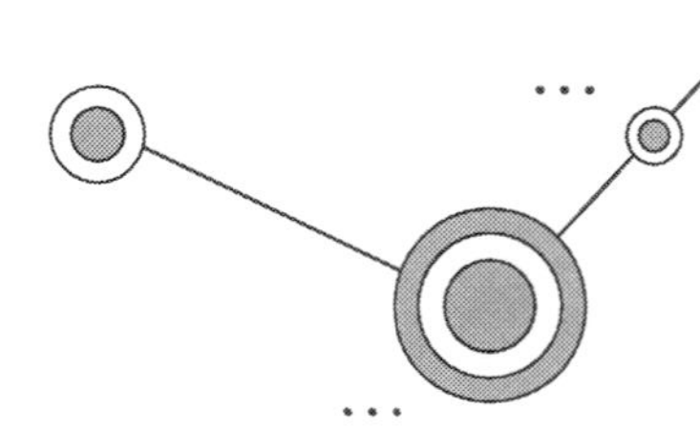

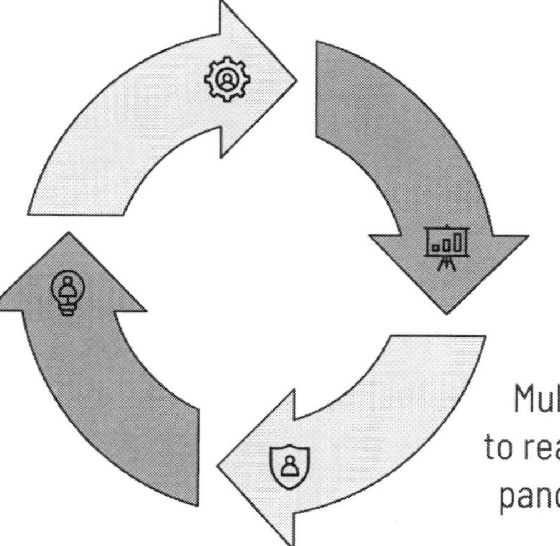

Proceedings of the 14th Conference of the Association for Machine Translation in the Americas
October 6 – 9, 2020, Workshop on the Impact of Machine Translation

Thanks!

Do you have any questions?

Vicent Briva-Iglesias
D-REAL, Dublin City University
vicent.brivaiglesias2@mail.dcu.ie
@VicentBriva

Proceedings of the 14th Conference of the Association for Machine Translation in the Americas
October 6 – 9, 2020, Workshop on the Impact of Machine Translation

Gender bias in Neural Machine Translation

Argentina Anna Rescigno
Eva Vanmassenhove
Johanna Monti
Andy Way

6th October 2020

This work has been supported by the Dublin City University Faculty of Engineering & Computing and the University of Naples "L'Orientale" Department of Literary, Linguistic and Comparative Studies under the Erasmus+ Traineeship project number 2019-1-IT02-KA103-061753

Proceedings of the 14th Conference of the Association for Machine Translation in the Americas
October 6 – 9, 2020, Workshop on the Impact of Machine Translation

Presentation Outline

- **Introduction**
  - A Note on Terminology
  - A Quick Problem Sketch

- **Experimental setup**
  - Compilation of Datasets
  - Description of the MT systems

- **Results & Analysis**

- **Three main points:**
  - Why does this kind of bias matter
  - What is its impact and on whom
  - Why we need to correct this bias

- **Conclusions and Future Work**

Proceedings of the 14th Conference of the Association for Machine Translation in the Americas
October 6 – 9, 2020, Workshop on the Impact of Machine Translation

Engaging Content
Engaging People

Introduction

Proceedings of the 14th Conference of the Association for Machine Translation in the Americas
October 6 - 9, 2020, Workshop on the Impact of Machine Translation

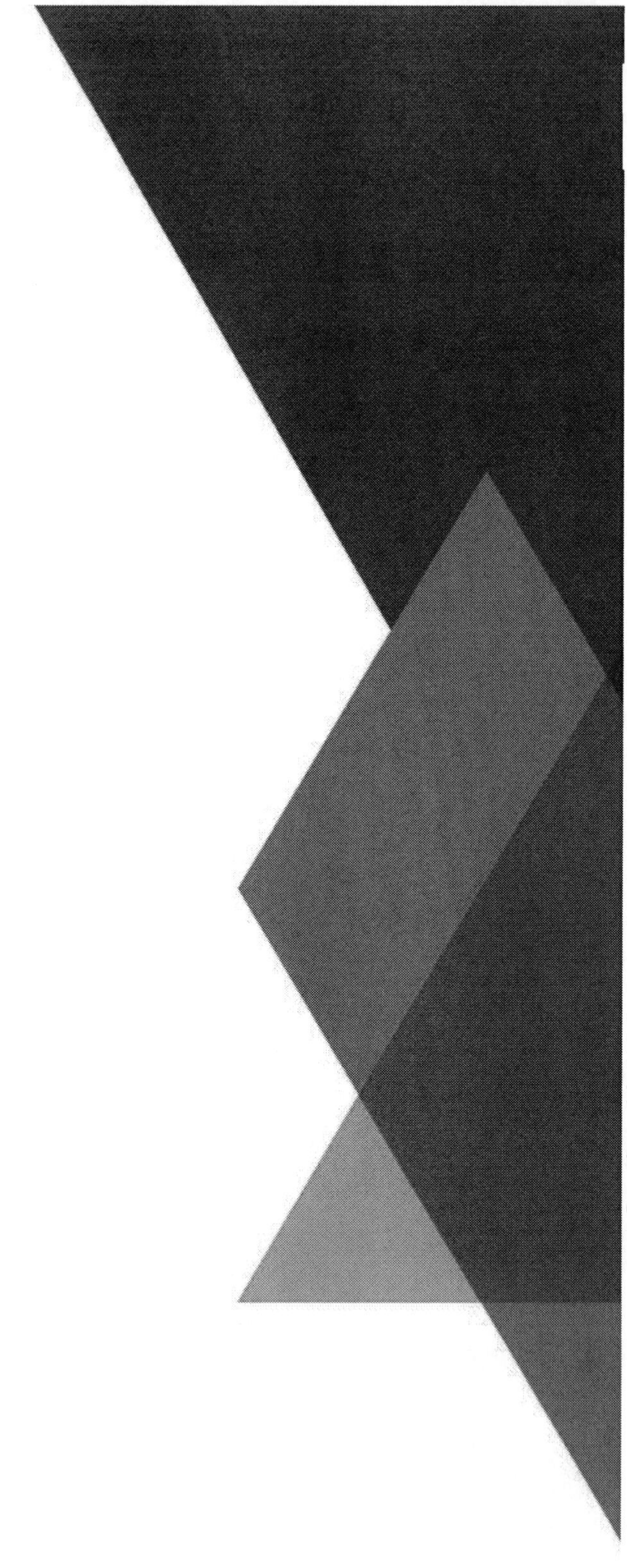

Introduction: a note on terminology

Natural Gender

*"Gender based on the **sex** or, for neuter, the lack of sex of the referent of a noun, as English girl (<u>feminine</u>) is referred to by the feminine pronoun she, boy (<u>masculine</u>) by the masculine pronoun he, and table (neuter) by the <u>neuter</u> pronoun it."*

Collins Dictionary 2018, HarperCollins, London,

viewed September 2020
http://www.collinsdictionary.com

Introduction: a note on terminology

Natural Gender	Grammatical Gender
*"Gender based on the **sex** or, for neuter, the lack of sex of the referent of a noun, as English girl (feminine) is referred to by the feminine pronoun she, boy (masculine) by the masculine pronoun he, and table (neuter) by the neuter pronoun it."*	*"Gender based on arbitrary assignment, without regard to the referent of a noun, as in French 'le livre' (masculine), "the book," and German 'das Mädchen' (neuter), "the girl."*
Collins Dictionary 2018, HarperCollins, London, viewed September 2020 http://www.collinsdictionary.com	*Collins Dictionary* 2018, HarperCollins, London, viewed September 2020 http://www.collinsdictionary.com

Proceedings of the 14th Conference of the Association for Machine Translation in the Americas
October 6 – 9, 2020, Workshop on the Impact of Machine Translation

Introduction: a note on terminology

Natural Gender	Grammatical Gender	Social Gender
*"Gender based on the **sex** or, for neuter, the lack of sex of the referent of a noun, as English girl (<u>feminine</u>) is referred to by the feminine pronoun she, boy (<u>masculine</u>) by the masculine pronoun he, and table (neuter) by the <u>neuter</u> pronoun it."*	*"Gender based on arbitrary assignment, without regard to the referent of a noun, as in French 'le livre' (masculine), "the book," and German 'das Mädchen' (neuter), "the girl."*	- *Embedded in the lexicon of many languages* - *Systematic structural bias.* - *Masculine forms the default for generic use.*
Collins Dictionary 2018, HarperCollins, London, viewed September 2020 http://www.collinsdictionary.com	*Collins Dictionary* 2018, HarperCollins, London, viewed September 2020 http://www.collinsdictionary.com	

Proceedings of the 14th Conference of the Association for Machine Translation in the Americas
October 6 – 9, 2020, Workshop on the Impact of Machine Translation

Introduction: a note on terminology

Romance Languages (e.g. ES, FR, IT)

- animate/persons/animals

  ↓

  grammatical gender = natural gender

- inanimate objects

  ↓

  grammatical gender = arbitrary

Proceedings of the 14th Conference of the Association for Machine Translation in the Americas
October 6 – 9, 2020, Workshop on the Impact of Machine Translation

Introduction: a note on terminology

Romance Languages (e.g. ES, FR, IT)	English
• animate/persons/animals ↓ grammatical gender = natural gender • inanimate objects ↓ grammatical gender = arbitrary	• grammatical gender is not inflectional • ***pronominal gender*** → gender expressed through the pronouns = natural gender • ***gender-neutralization*** of the language

Proceedings of the 14th Conference of the Association for Machine Translation in the Americas
October 6 – 9, 2020, Workshop on the Impact of Machine Translation

www.adaptcentre.ie

A simple example:

I am happy!

Io sono
content**o**!

Io sono
content**a**!

[Natural Gender]

[Grammatical Gender]

I am happy!

Je suis
heureu**x**!

Je suis
heureu**se**!

[Natural Gender]

[Grammatical Gender]

Proceedings of the 14th Conference of the Association for Machine Translation in the Americas
October 6 – 9, 2020, Workshop on the Impact of Machine Translation

Introduction: a quick problem sketch

		Subject gender	Predicative nominative gender	Agreement?
English	Mark is an efficient nurse.	M	covered	/
Italian	Mark è un'infermiera efficiente.	M	F	X
French	Mark est une infirmière efficace.	M	F	X
Spanish	Mark es una enfermera eficiente.	M	F	X

Nov 2019

➤ **Lack of diversity** → preference for masculine & gender-bias exemptions

➤ **Agreement errors**

Proceedings of the 14th Conference of the Association for Machine Translation in the Americas
October 6 - 9, 2020, Workshop on the Impact of Machine Translation

Experimental Setup

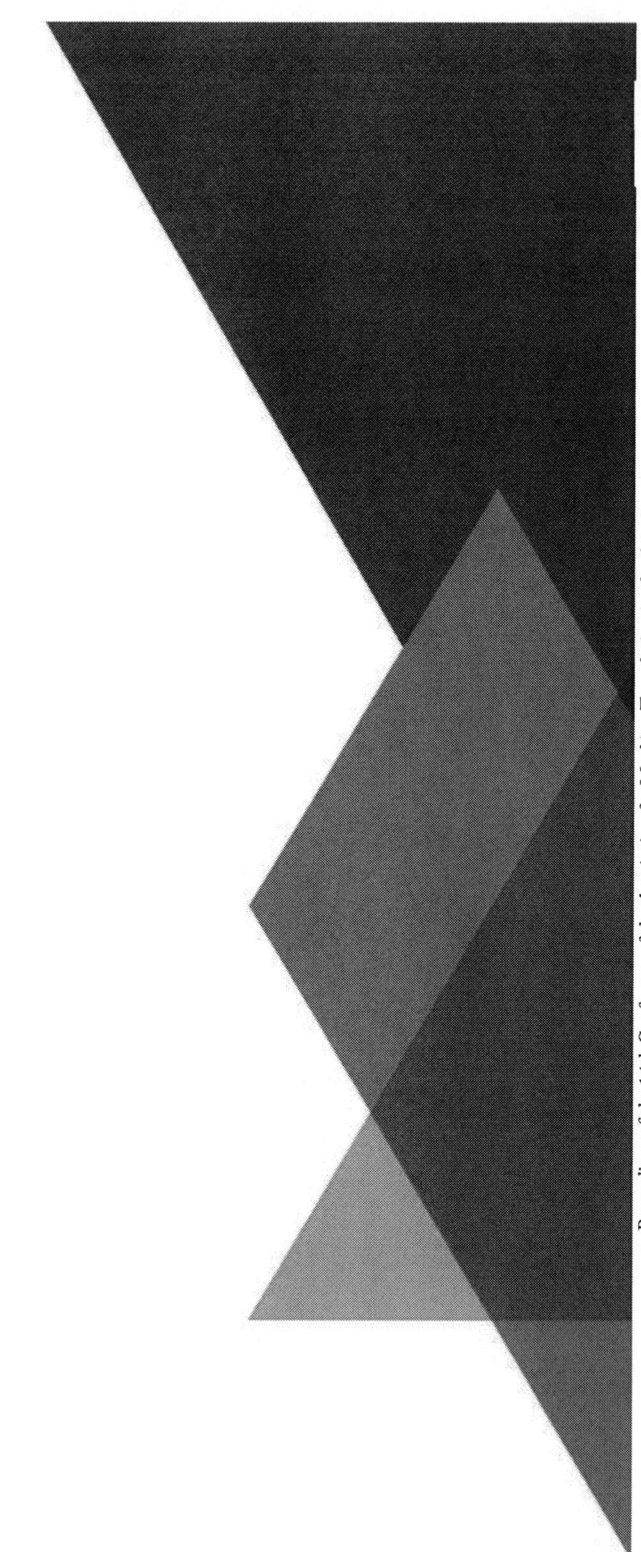

Proceedings of the 14th Conference of the Association for Machine Translation in the Americas
October 6 - 9, 2020, Workshop on the Impact of Machine Translation

Gender bias in MT

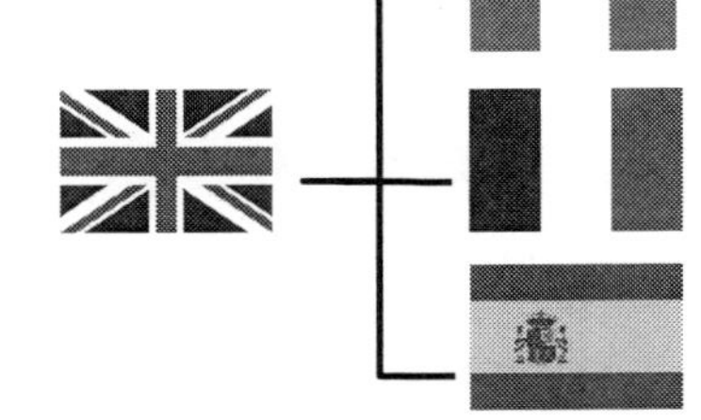

- personality adjectives
- profession nouns
- bigender nouns (in Italian)
  - minimal sentence "I am a(n)..."
  - sentence with a referring adjective

	#	Sources
Adjectives	136	(I, 2019a); (II, 2019a);(III, 2019)
Professions	107	(I, 2019b); (II, 2019b)
Bigender	30	(Cacciari et al., 1997); (Cacciari et al., 2011) (Thornton and Anna, 2004)

Table 1: Overview of adjectives, profession and bigender nouns along with the sources from which they were retrieved

Proceedings of the 14th Conference of the Association for Machine Translation in the Americas
October 6 – 9, 2020, Workshop on the Impact of Machine Translation

Compilation of Datasets

	#	Sources
Adjectives	136	(I, 2019a); (II, 2019a);(III, 2019)
Professions	107	(I, 2019b); (II, 2019b)
Bigender	30	(Cacciari et al., 1997); (Cacciari et al., 2011) (Thornton and Anna, 2004)

Table 1: Overview of adjectives, profession and bigender nouns along with the sources from which they were retrieved

English	Italian		French		Spanish	
I am an assistant.	Sono un assistente.	M	Je suis un assistant.	M	Soy asistente.	*
I am a beautiful assistant.	**Sono una bellissima assistente.**	F	**Je suis une belle assistante.**	F	**Soy una bella asistente.**	F
I am an efficient assistant.	Sono un assistente efficiente.	M	Je suis un assistant efficace.	M	Soy un asistente eficiente.	M
I am a translator.	Sono un traduttore.	M	Je suis un traducteur.	M	Soy un traductor.	M
I am a beautiful translator.	**Sono una bellissima traduttrice.**	F	**Je suis une belle traductrice.**	F	**Soy una bella traductora.**	F
I am an efficient translator.	Sono un traduttore efficiente.	M	Je suis un traducteur efficace.	M	Soy un traductor eficiente.	M

Proceedings of the 14th Conference of the Association for Machine Translation in the Americas
October 6 – 9, 2020, Workshop on the Impact of Machine Translation

Description of MT systems

Google Translate

- 2003
- statistical MT system
- 2016 → neural MT system
- 2018 → double alternatives on word level

Proceedings of the 14th Conference of the Association for Machine Translation in the Americas
October 6 – 9, 2020, Workshop on the Impact of Machine Translation

Description of MT systems

 Google Translate

 **DeepL** DeepL Translator

- 2017
- convolutional neural networks
- Linguee database (dictionary)
- nine languages supported
- provides not morphological alternatives
- serves also as glossary

Proceedings of the 14th Conference of the Association for Machine Translation in the Americas
October 6 – 9, 2020, Workshop on the Impact of Machine Translation

Description of MT systems

 Google Translate

 **DeepL** DeepL Translator

 **Bing Microsoft Translator**

- originally a statistical MT system
- switched to a neural system
- does not provides alternatives but
- provides examples of usage

Proceedings of the 14th Conference of the Association for Machine Translation in the Americas
October 6 – 9, 2020, Workshop on the Impact of Machine Translation

Results & Analysis

Proceedings of the 14th Conference of the Association for Machine Translation in the Americas
October 6 - 9, 2020, Workshop on the Impact of Machine Translation

Results & Analysis

- ADJECTIVES

ADJ	GT	BMT	DL
F	37.3	1.5	22.8
M	**39.2**	**58.8**	**45.6**
N	20.7	33.1	26.5
Other	2.8	6.5	5.1
Total	100	100	100

Table 2: Results in % for male (M), female (F) and neutral (N) adjectives generated for EN $\rightarrow$ IT for GT, BMT and DL. The "Other" label includes all results obtained that do not correspond to the "adjective" category

Proceedings of the 14th Conference of the Association for Machine Translation in the Americas
October 6 – 9, 2020, Workshop on the Impact of Machine Translation

Results & Analysis

❑ NOUNS

NOUN	GT	BMT	DL
F	35.8	0.9	7.5
M	**46.1**	**60.4**	**60.4**
N	17.6	28.3	28.3
Other	0.6	10.5	3.7
Total	100	100	100

Table 3: Results in % for male (M), female (F) and neutral (N) nouns generated for EN → IT for GT, BMT and DL. The "Other" label includes all results obtained that do not correspond to the "noun" category

Proceedings of the 14th Conference of the Association for Machine Translation in the Americas
October 6 – 9, 2020, Workshop on the Impact of Machine Translation

Results & Analysis

BMT	IT			FR			ES		
	F	M	N	F	M	N	F	M	N
no adj.	10.0	**86.7**	Q^*	10.0	**63.3**	26.7	3.3	**66.7**	30.0
beautiful	**63.3**	36.7	0.0	43.3	**56.7**	0.0	**66.7**	33.3	0.0
other adj.	13.3	**83.3**	Q^*	3.3	**96.7**	0.0	6.7	**93.3**	0.0

DL	IT			FR			ES		
	F	M	N	F	M	N	F	M	N
no adj	30.0	**70.0**	0.0	20.0	**63.3**	16.7	3.3	**76.6**	20.0
beautiful	**83.3**	16.7	0.0	**73.3**	26.7	0.0	**96.7**	3.3	0.0
other adj.	**53.3**	43.3	Q^*	13.3	**83.3**	3.3	6.7	**93.3**	0.0

GT	IT			FR			ES		
	F	M	N	F	M	N	F	M	N
no adj.	6.7	**93.3**	0.0	6.7	**90.0**	3.3	3.3	**66.7**	30.0
beautiful	43.3	**56.7**	0.0	**80.**	20.0	0.0	**80.0**	20.0	0.0
other adj.	3.3	**96.7**	0.0	3.3	**96.7**	0.0	3.3	**96.7**	0.0

Table 4: Results in % for male (M), female (F) and neutral (N) forms generated for EN → IT, FR and ES for BMT, DL and GT

- *beautiful*

other adjectives:

- *efficient*
- *intelligent*
- *sad*
- *famous*

Proceedings of the 14th Conference of the Association for Machine Translation in the Americas
October 6 - 9, 2020, Workshop on the Impact of Machine Translation

BMT	IT			FR			ES		
	F	M	N	F	M	N	F	M	N
no adj.	10.0	**86.7**	Q^*	10.0	**63.3**	26.7	3.3	**66.7**	30.0
beautiful	**63.3**	36.7	0.0	43.3	**56.7**	0.0	**66.7**	33.3	0.0
other adj.	13.3	**83.3**	Q^*	3.3	**96.7**	0.0	6.7	**93.3**	0.0
DL	IT			FR			ES		
	F	M	N	F	M	N	F	M	N
no adj	30.0	**70.0**	0.0	20.0	**63.3**	16.7	3.3	**76.6**	20.0
beautiful	**83.3**	16.7	0.0	**73.3**	26.7	0.0	**96.7**	3.3	0.0
other adj.	**53.3**	43.3	Q^*	13.3	**83.3**	3.3	6.7	**93.3**	0.0
GT	IT			FR			ES		
	F	M	N	F	M	N	F	M	N
no adj.	6.7	**93.3**	0.0	6.7	**90.0**	3.3	3.3	**66.7**	30.0
beautiful	43.3	**56.7**	0.0	**80.**	20.0	0.0	**80.0**	20.0	0.0
other adj.	3.3	**96.7**	0.0	3.3	**96.7**	0.0	3.3	**96.7**	0.0

Table 4: Results in % for male (M), female (F) and neutral (N) forms generated for EN $\rightarrow$ IT, FR and ES for BMT, DL and GT

- *beautiful*

other adjectives:

- *efficient*
- *intelligent*
- *sad*
- *famous*

Proceedings of the 14th Conference of the Association for Machine Translation in the Americas
October 6 – 9, 2020, Workshop on the Impact of Machine Translation

iMpacT

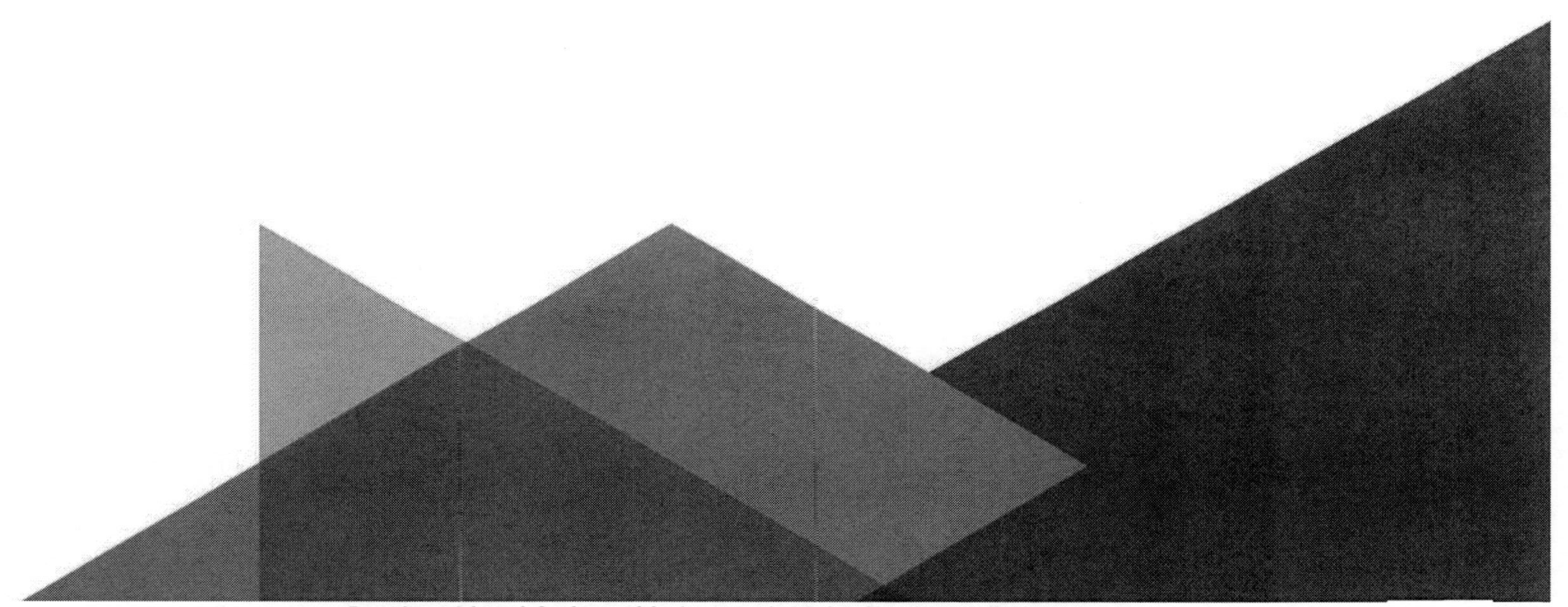

Proceedings of the 14th Conference of the Association for Machine Translation in the Americas
October 6 – 9, 2020, Workshop on the Impact of Machine Translation

iMpacT

- **From a linguistic point of view:**
    - Avoiding basic gender agreement mistakes

- **From a technological point of view:**
    - Solving these issues is not trivial (see attempts Google)

    - Black box of NLP (we have no/little control over the actual output that are being generated)

- **From a societal/ethical point of view:**
    - Identifying biases in current state-of-the-art systems is important so they don't end up getting mistaken for 'objective' translations

    - if an MT system is being used without human in the loop: real-world consequences

Proceedings of the 14th Conference of the Association for Machine Translation in the Americas
October 6 – 9, 2020, Workshop on the Impact of Machine Translation

Break the cycle

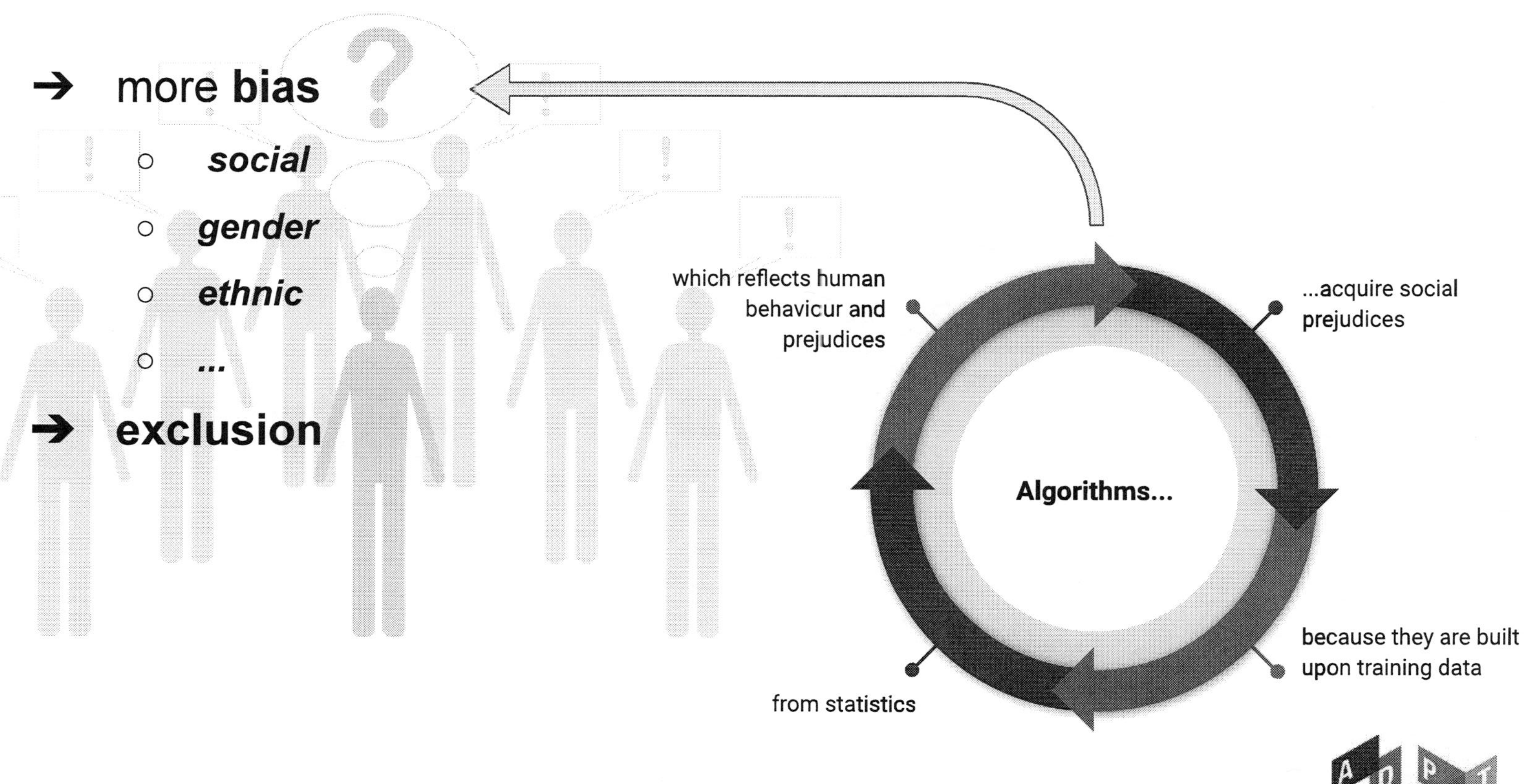

Proceedings of the 14th Conference of the Association for Machine Translation in the Americas
October 6 – 9, 2020, Workshop on the Impact of Machine Translation

Conclusion and Future Work

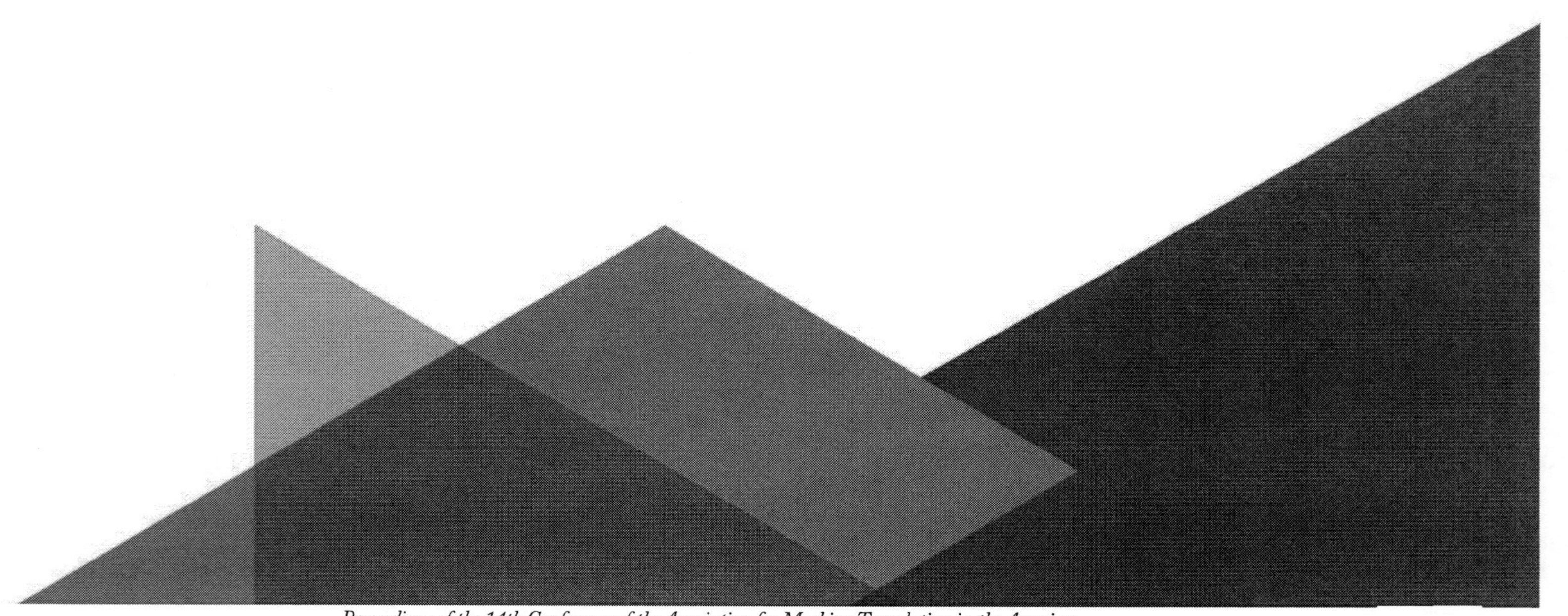

Proceedings of the 14th Conference of the Association for Machine Translation in the Americas
October 6 – 9, 2020, Workshop on the Impact of Machine Translation

Conclusion and Future Work

Conclusion:

- Remove gender bias in training data

- Train algorithms to address the problem

- Stop using masculine "neutral" in machine learning texts

- Evaluation of gender phenomena is challenging

Future Work:

- Extend to other language pairs (different languages → different gender phenomena)

- Larger evaluation of more diverse set of words

- Create language specific challenge sets to evaluate how biased is an MT system

- Train our own MT system to verify whether machine bias influences the output of the translation

Proceedings of the 14th Conference of the Association for Machine Translation in the Americas
October 6 – 9, 2020, Workshop on the Impact of Machine Translation

Thank you for your attention!

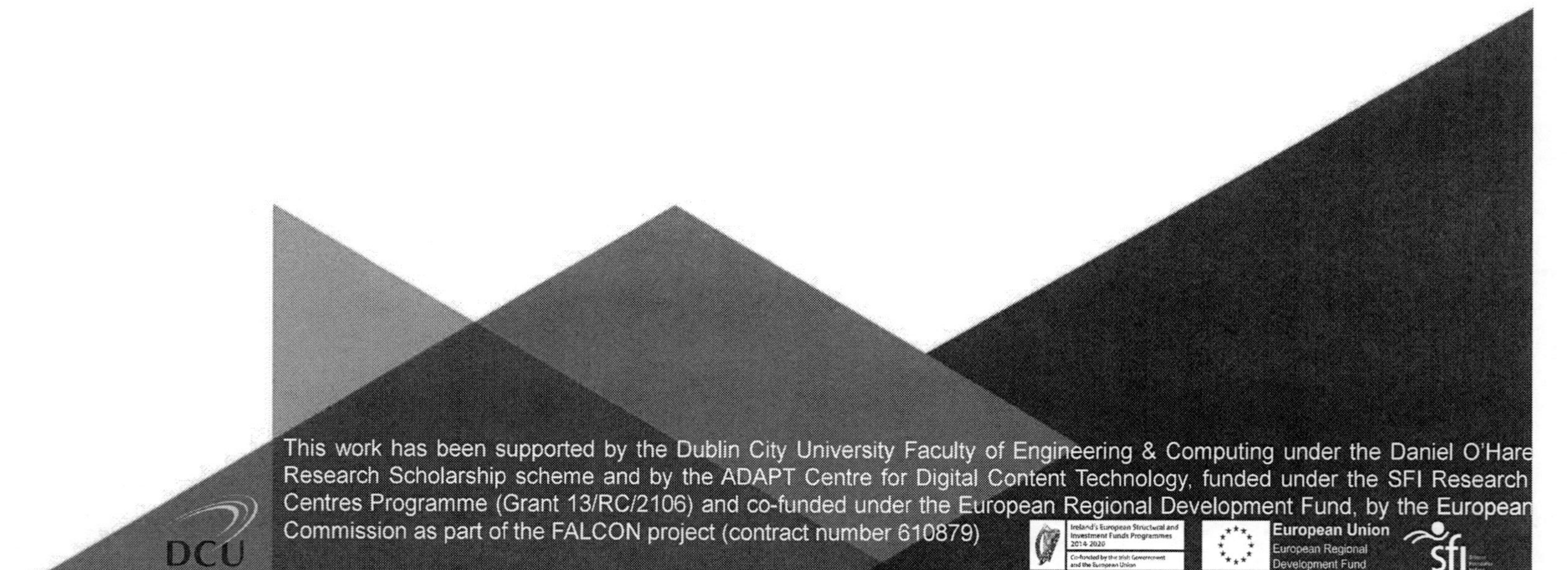

Proceedings of the 14th Conference of the Association for Machine Translation in the Americas
October 6 – 9, 2020, Workshop on the Impact of Machine Translation

References

Bond, E., 2020. Cambridge Researchers Tackle Neural Machine Translation'S Gender Bias | Slator. [online] Slator. Available at: <https://slator.com/machine-translation/cambridge-researchers-tackle-neural-machine-translations-gender-bias/> [Accessed 29 September 2020].

Caliskan, A., Bryson, J. and Narayanan, A., 2017. Semantics derived automatically from language corpora contain human-like biases. Science, 356(6334), pp.183-186.

Devlin, H., 2017. AI Programs Exhibit Racial And Gender Biases, Research Reveals. [online] the Guardian. Available at: <https://www.theguardian.com/technology/2017/apr/13/ai-programs-exhibit-racist-and-sexist-biases-research-reveals> [Accessed 29 September 2020].

Monti, J., 2017. Questioni di genere in traduzione automatica. In: A. de Meo, L. di Pace, A. Manco and J. Monti, ed., Al femminile. Scritti linguistici in onore di Cristina Vallini. Firenze: Cesati, pp.411-431.

Prates, M., Avelar, P. and Lamb, L., 2019. Assessing gender bias in machine translation: a case study with Google Translate. Neural Computing and Applications, 32(10), pp.1-19.

Saunders, D. and Byrne, B., 2020. Reducing Gender Bias in Neural Machine Translation as a Domain Adaptation Problem. *arXiv: 2004.04498v3*

Vanmassenhove, E., Shterionov, D. and Way, A., 2019. Lost in Translation: Loss and Decay of Linguistic Richness in Machine Translation. *arXiv: 1906.12068*

Zou, J. and Schiebinger, L., 2018. AI can be sexist and racist — it's time to make it fair. Nature, 559(7714), pp.324-326.

Proceedings of the 14th Conference of the Association for Machine Translation in the Americas
October 6 – 9, 2020, Workshop on the Impact of Machine Translation

Contact info

Argentina A. Rescigno: argentina.res@gmail.com

Eva Vanmassenhove: vanmassenhove.eva@gmail.com

Johanna Monti: johmonti@gmail.com

Andy Way: andy.way@adaptcentre.ie

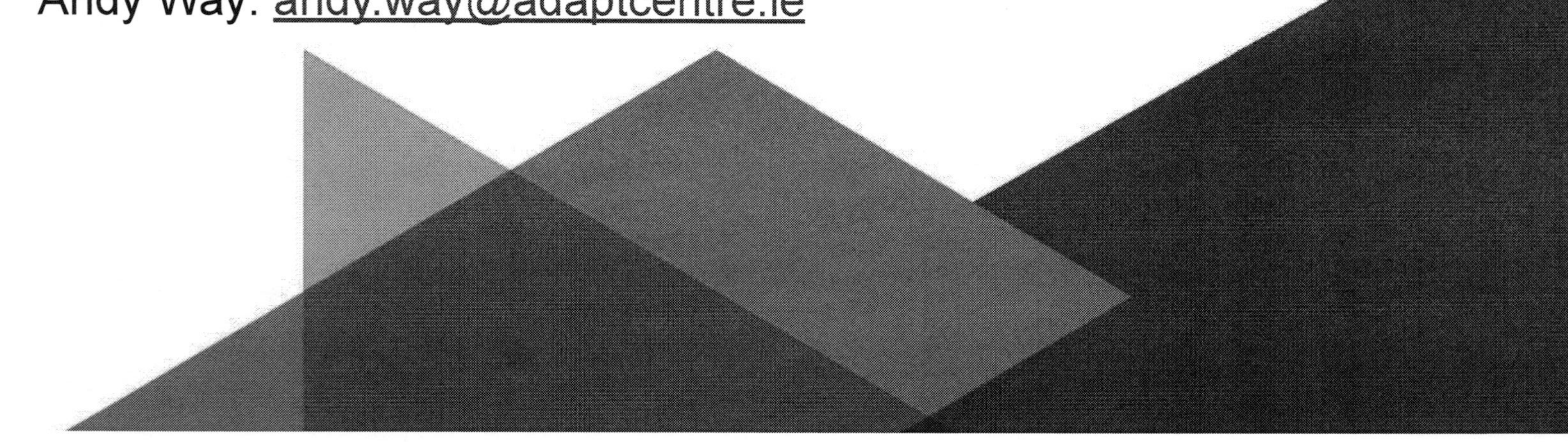

Proceedings of the 14th Conference of the Association for Machine Translation in the Americas
October 6 – 9, 2020, Workshop on the Impact of Machine Translation

Proceedings of the 14th Conference of the Association for Machine Translation in the Americas
October 6 – 9, 2020, Workshop on the Impact of Machine Translation

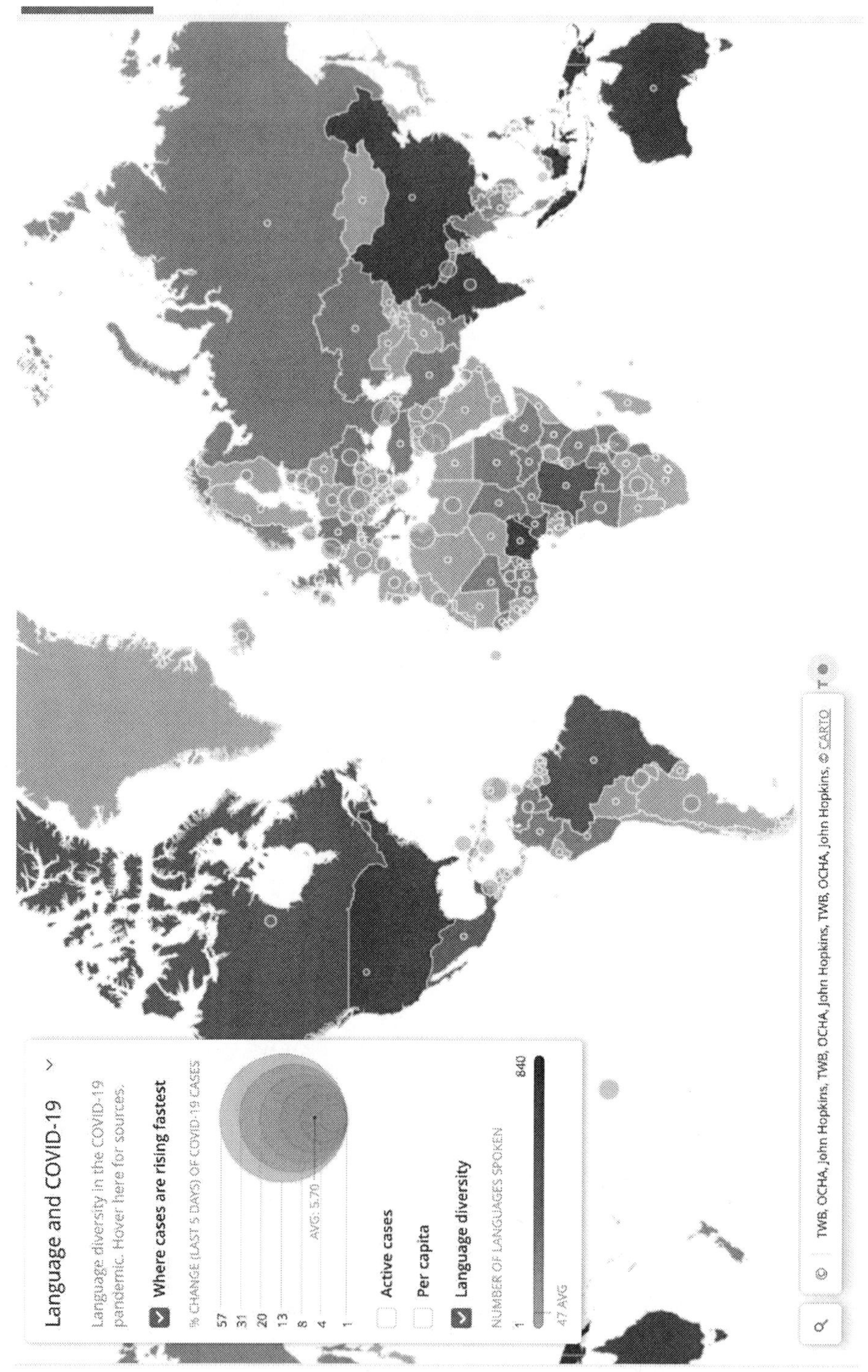

Language and COVID-19
Language diversity in the COVID-19 pandemic. Hover here for sources.
Where cases are rising fastest
% CHANGE (LAST 5 DAYS) OF COVID-19 CASES
57
31
20
13
8
4
1
AVG: 5.70
Active cases
Per capita
Language diversity
NUMBER OF LANGUAGES SPOKEN
1
840
47 AVG
TWB, OCHA, John Hopkins, TWB, OCHA, John Hopkins, © CARTO

Linguistic crisis response

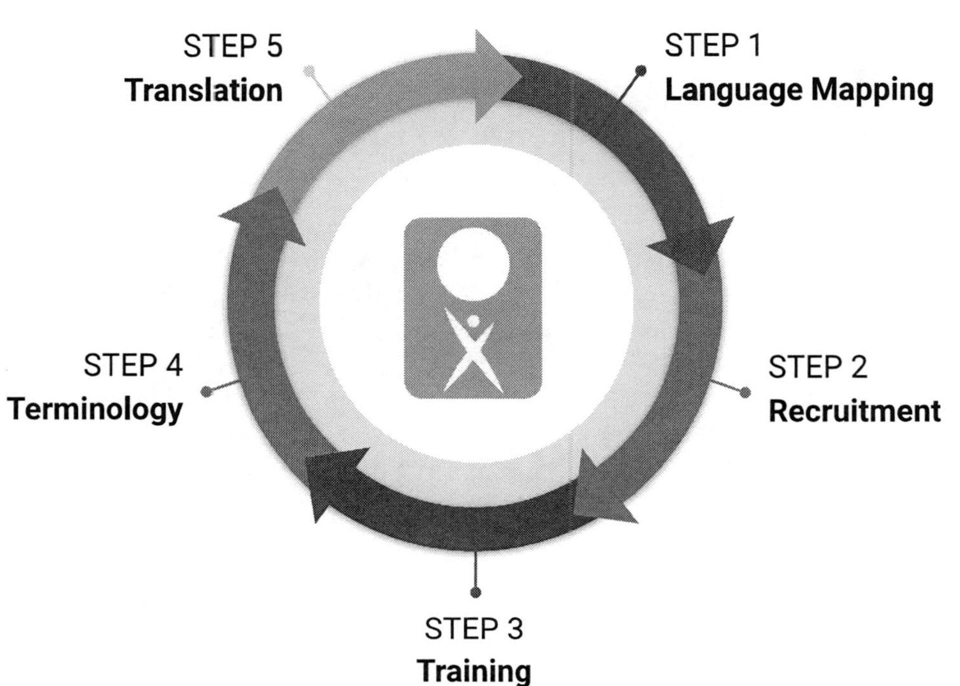

Proceedings of the 14th Conference of the Association for Machine Translation in the Americas
October 6 - 9, 2020, Workshop on the Impact of Machine Translation

Linguistic crisis response

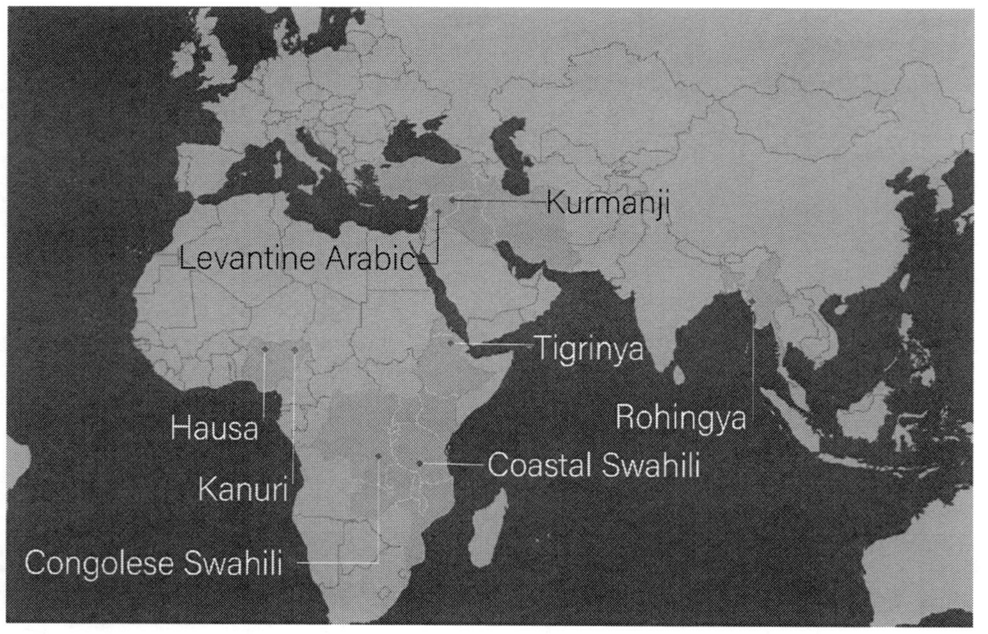

Hausa vs. French

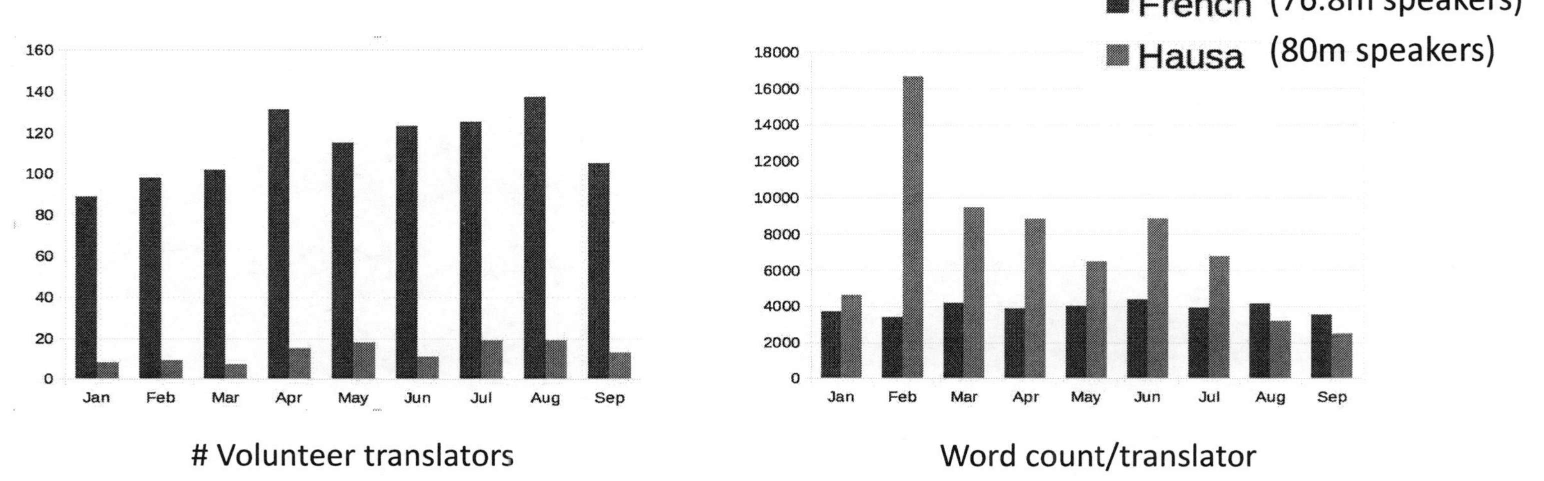

Data from Kato: TWB's translation platform during Covid-19 pandemic

How can **language technology** help to empower translators of **marginalized languages?**

Proceedings of the 14th Conference of the Association for Machine Translation in the Americas
October 6 - 9, 2020, Workshop on the Impact of Machine Translation

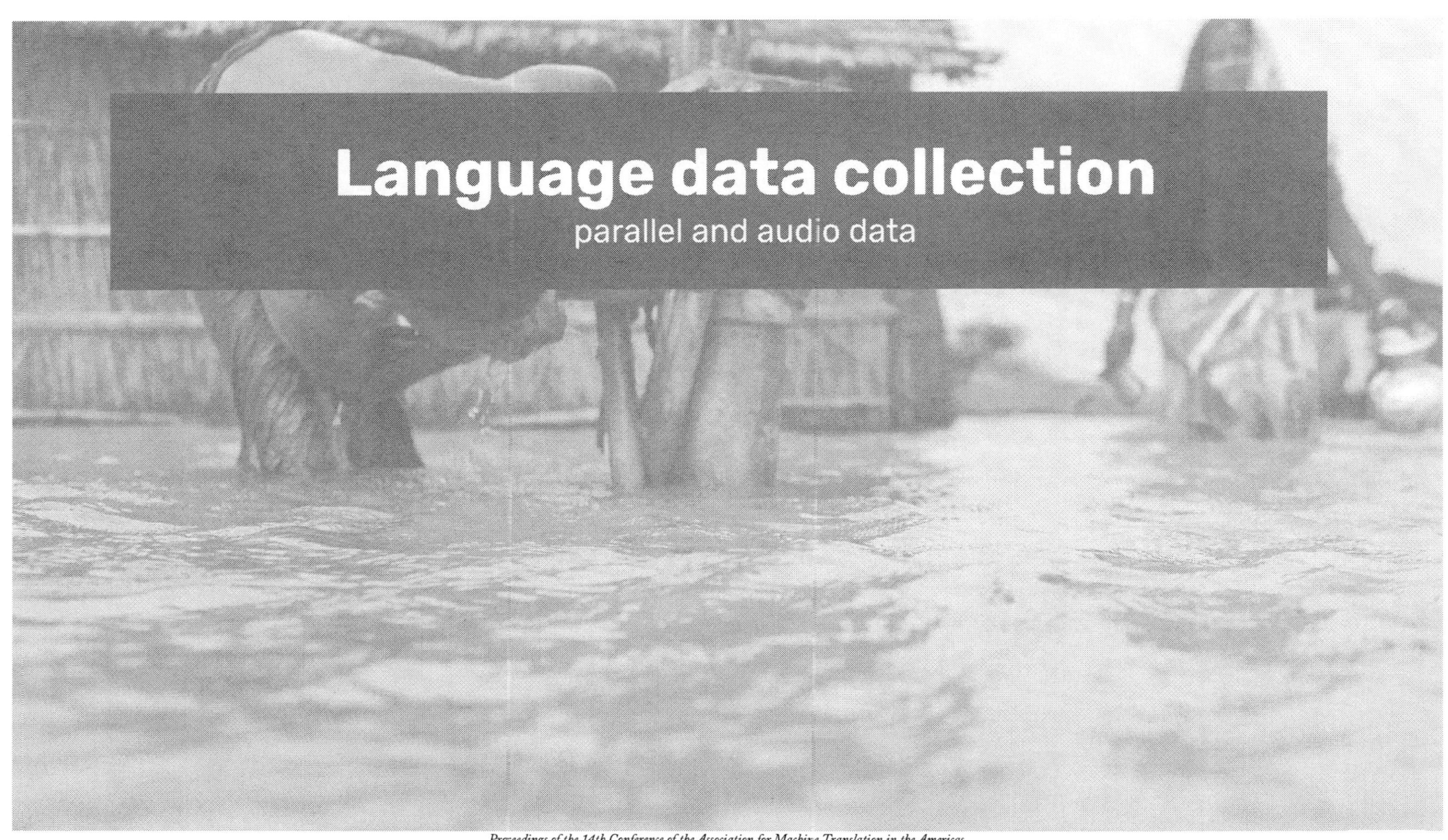

Proceedings of the 14th Conference of the Association for Machine Translation in the Americas
October 6 - 9, 2020, Workshop on the Impact of Machine Translation

97

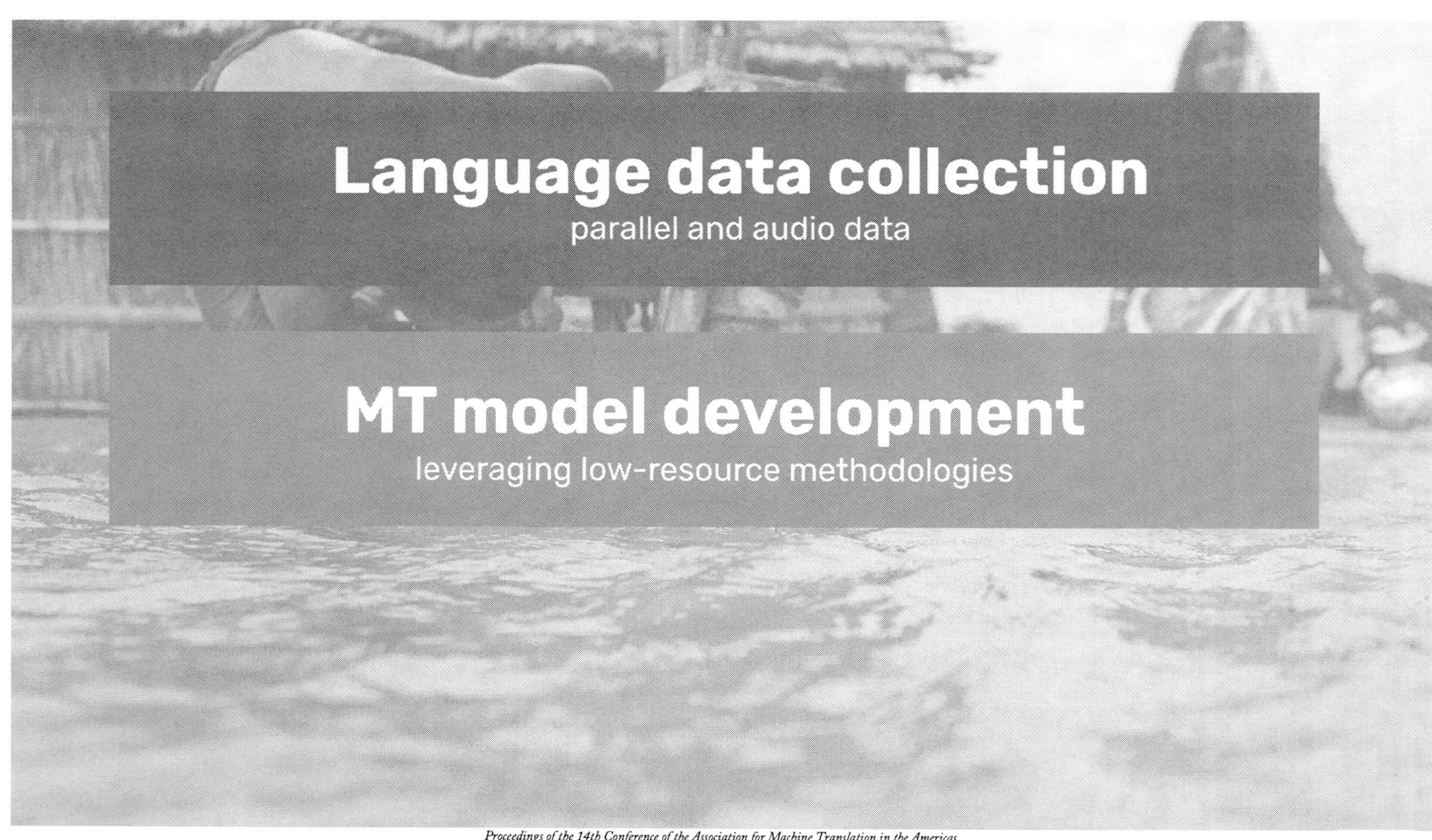

Language data collection
parallel and audio data
MT model development
leveraging low-resource methodologies

Proceedings of the 14th Conference of the Association for Machine Translation in the Americas
October 6 - 9, 2020, Workshop on the Impact of Machine Translation

Language data collection

NMT for humanitarian impact

Language Data Disparity

Data has been consolidated from the OPUS collection of pub icly available parallel corpora paired with English.

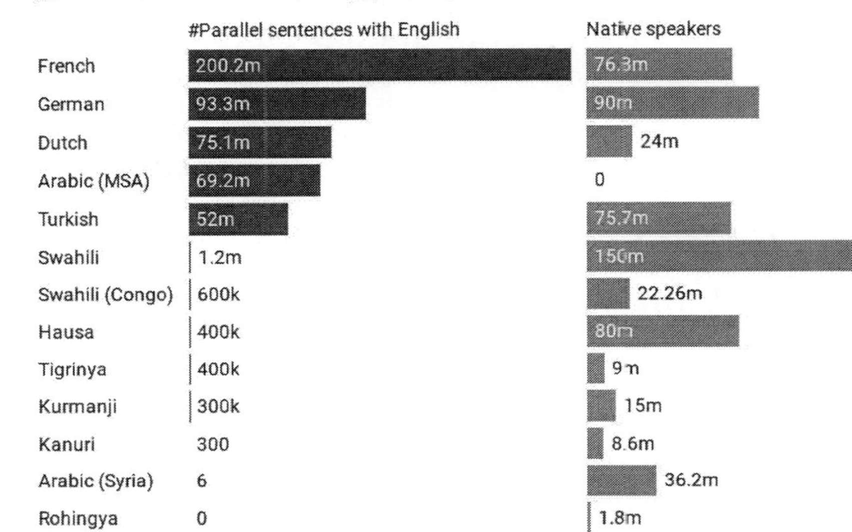

	#Parallel sentences with English	Native speakers
French	200.2m	76.3m
German	93.3m	90m
Dutch	75.1m	24m
Arabic (MSA)	69.2m	0
Turkish	52m	75.7m
Swahili	1.2m	150m
Swahili (Congo)	600k	22.26m
Hausa	400k	80m
Tigrinya	400k	9m
Kurmanji	300k	15m
Kanuri	300	8.6m
Arabic (Syria)	6	36.2m
Rohingya	0	1.8m

Gamayun kits

- Starting point for developing audio and text corpora for languages without pre-existing data resources.
- Four dataset versions:
  - Mini-kit - 5,000 sentences
  - Small-kit - 10,000 sentences
  - Medium-kit - 15,000 sentences
  - Large-kit - 30,000 sentences.
- Source sentences in English, Spanish, French
- Freely available from https://gamayun.translatorswb.org/
  - Currently mini-kits in Hausa, Kanuri, Rohingya, Swahili, Nande

Data > MT > Application

Proceedings of the 14th Conference of the Association for Machine Translation in the Americas
October 6 – 9, 2020, Workshop on the Impact of Machine Translation

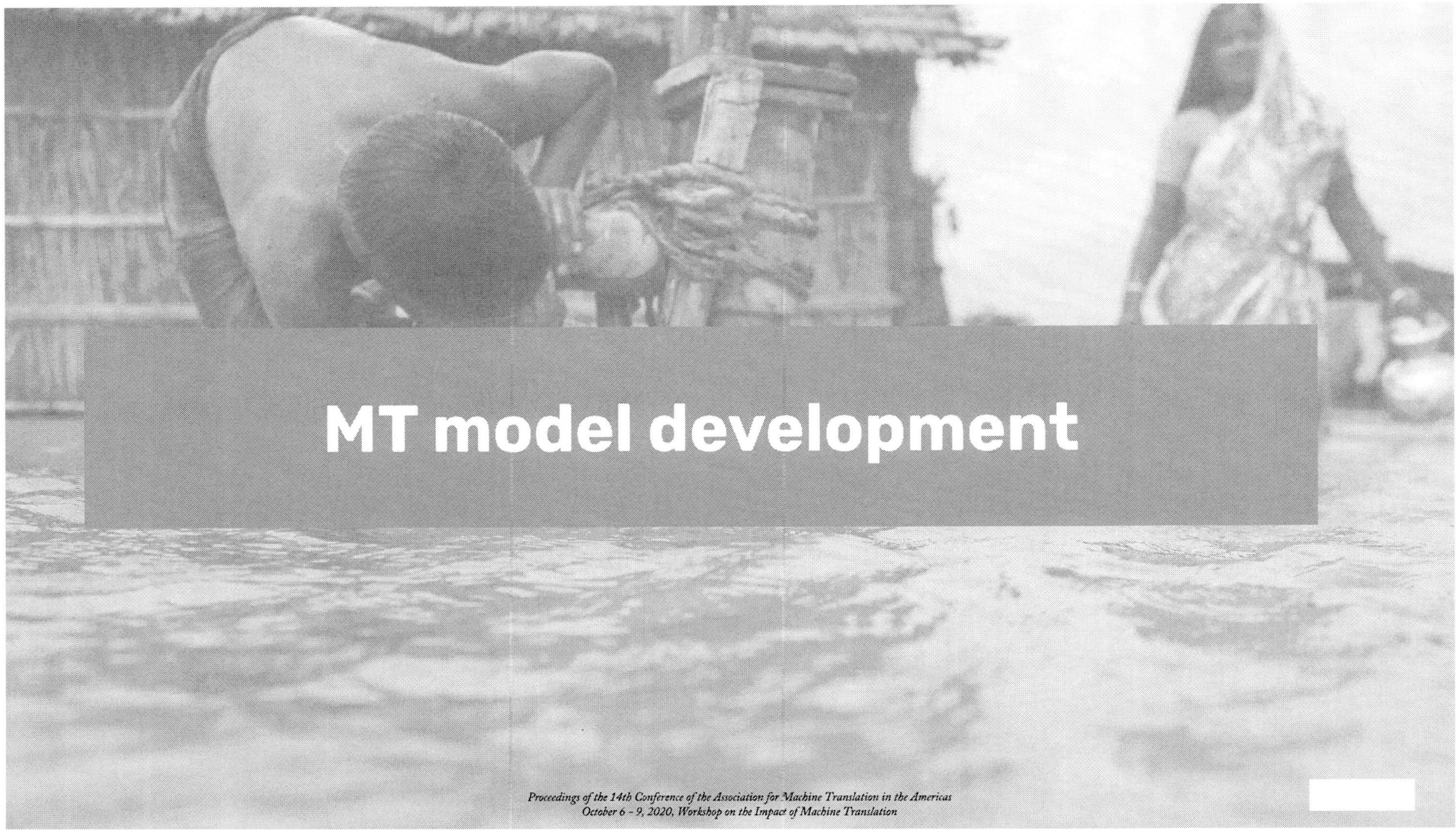

Proceedings of the 14th Conference of the Association for Machine Translation in the Americas
October 6 – 9, 2020, Workshop on the Impact of Machine Translation

MT model development

- Languages: Levantine Arabic, Tigrinya, Congolese Swahili
- Main techniques employed:
  - Domain adaptation
  - Dialect adaptation
  - Cross-lingual transfer learning
  - Back-translation

Proceedings of the 14th Conference of the Association for Machine Translation in the Americas
October 6 - 9, 2020, Workshop on the Impact of Machine Translation

Domain/dialect adaptation

- Levantine Arabic to English machine translation
- For social media content by Syrian refugees in Jordan
- Small in-domain data (5200 sentences)
- Modern Standard Arabic as base model

Domain/dialect adaptation

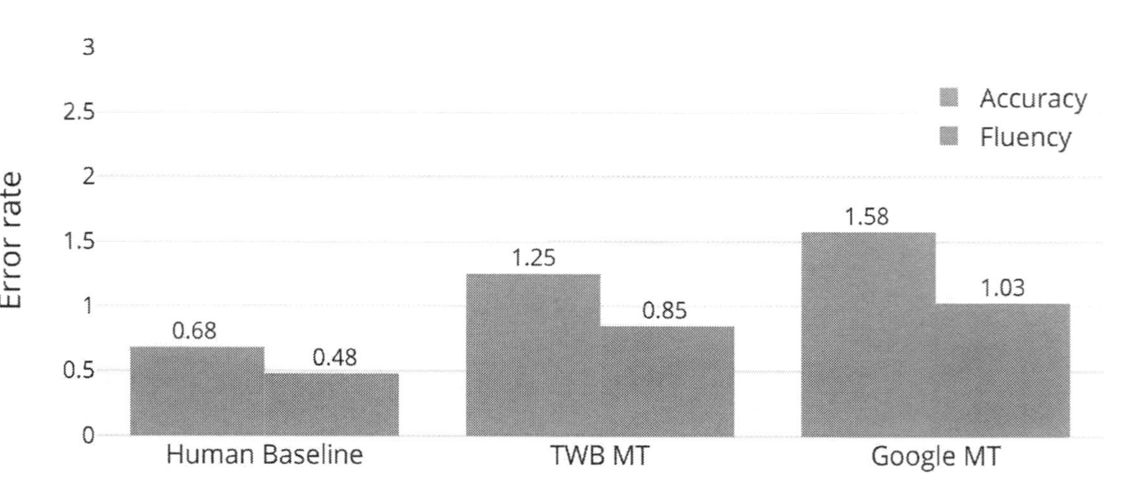

Manual evaluation of TWB's Levantine Arabic MT for usability in social media monitoring

Proceedings of the 14th Conference of the Association for Machine Translation in the Americas
October 6 - 9, 2020, Workshop on the Impact of Machine Translation

Domain/dialect adaptation

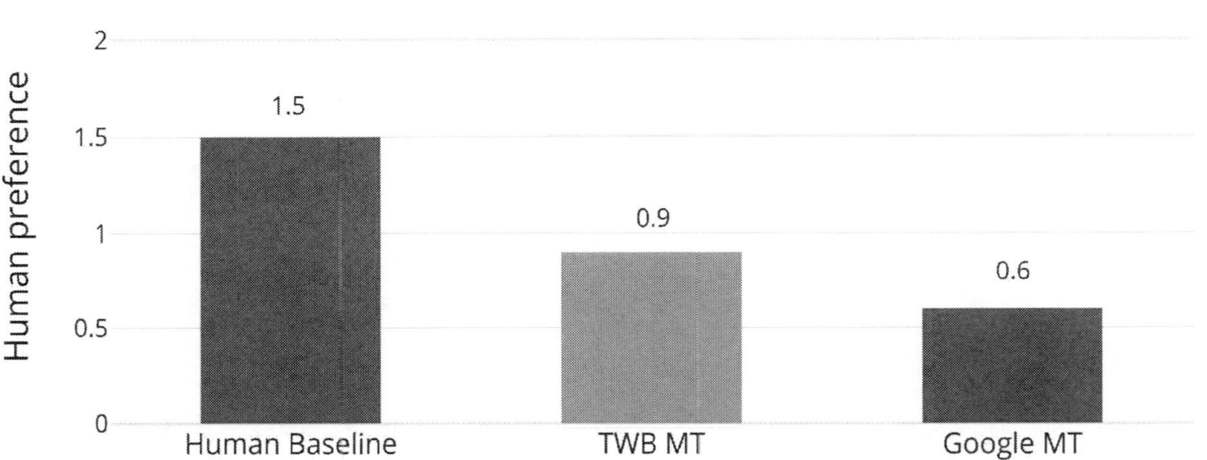

Proceedings of the 14th Conference of the Association for Machine Translation in the Americas
October 6 - 9, 2020, Workshop on the Impact of Machine Translation

Tigrinya NMT

- Semitic language with estimate # speakers of 7.9 million
- Refugee language in Europe and USA
- Hard-to-resource for translation
  - 3 active translators
  - %81 claimed in 2020
  - 72-day average delay
- Transfer learning from Amharic

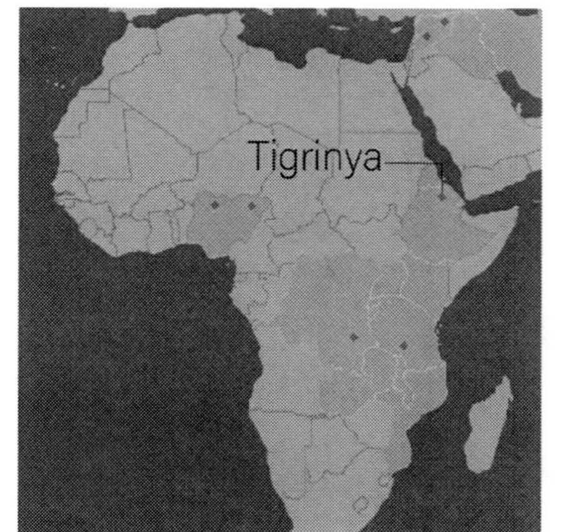

Data | MT | Application

Tigrinya NMT

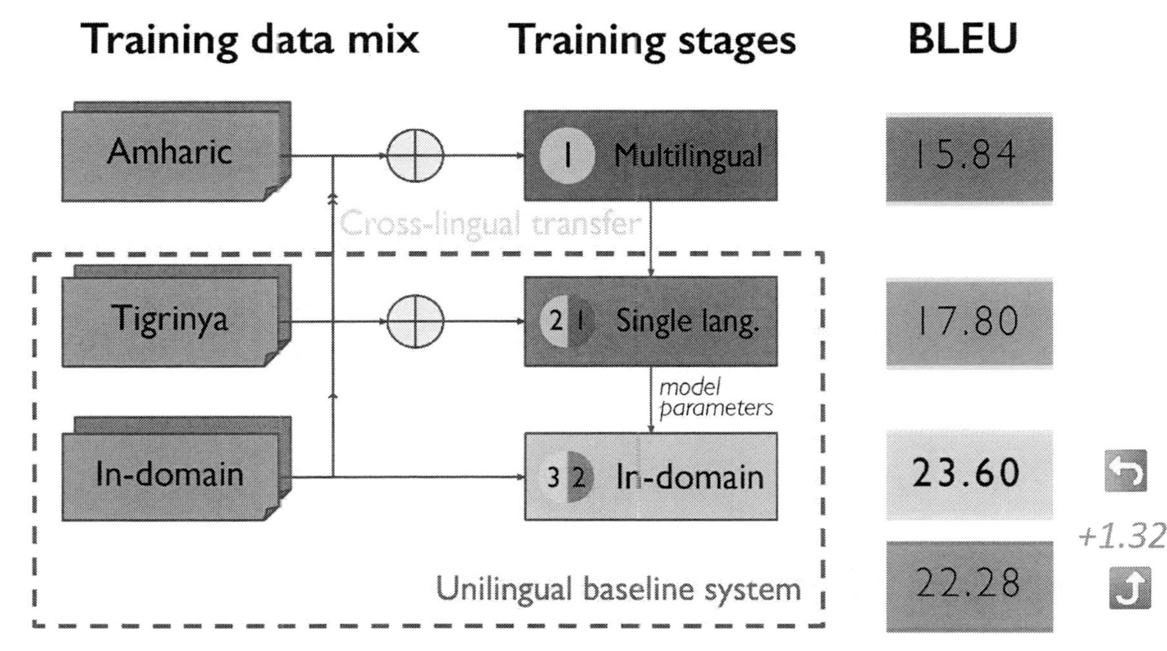

Cross-lingual transfer learning and domain adaptation

Proceedings of the 14th Conference of the Association for Machine Translation in the Americas
October 6 - 9, 2020, Workshop on the Impact of Machine Translation

Tigrinya NMT

- Bidirectionality challenge:
  - Tigrinya-to-English: 23.60 BLEU
  - English-to-Tigrinya: 9.92 BLEU
- More details on paper:
  - A. Öktem, M. Plitt, G. Tang. *Tigrinya neural machine translation with transfer learning for humanitarian response.* AfricaNLP Workshop organized within ICLR, Addis Ababa, Ethiopia, April 2020.

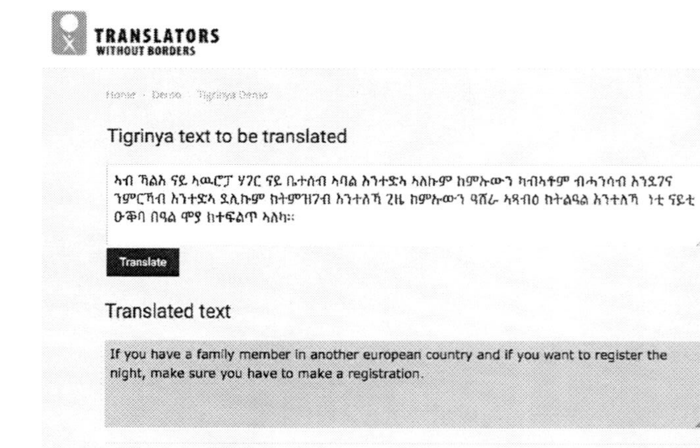

https://gamayun.translatorswb.org/

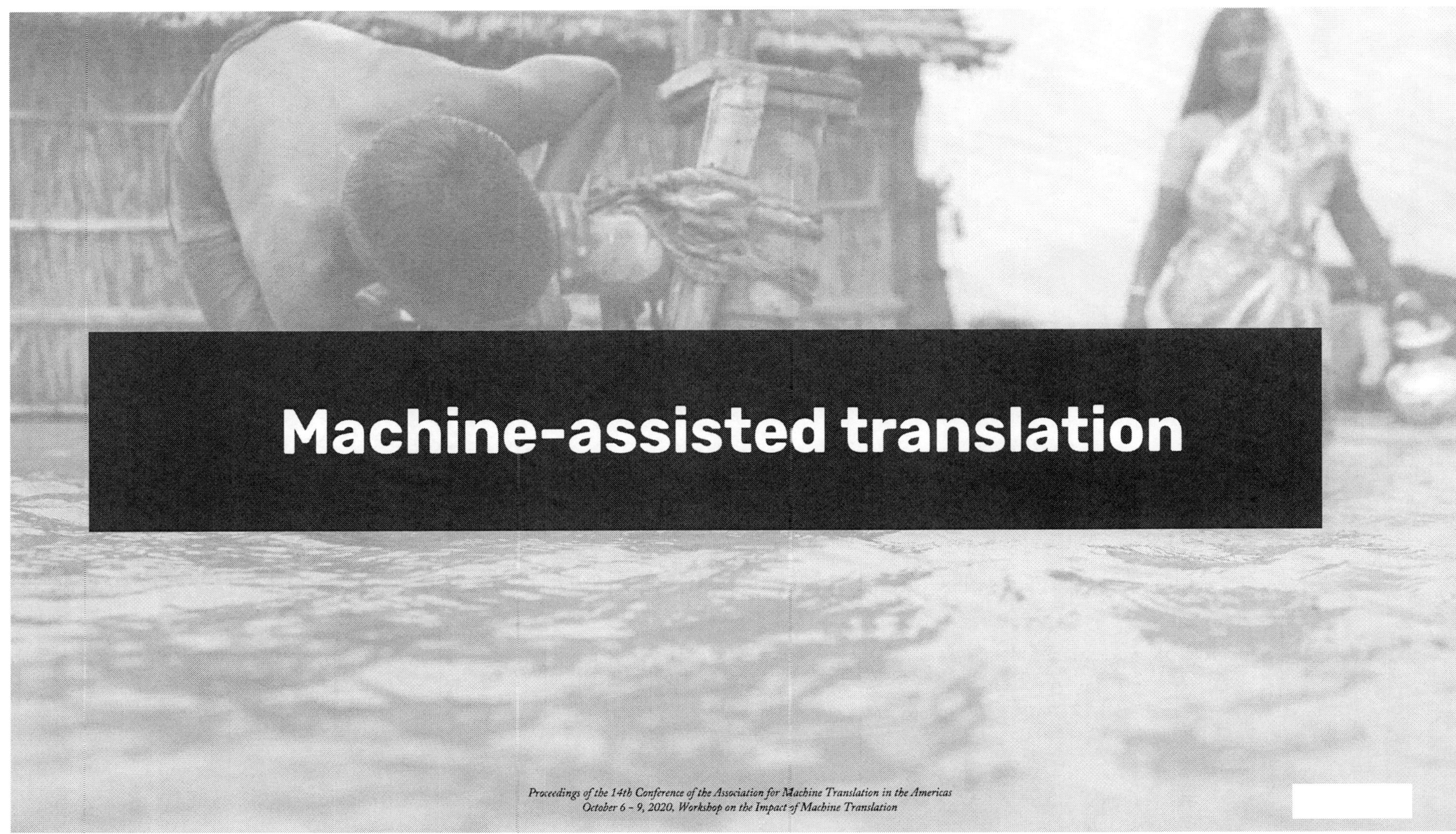

Proceedings of the 14th Conference of the Association for Machine Translation in the Americas
October 6 – 9, 2020, Workshop on the Impact of Machine Translation

Interactive Machine Translation

- Proof-of-concept by Microsoft Research India
- Assisted translation through:
  - on-the-fly hints
  - suggestions
- Alternative to post-editing

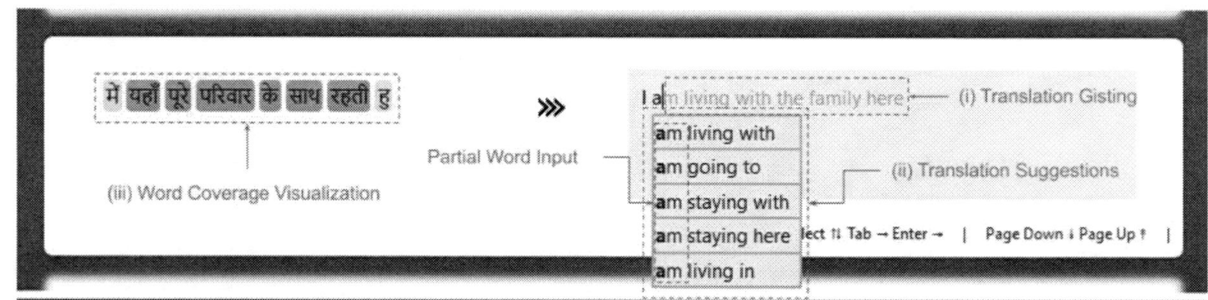

Santy, Dandapat, Choudhury, Bali. "INMT: Interactive Neural Machine Translation Prediction". EMNLP 2019

Proceedings of the 14th Conference of the Association for Machine Translation in the Americas
October 6 – 9, 2020, Workshop on the Impact of Machine Translation

Interactive Machine Translation

- Faster turnaround of document translations
  - compared to manual, and post-edited

Word Coverage and Translation Gisting	Suggestions	Keystrokes
उसी प्रकार मानसिक स्वास्थ्य के लिए ज्ञान की प्राप्ति आवश्यक है Similarly , knowledge for mental health is necessary .	Similarly , In the The knowledge Thus , So the	↓ ↓ Enter ↵
उसी प्रकार मानसिक स्वस्थ्य के लिए ज्ञान की प्राप्ति आवश्यक है **In the** same way , knowledge of knowledge is essential for mental health	same way	Tab Tab Tab Tab
उसी प्रकार मानसिक स्वस्थ्य के लिए ज्ञान की प्राप्ति आवश्यक है **In the same way , knowledge** of knowledge is essential for mental health	of knowledge is essential is necessary for mental	i
उसी प्रकार मानसिक स्वस्थ्य के लिए ज्ञान की प्राप्ति आवश्यक है **In the same way , knowledge is** essential for mental health	is essential for is necessary for is required to	Enter ↵
उसी प्रकार मानसिक स्वस्थ्य के लिए ज्ञान की प्राप्ति आवश्यक है **In the same way , knowledge is essential for mental health**		Page ↓

Santy, Dandapat, Choudhury, Bali. "INMT: Interactive Neural Machine Translation Prediction". EMNLP 2019

Proceedings of the 14th Conference of the Association for Machine Translation in the Americas
October 6 – 9, 2020, Workshop on the Impact of Machine Translation

Interactive Machine Translation

- Faster turnaround of document translations
  - compared to manual, and post-edited
- Human-machine collaboration to best leverage low-resource models

	Data Size	0%	10%	20%	40%
bn-en	1.1M	25.31	27.54	35.68	54.03
hi-en	1.5M	40.64	42.06	47.90	62.18
ml-en	897K	19.76	21.95	29.84	49.88
ta-en	428K	18.71	20.90	27.05	44.55
te-en	104K	11.92	14.57	21.17	41.98

Table 2: Multi-BLEU Score with x% of partial input

Santy, Dandapat, Choudhury, Bali. "INMT: Interactive Neural Machine Translation Prediction". EMNLP 2019

Proceedings of the 14th Conference of the Association for Machine Translation in the Americas
October 6 - 9, 2020, Workshop on the Impact of Machine Translation

Interactive Machine Translation

- Faster turnaround of document translations
  - compared to manual, and post-edited
- Human-machine collaboration to best leverage low-resource models
- Boost for hard-to-source languages
  - for translation by non-experts
  - for crowdsourced data collection

Proceedings of the 14th Conference of the Association for Machine Translation in the Americas
October 6 - 9, 2020, Workshop on the Impact of Machine Translation

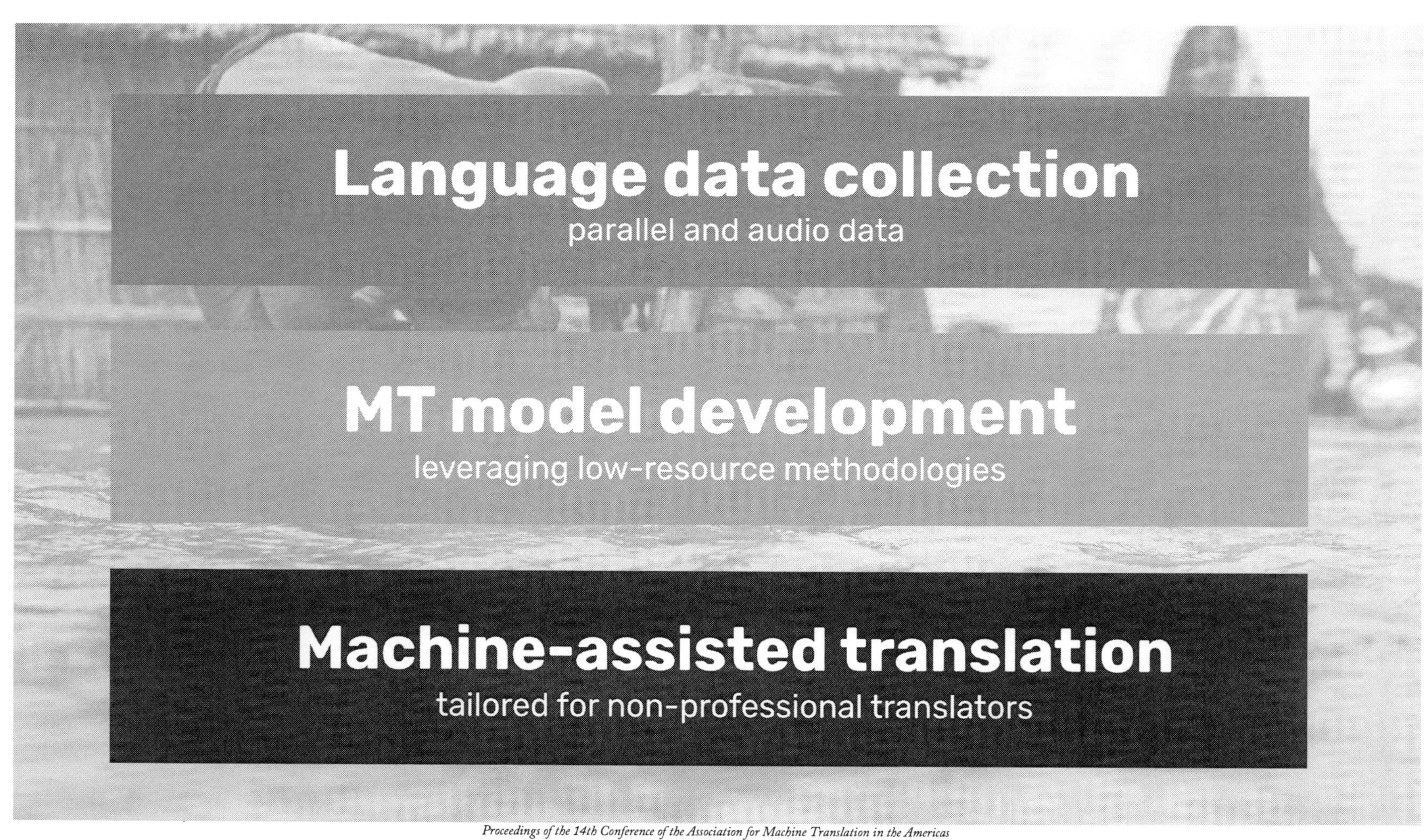

Proceedings of the 14th Conference of the Association for Machine Translation in the Americas
October 6 - 9, 2020, Workshop on the Impact of Machine Translation

Proceedings of the 14th Conference of the Association for Machine Translation in the Americas
October 6 - 9, 2020, Workshop on the Impact of Machine Translation

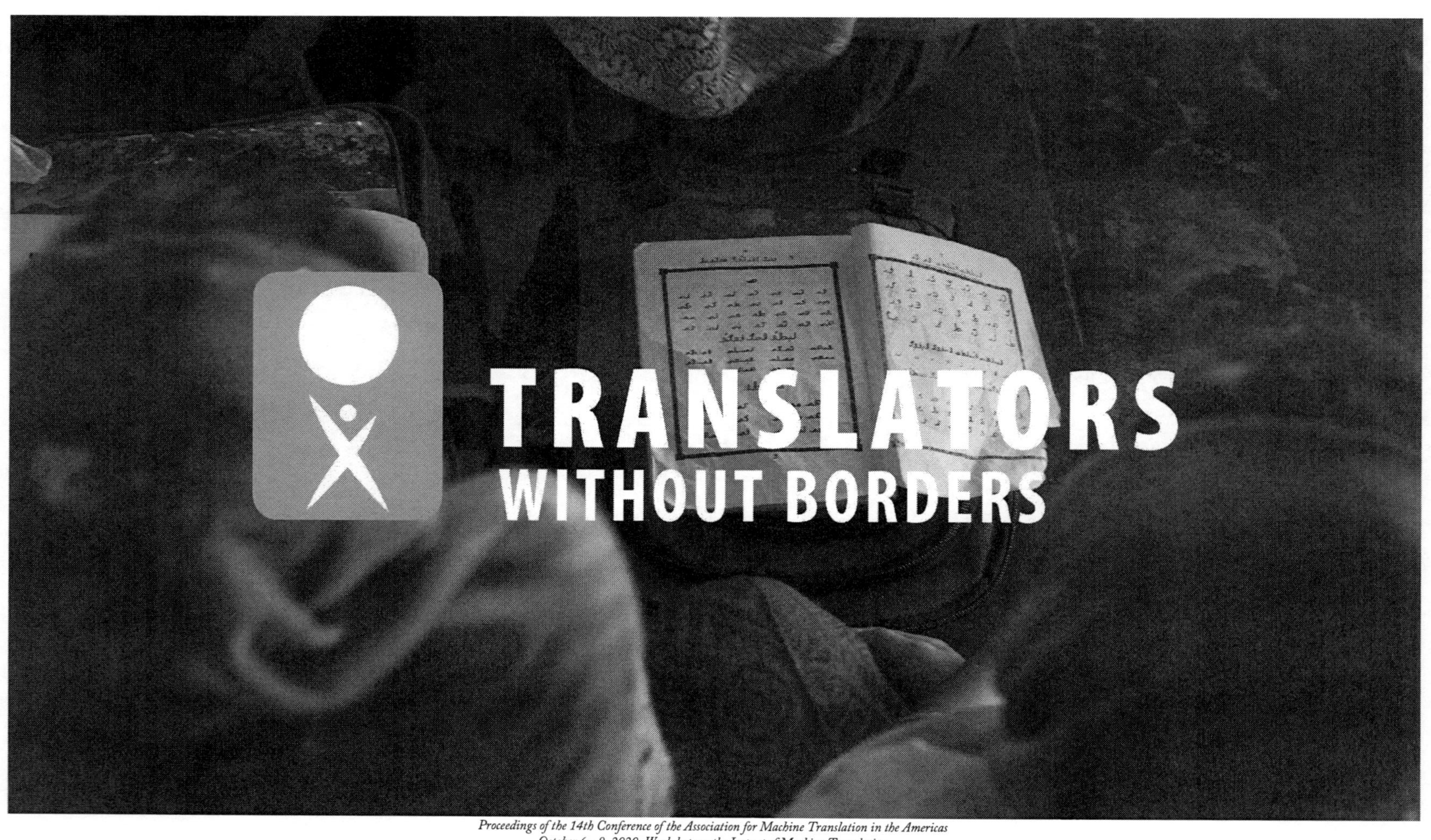

Proceedings of the 14th Conference of the Association for Machine Translation in the Americas
October 6 – 9, 2020, Workshop on the Impact of Machine Translation

MT for humanitarian impact

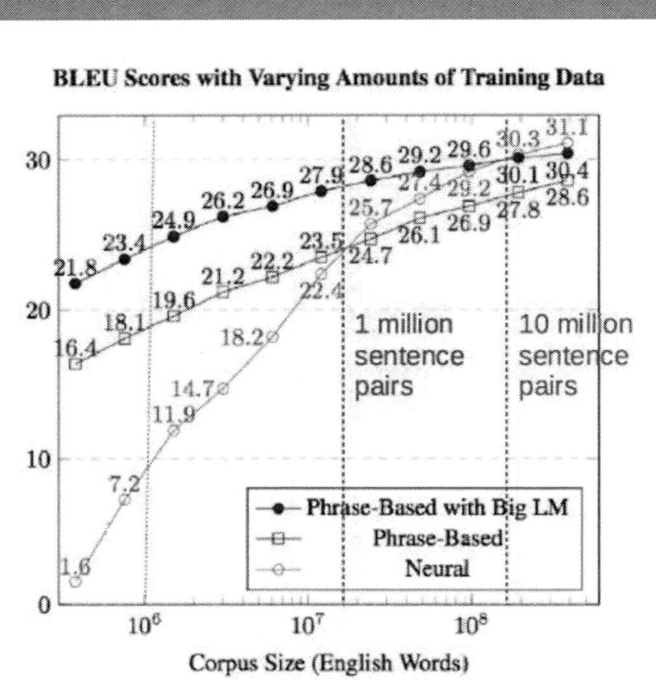

Diagram edited from Koehn and Knowles (2017)

Proceedings of the 14th Conference of the Association for Machine Translation in the Americas
October 6 – 9, 2020, Workshop on the Impact of Machine Translation

Tigrinya NMT

SMT on 7 Ethiopian languages (Teferra Abate et al., 2018)

Parallel corpus of 300+ languages from *jw.org* (Agić and Vulić, 2019)

Available on OPUS repository (Tiedemann, 2012)

TWB's translation memories

	Ethiopian corpus	JW300	Bible-uedin	Global voices	GNOME	Tanzil	TWB	**TOTAL**
Amharic	66K	722K	61K	1.6K	57K	94K	-	1M
Ge'ez	11K	-	-	-	-	-	-	11K
Tigrinya	36K	400K	-	-	-	-	2.5K	439K

Dataset sizes (#sentences) for Ge'ez scripted languages

Data   MT   Application

Proceedings of the 14th Conference of the Association for Machine Translation in the Americas
October 6 - 9, 2020, Workshop on the Impact of Machine Translation

Gamayun kits

Language	kit-5k	Audio	Language tech development goals
Hausa	✓	⚙	Machine-assisted data collection
Kanuri	✓	⚙	Machine-assisted data collection
Kurmanji Kurdish		⚙	Machine-assisted survey transcription
Rohingya	✓	✓	Glossary with voice search
Coastal Swahili	✓	✓	MT and audio keyword detection
Congolese Swahili	✓		Interactive neural machine translation
Tigrinya	⚙		Interactive neural machine translation

Data > MT > Application

Proceedings of the 14th Conference of the Association for Machine Translation in the Americas
October 6 – 9, 2020, Workshop on the Impact of Machine Translation

Interactive Machine Translation

How?

- Constrained decoding on top of *OpenNMT* models
- Latest development: BPE integration
- Work-in-progress: Evaluation with our volunteer translators

Demo

- https://microsoft.github.io/inmt/

Data | MT | Application

Proceedings of the 14th Conference of the Association for Machine Translation in the Americas
October 6 – 9, 2020, Workshop on the Impact of Machine Translation

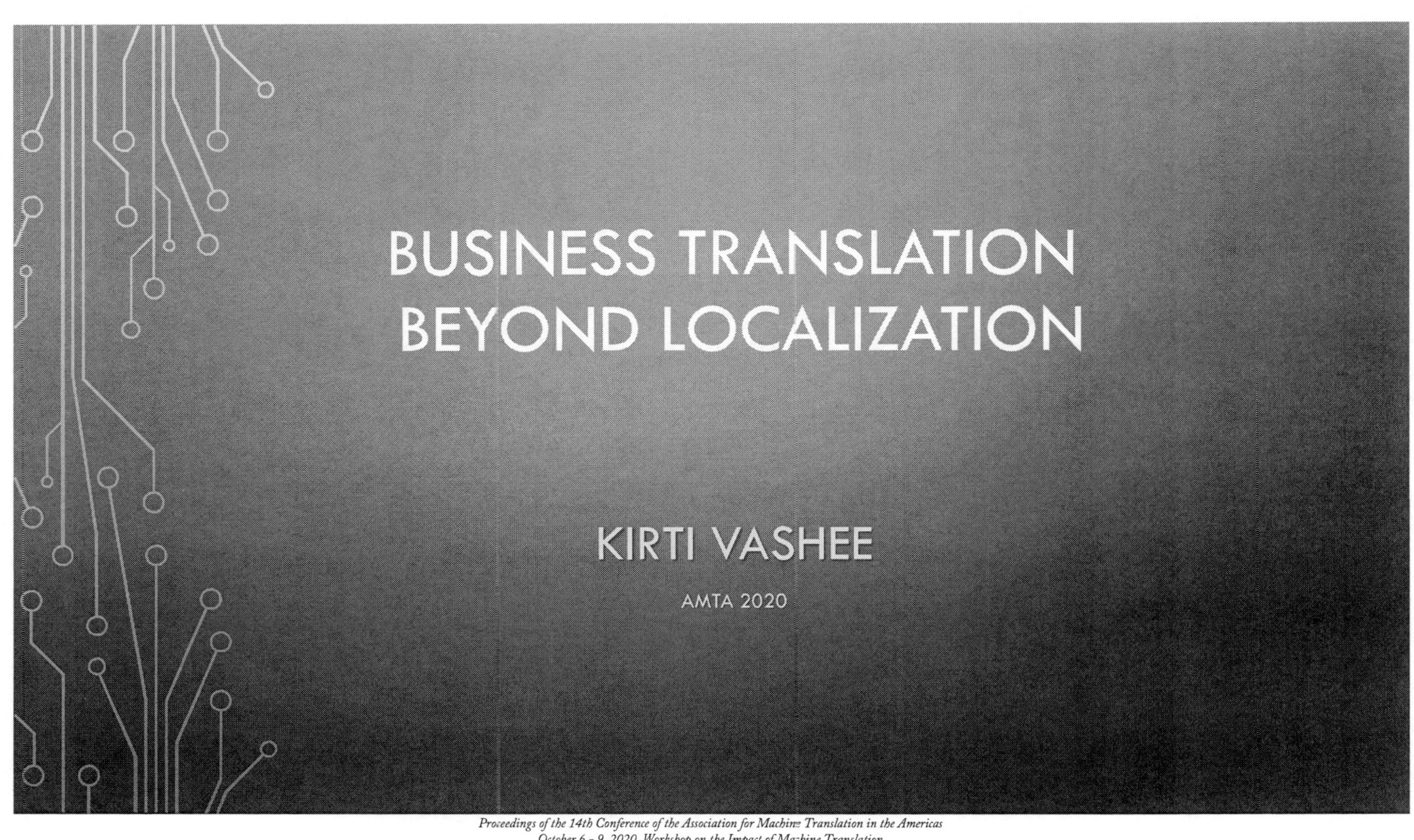

Proceedings of the 14th Conference of the Association for Machine Translation in the Americas
October 6 - 9, 2020, Workshop on the Impact of Machine Translation

Proceedings of the 14th Conference of the Association for Machine Translation in the Americas
October 6 - 9, 2020, Workshop on the Impact of Machine Translation

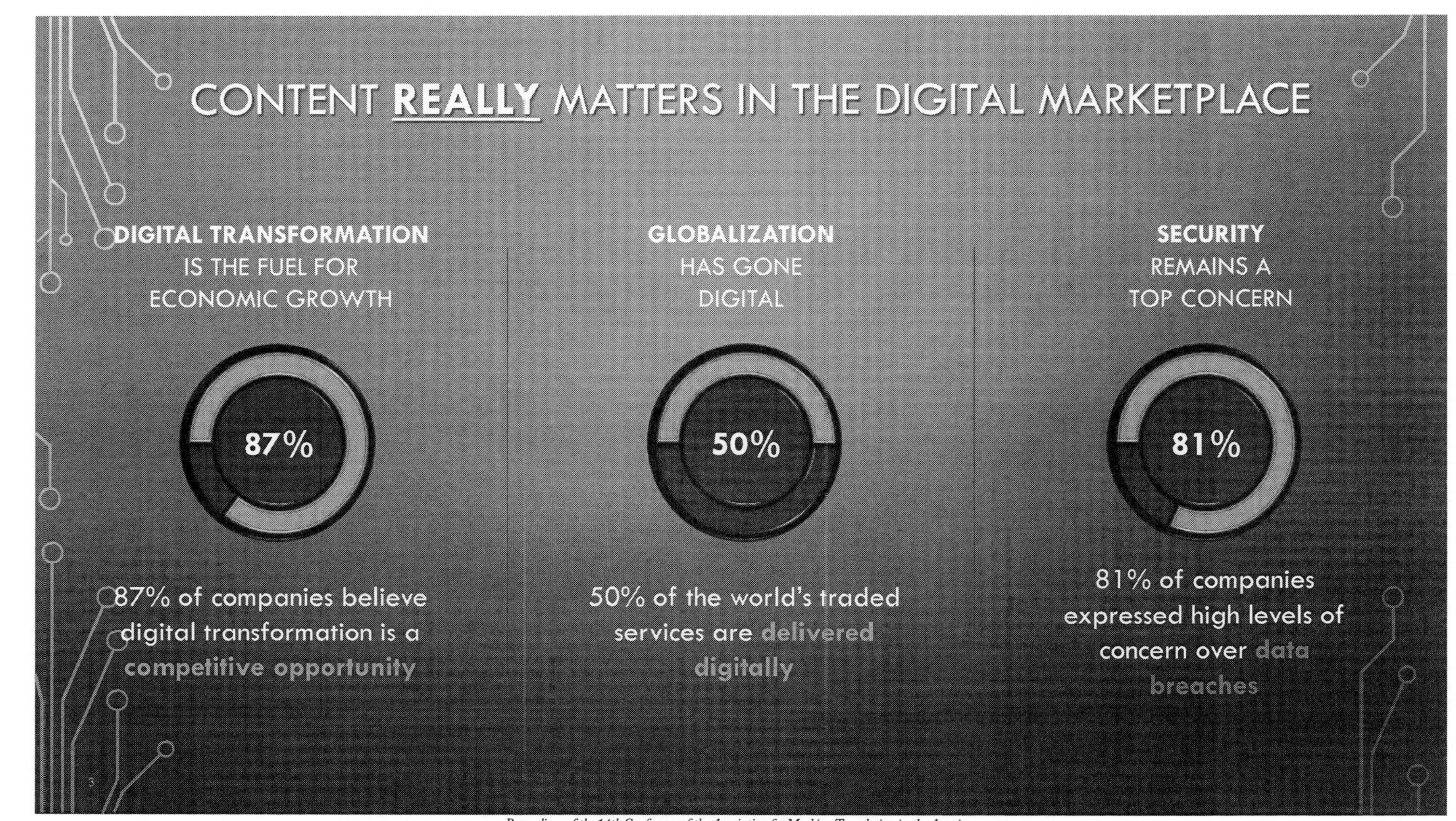

Proceedings of the 14th Conference of the Association for Machine Translation in the Americas
October 6 – 9, 2020, Workshop on the Impact of Machine Translation

Proceedings of the 14th Conference of the Association for Machine Translation in the Americas
October 6 - 9, 2020, Workshop on the Impact of Machine Translation

Large volumes of multilingual data flows have created
a huge and growing need for rapid translation

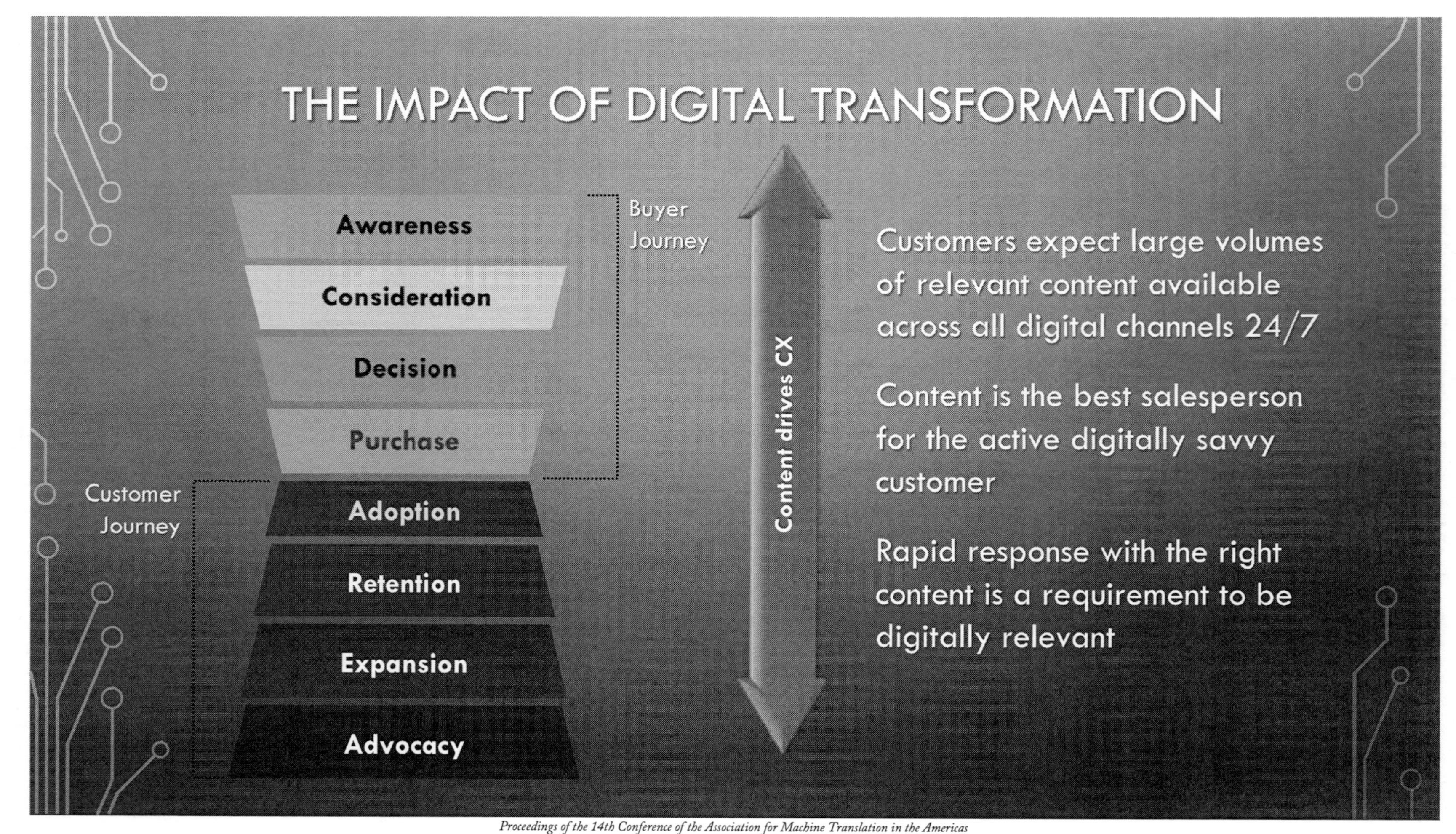

THE IMPACT OF DIGITAL TRANSFORMATION
Awareness
Consideration
Decision
Purchase
Adoption
Retention
Expansion
Advocacy
Buyer Journey
Customer Journey
Content drives CX
Customers expect large volumes of relevant content available across all digital channels 24/7
Content is the best salesperson for the active digitally savvy customer
Rapid response with the right content is a requirement to be digitally relevant

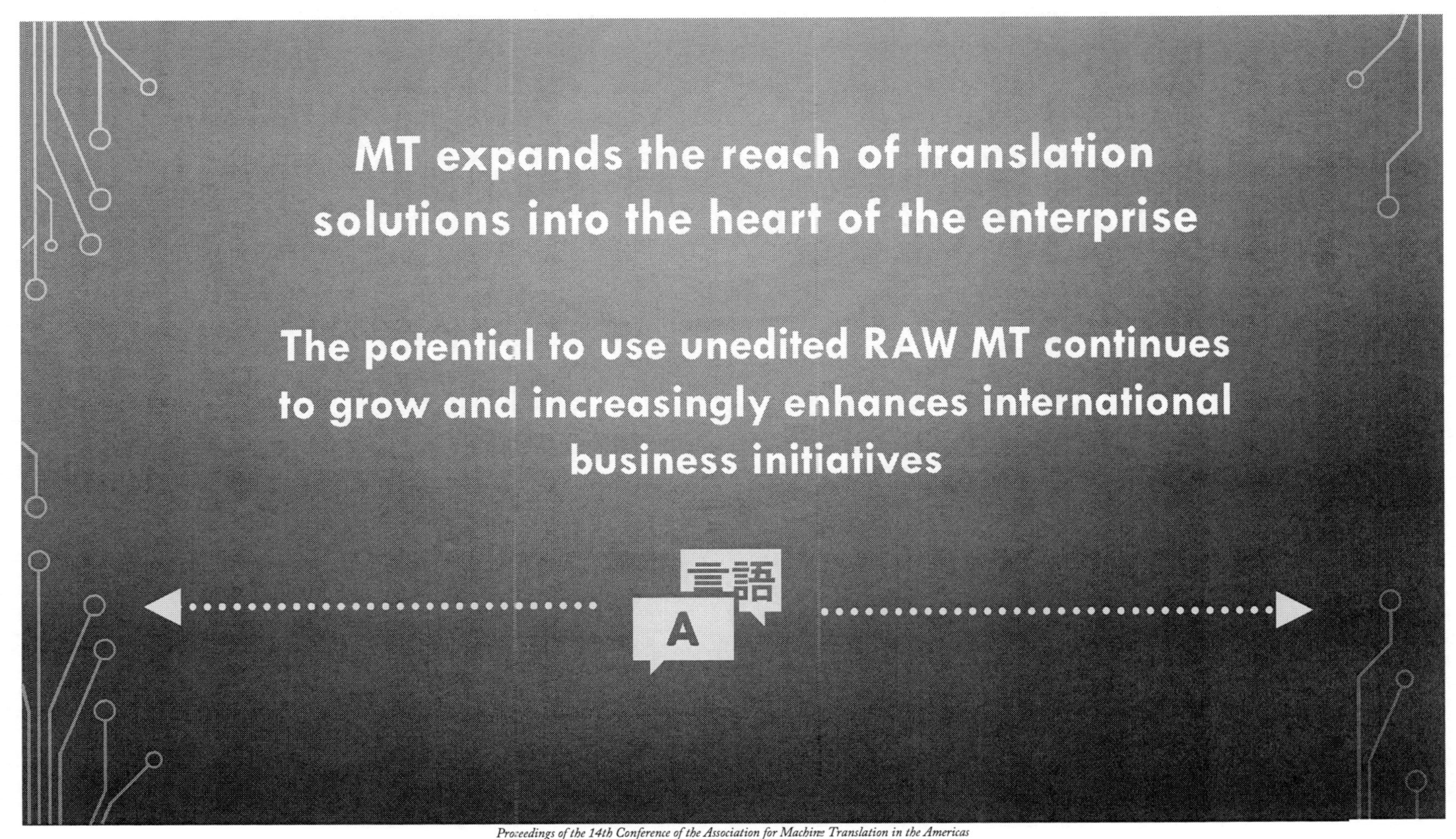

MT expands the reach of translation solutions into the heart of the enterprise
The potential to use unedited RAW MT continues to grow and increasingly enhances international business initiatives
言語
A

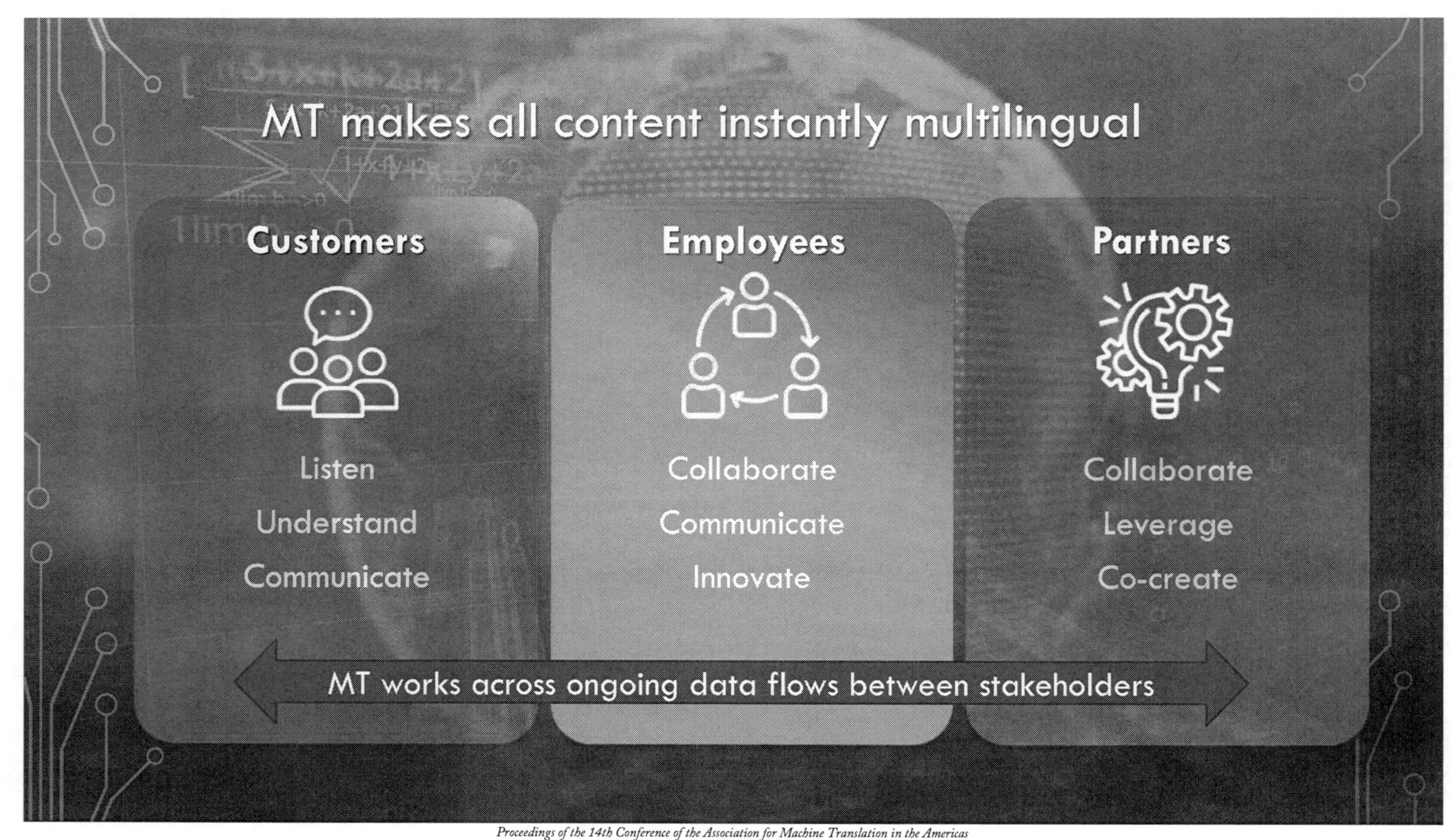

Proceedings of the 14th Conference of the Association for Machine Translation in the Americas
October 6 – 9, 2020, Workshop on the Impact of Machine Translation

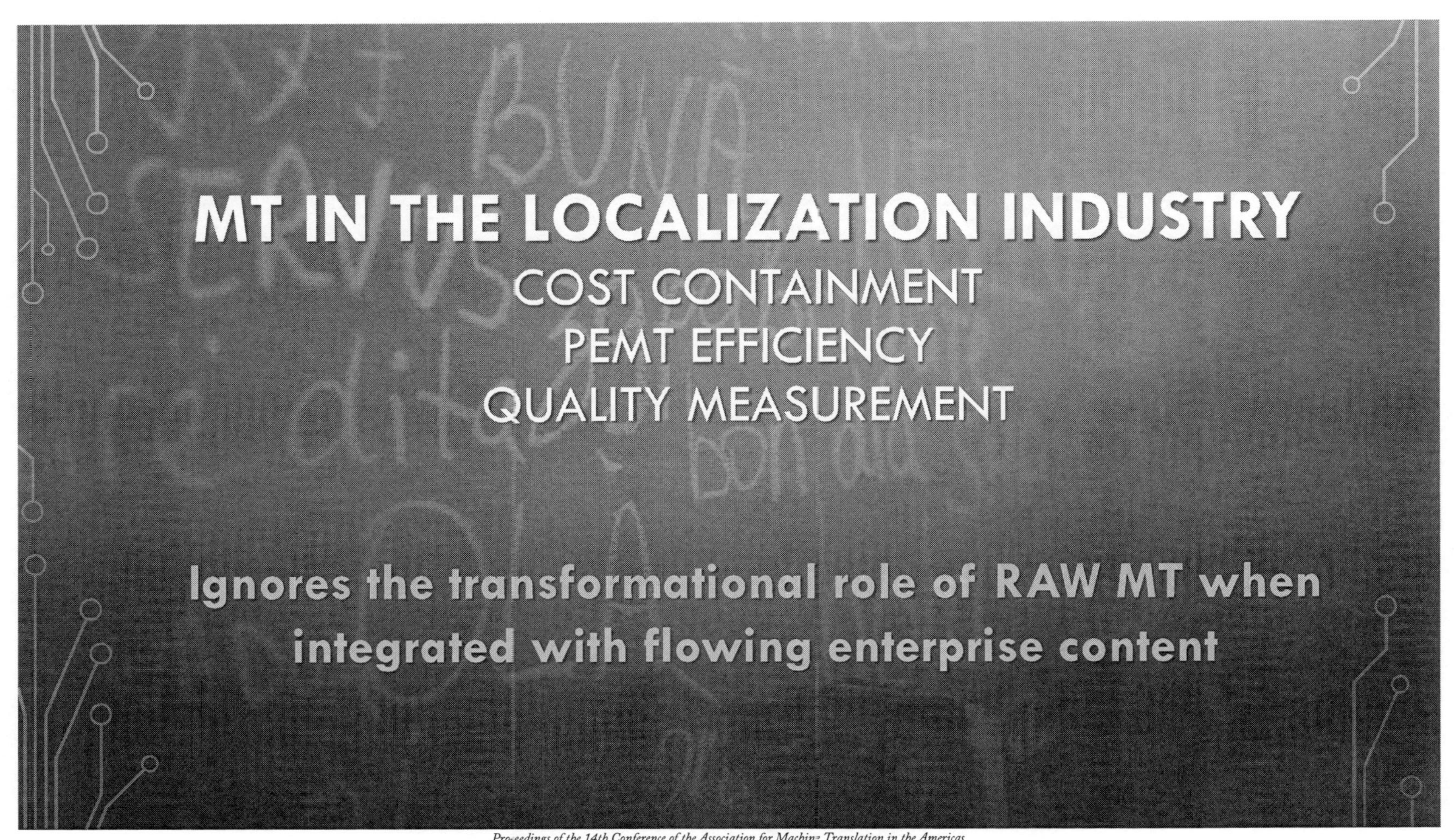

Proceedings of the 14th Conference of the Association for Machine Translation in the Americas
October 6 - 9, 2020, Workshop on the Impact of Machine Translation

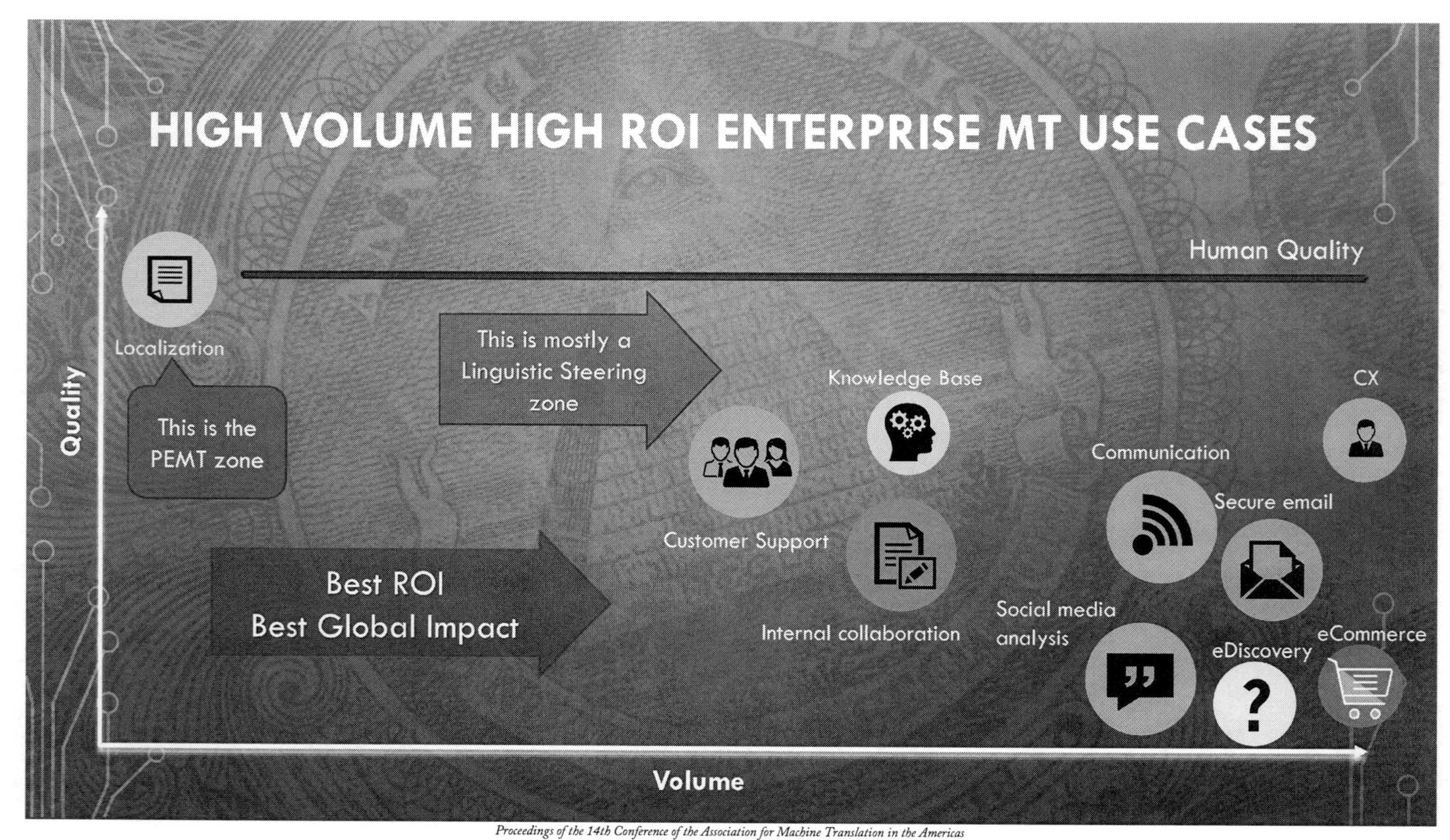

Proceedings of the 14th Conference of the Association for Machine Translation in the Americas
October 6 - 9, 2020, Workshop on the Impact of Machine Translation

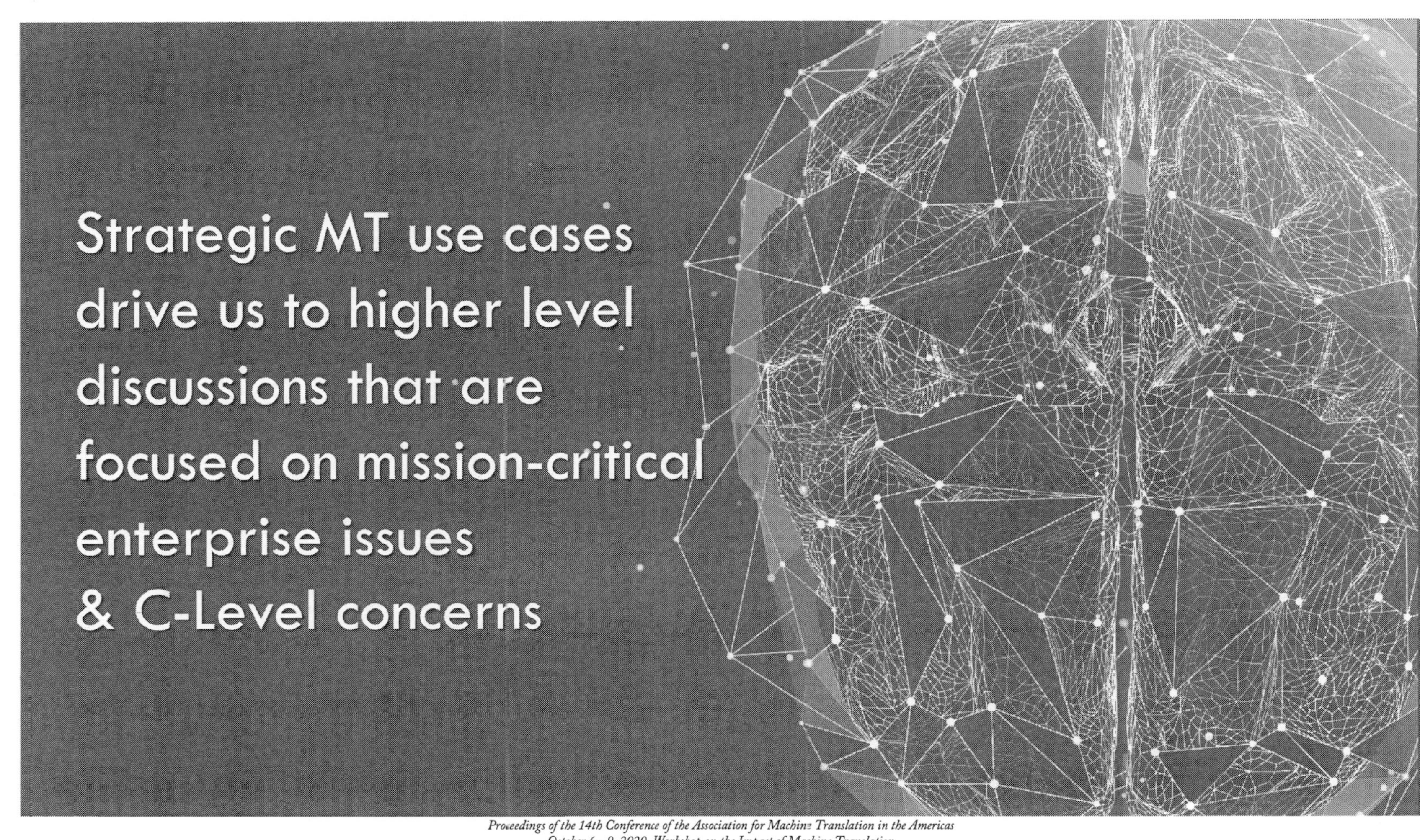

Proceedings of the 14th Conference of the Association for Machine Translation in the Americas
October 6 - 9, 2020, Workshop on the Impact of Machine Translation

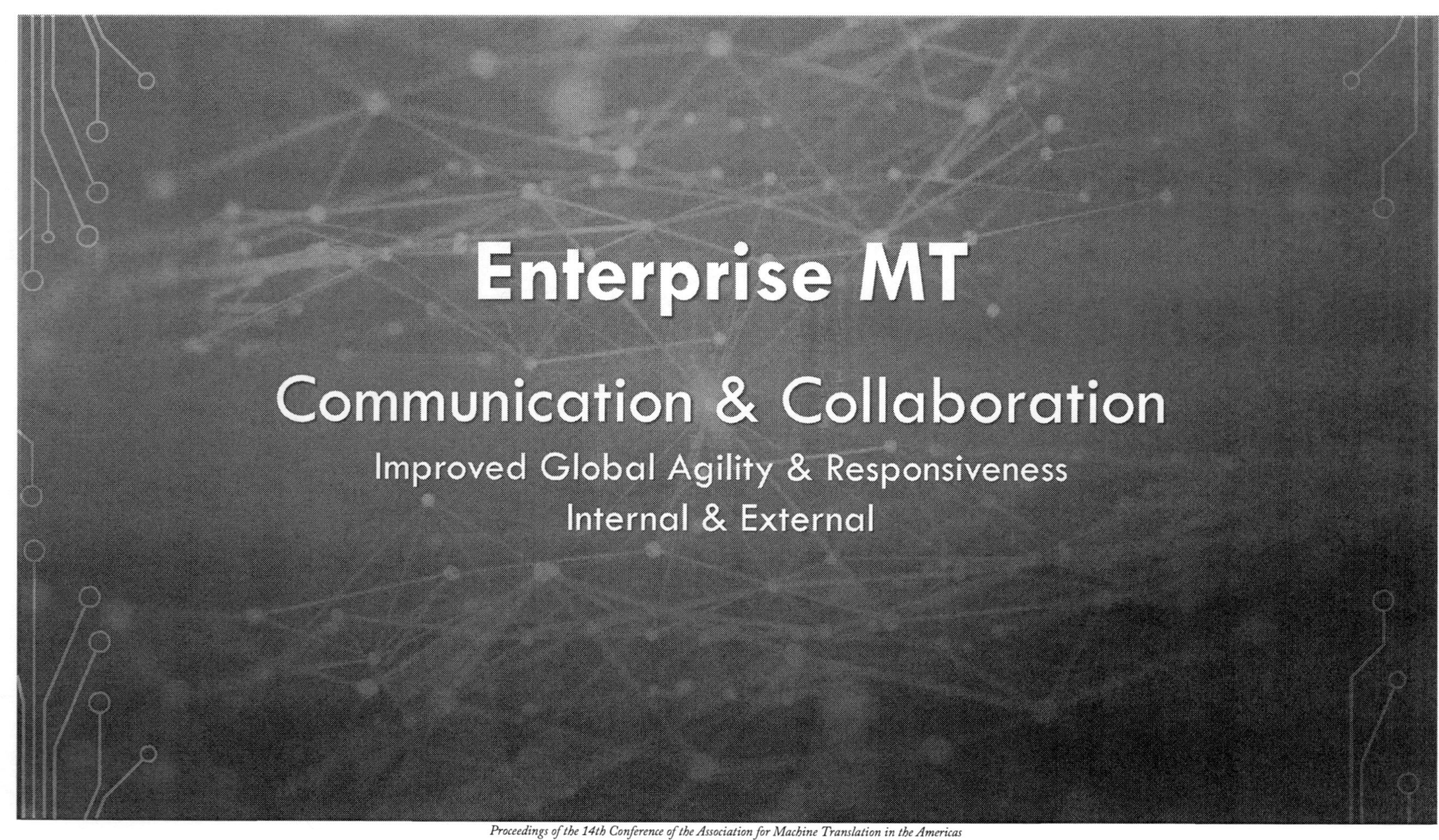

Proceedings of the 14th Conference of the Association for Machine Translation in the Americas
October 6 – 9, 2020, Workshop on the Impact of Machine Translation

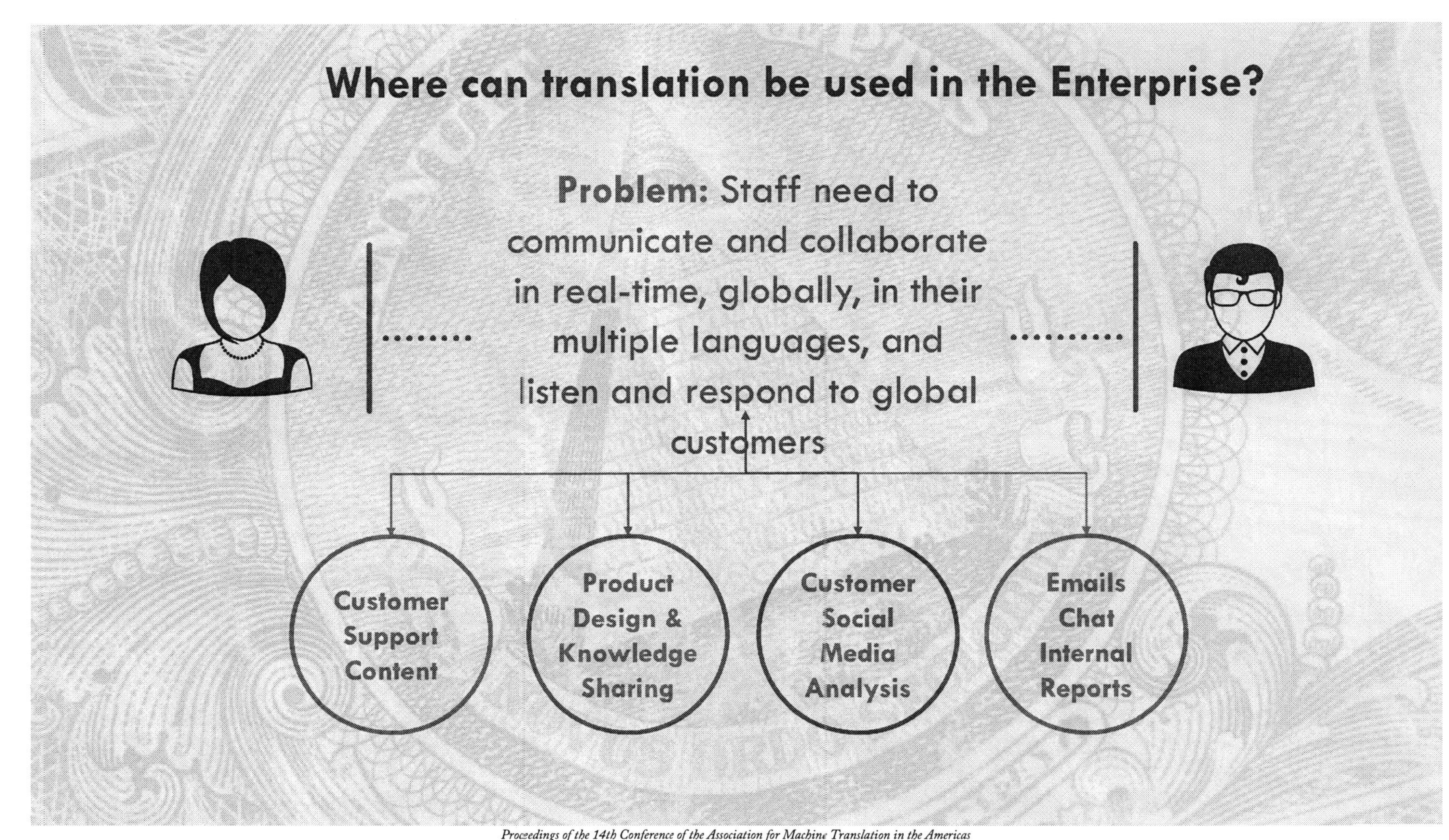

Proceedings of the 14th Conference of the Association for Machine Translation in the Americas
October 6 - 9, 2020, Workshop on the Impact of Machine Translation

Content drives revenue and is critical to overall customer experience

Proceedings of the 14th Conference of the Association for Machine Translation in the Americas
October 6 - 9, 2020, Workshop on the Impact of Machine Translation

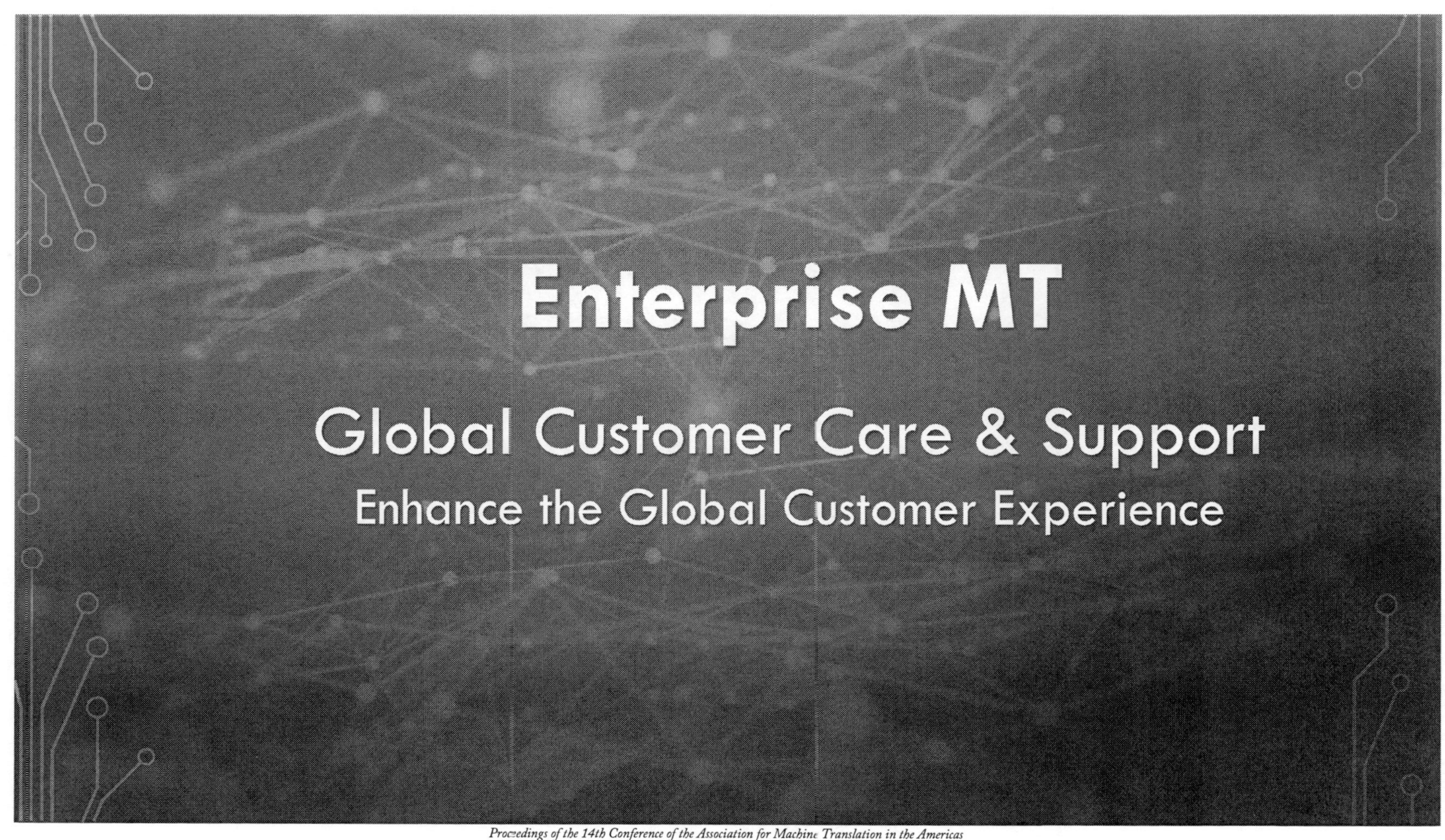

Proceedings of the 14th Conference of the Association for Machine Translation in the Americas
October 6 - 9, 2020, Workshop on the Impact of Machine Translation

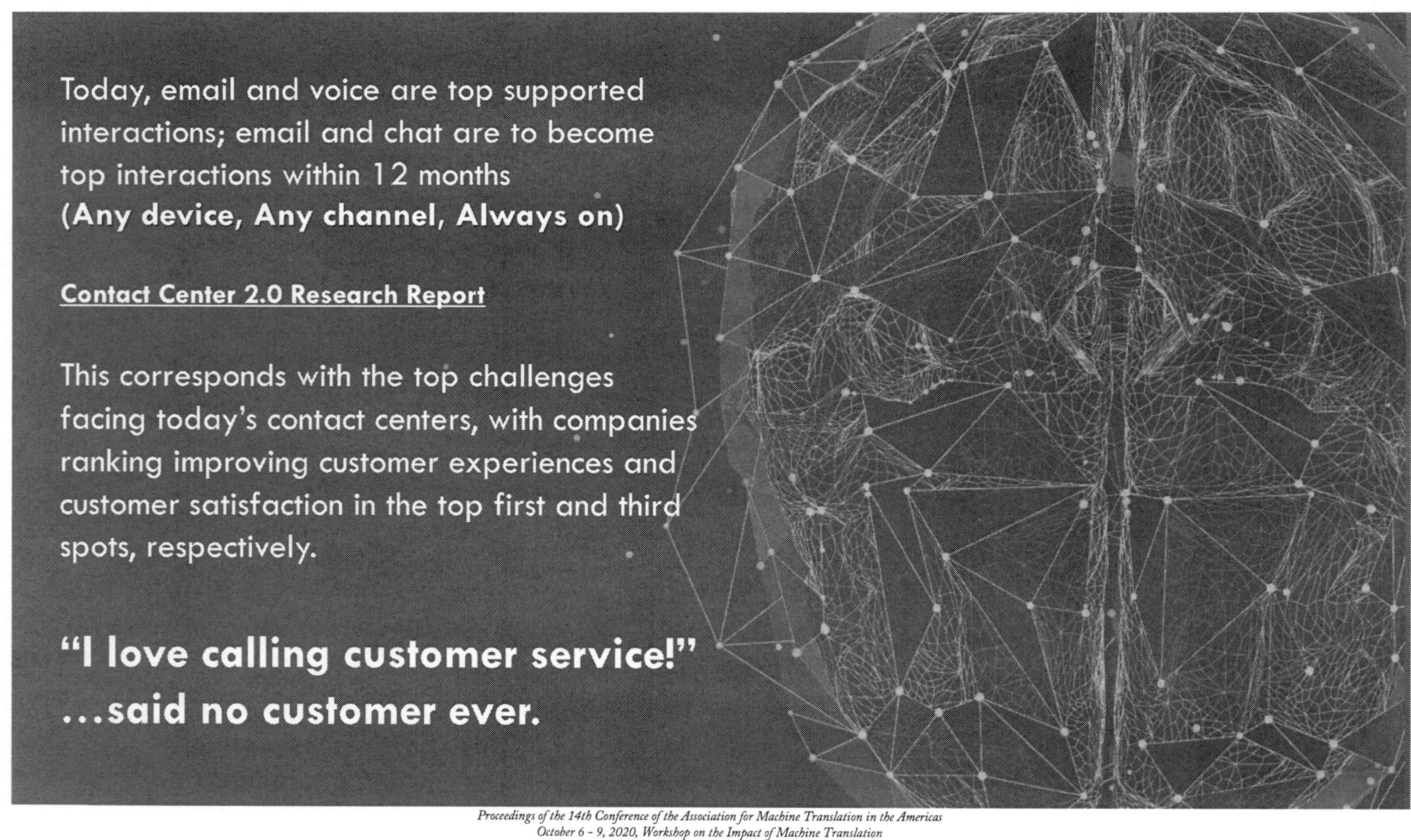

Proceedings of the 14th Conference of the Association for Machine Translation in the Americas
October 6 - 9, 2020, Workshop on the Impact of Machine Translation

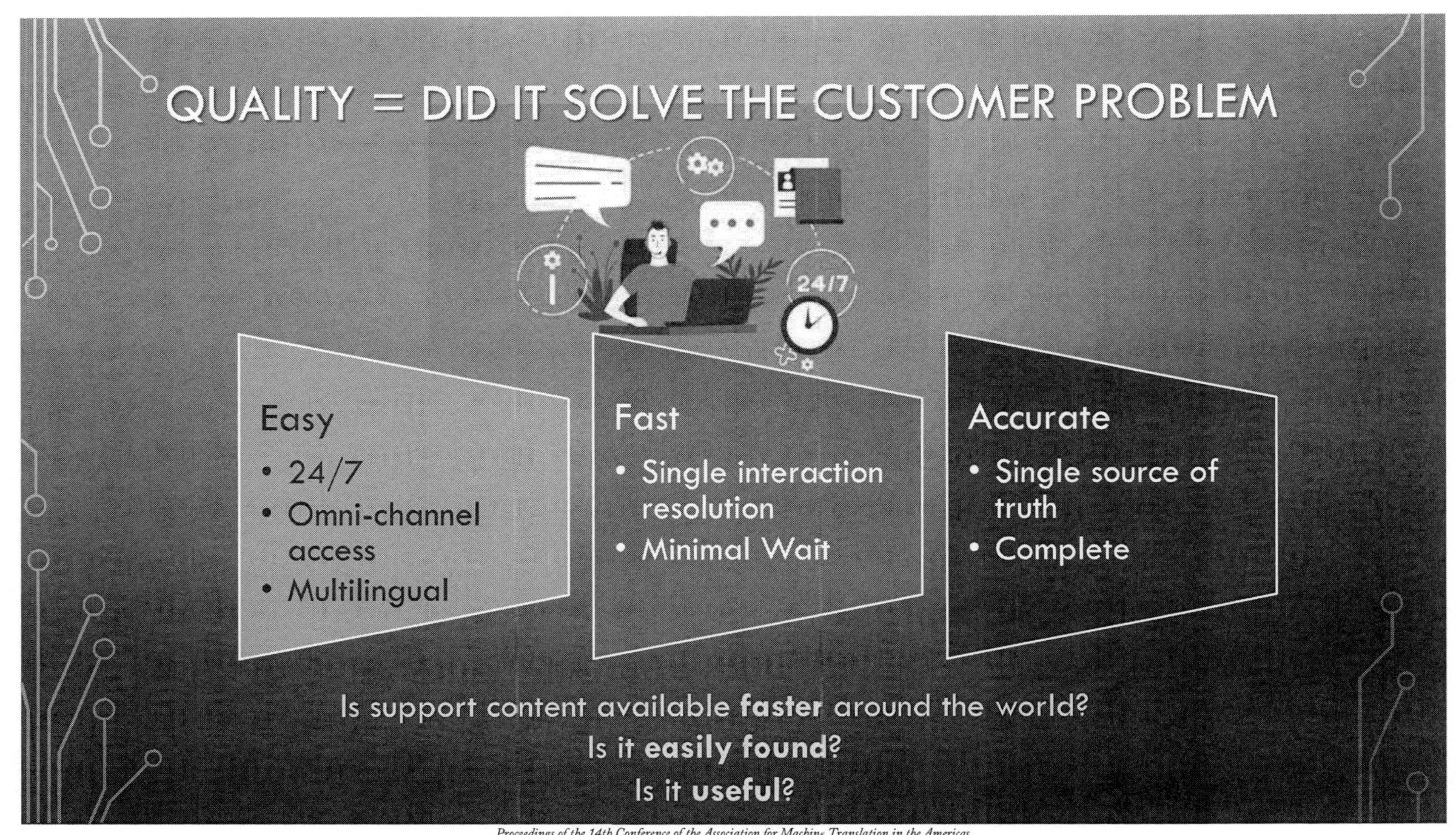

Proceedings of the 14th Conference of the Association for Machine Translation in the Americas
October 6 – 9, 2020, Workshop on the Impact of Machine Translation

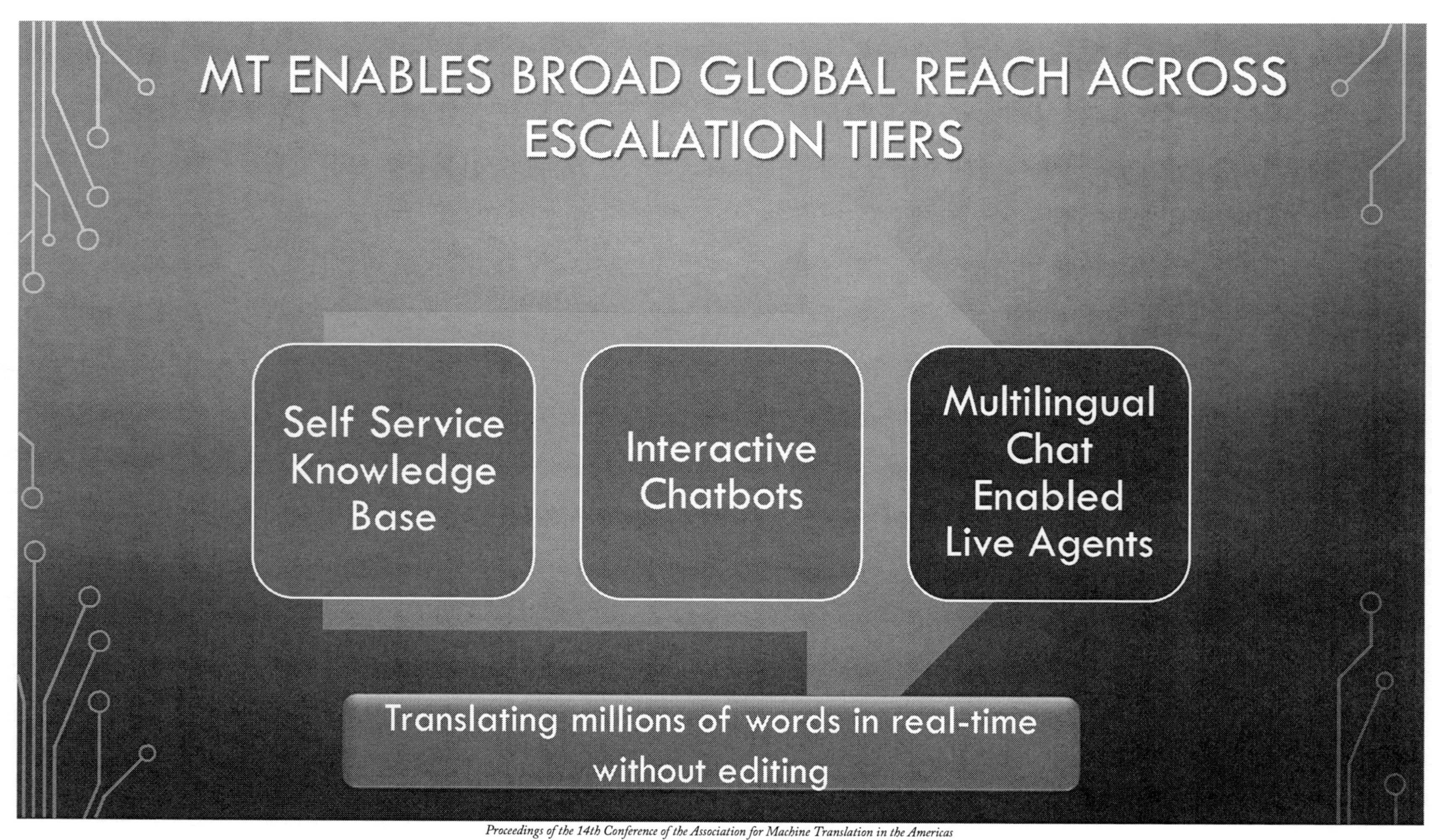

Proceedings of the 14th Conference of the Association for Machine Translation in the Americas
October 6 - 9, 2020, Workshop on the Impact of Machine Translation

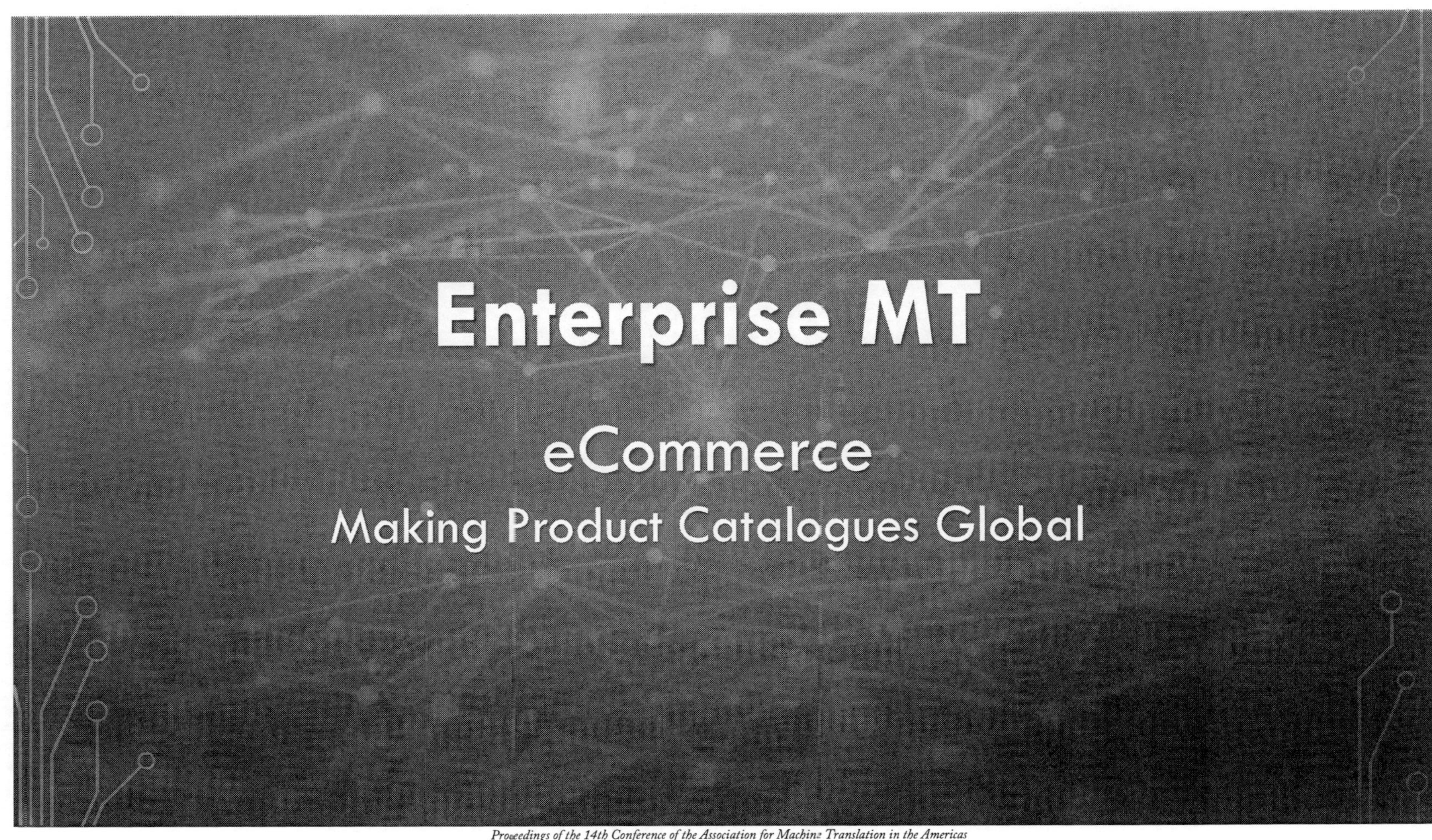

Proceedings of the 14th Conference of the Association for Machine Translation in the Americas
October 6 - 9, 2020, Workshop on the Impact of Machine Translation

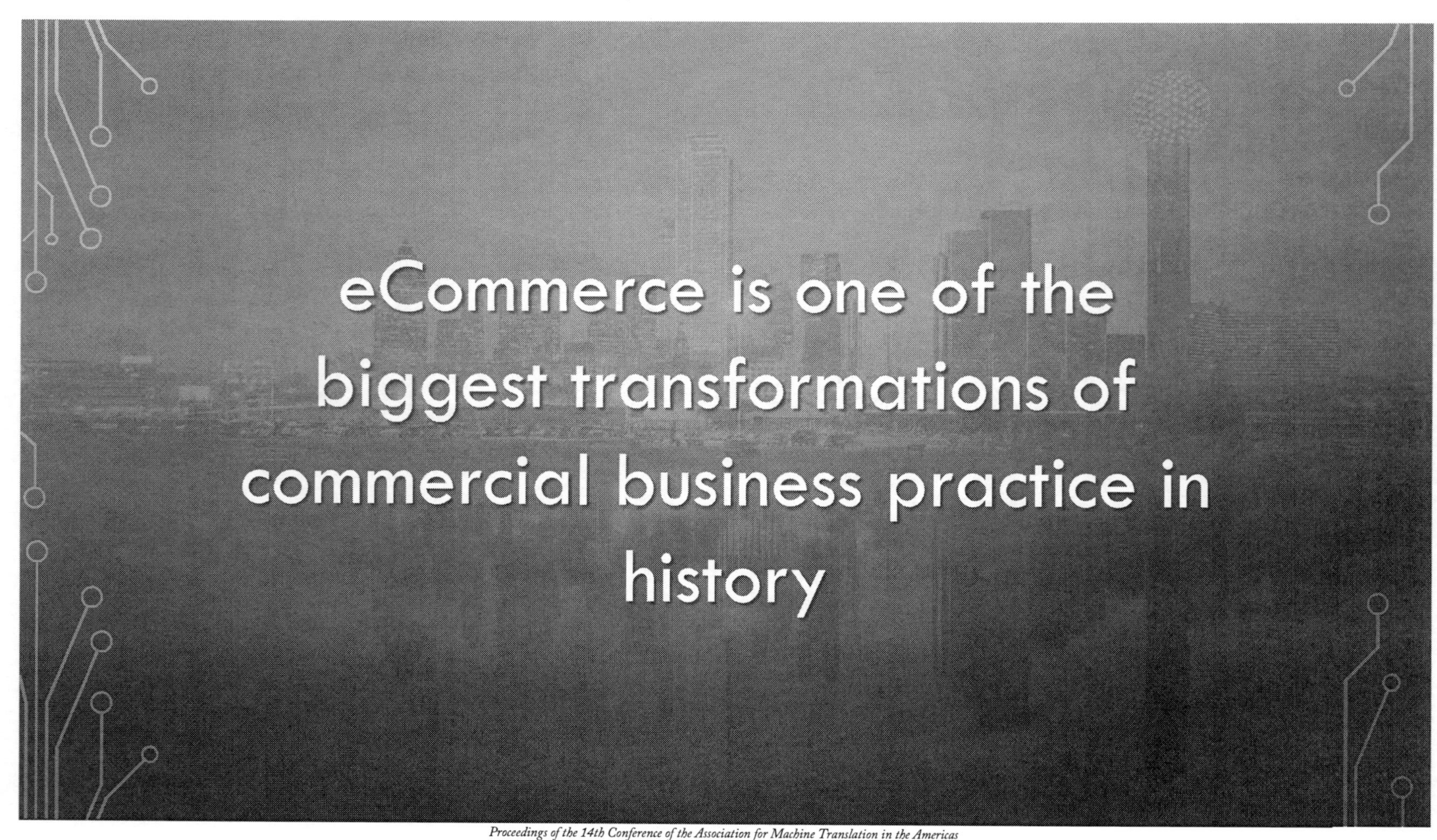

eCommerce is one of the
biggest transformations of
commercial business practice in
history

Multilingual eCommerce
Online eCommerce Product Portfolios
Allow rapid expansion of global buyers with multilingual Product Catalogues
Rapidly expand global customer base
Expand into global markets in a cost effective way
Product Title
Product Description
Global User Reviews
Buyer <> Seller Communications
Transaction Related Pricing, Policies & Procedures

Proceedings of the 14th Conference of the Association for Machine Translation in the Americas
October 6 - 9, 2020, Workshop on the Impact of Machine Translation

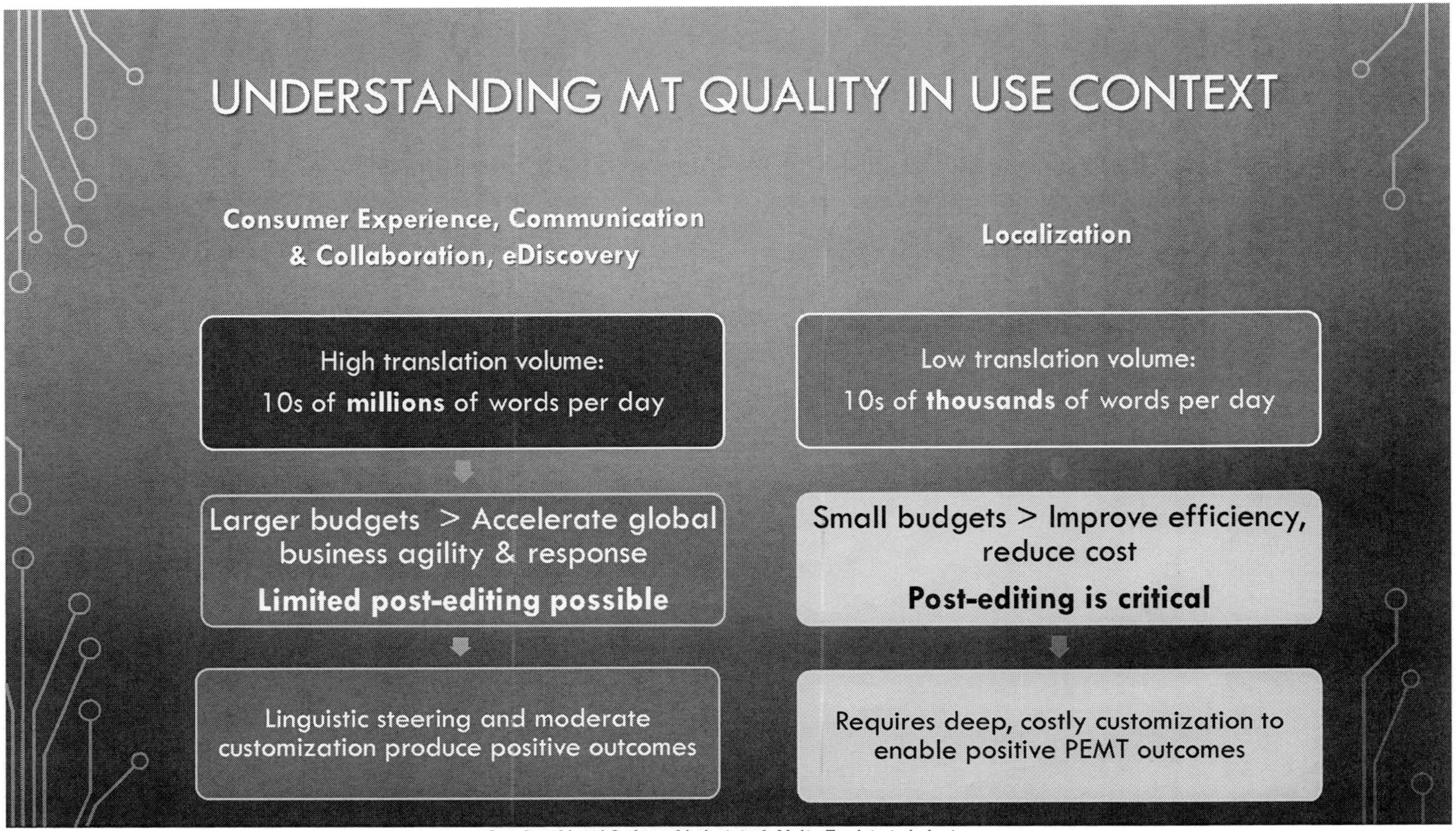
UNDERSTANDING MT QUALITY IN USE CONTEXT
Consumer Experience, Communication & Collaboration, eDiscovery
Localization
High translation volume:
10s of millions of words per day
Low translation volume:
10s of thousands of words per day
Larger budgets > Accelerate global business agility & response
Limited post-editing possible
Small budgets > Improve efficiency, reduce cost
Post-editing is critical
Linguistic steering and moderate customization produce positive outcomes
Requires deep, costly customization to enable positive PEMT outcomes

Proceedings of the 14th Conference of the Association for Machine Translation in the Americas
October 6 - 9, 2020, Workshop on the Impact of Machine Translation

Proceedings of the 14th Conference of the Association for Machine Translation in the Americas
October 6 - 9, 2020, Workshop on the Impact of Machine Translation

The Translation Opportunity Beyond Localization

Develop large-scale translation ability

- Understand Linguistic Steering vs PEMT
- Understand how to solve dynamic, big-data translation challenges
- Understand corpus level linguistic profiling
- Identify internal and external high value content

Leverage multilingual content production

Proceedings of the 14th Conference of the Association for Machine Translation in the Americas
October 6 - 9, 2020, Workshop on the Impact of Machine Translation

Proceedings of the 14th Conference of the Association for Machine Translation in the Americas
October 6 - 9, 2020, Workshop on the Impact of Machine Translation

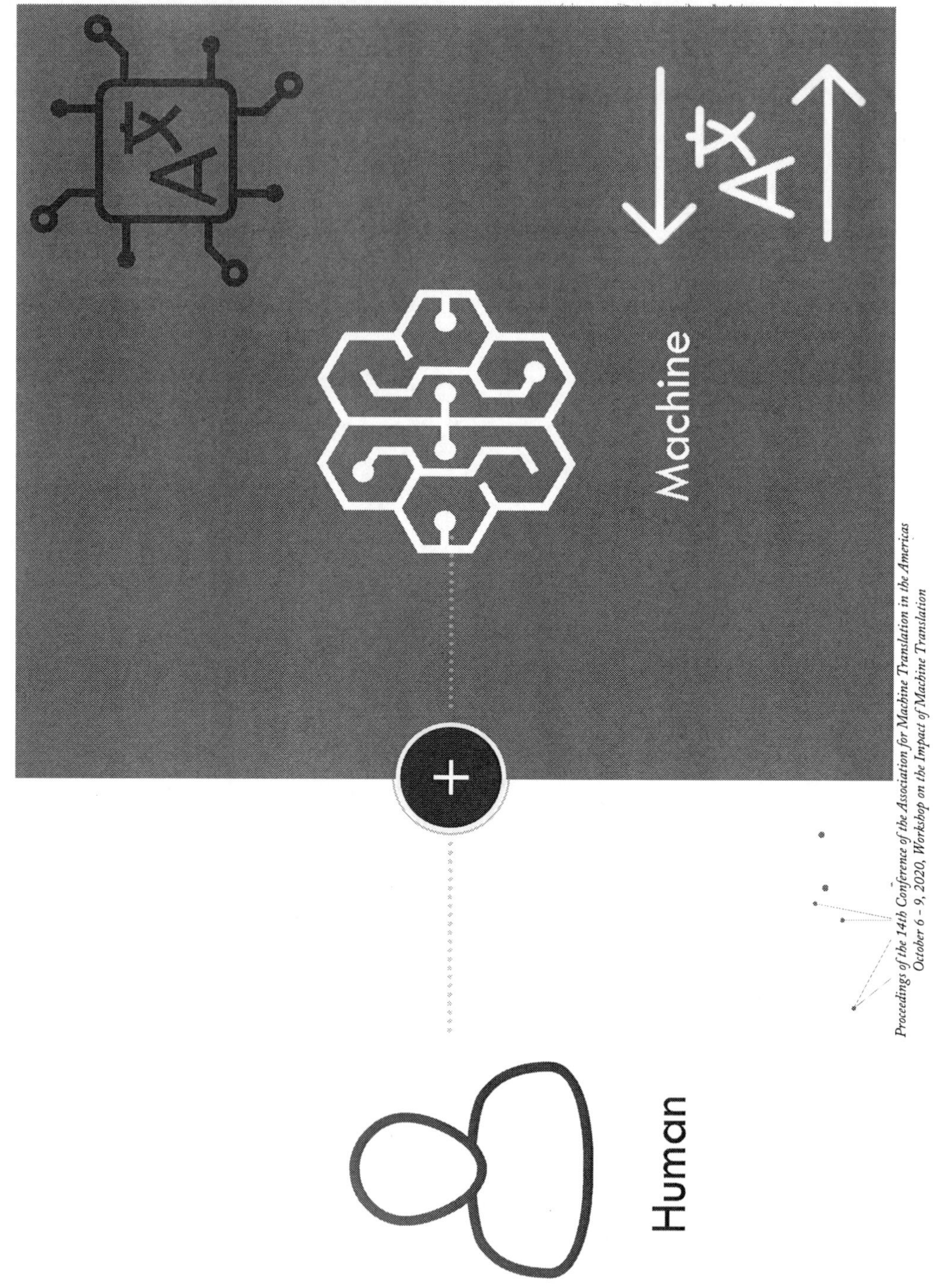

Proceedings of the 14th Conference of the Association for Machine Translation in the Americas
October 6 – 9, 2020, Workshop on the Impact of Machine Translation

Proceedings of the 14th Conference of the Association for Machine Translation in the Americas
October 6 - 9, 2020, Workshop on the Impact of Machine Translation

Predictive Translation Memory in the Wild: A Study of Interactive Machine Translation Use on Lilt

Geza Kovacs
geza@lilt.com

Proceedings of the 14th Conference of the Association for Machine Translation in the Americas
October 6 - 9, 2020, Workshop on the Impact of Machine Translation

Why Interactive MT?

- **Problem**: MT systems cannot guarantee correctness. Errors can affect business reputation

- A **human in the loop** is needed to ensure correctness

- **Interactive MT**: optimizing interactions between the translator and MT system

Proceedings of the 14th Conference of the Association for Machine Translation in the Americas
October 6 - 9, 2020, Workshop on the Impact of Machine Translation

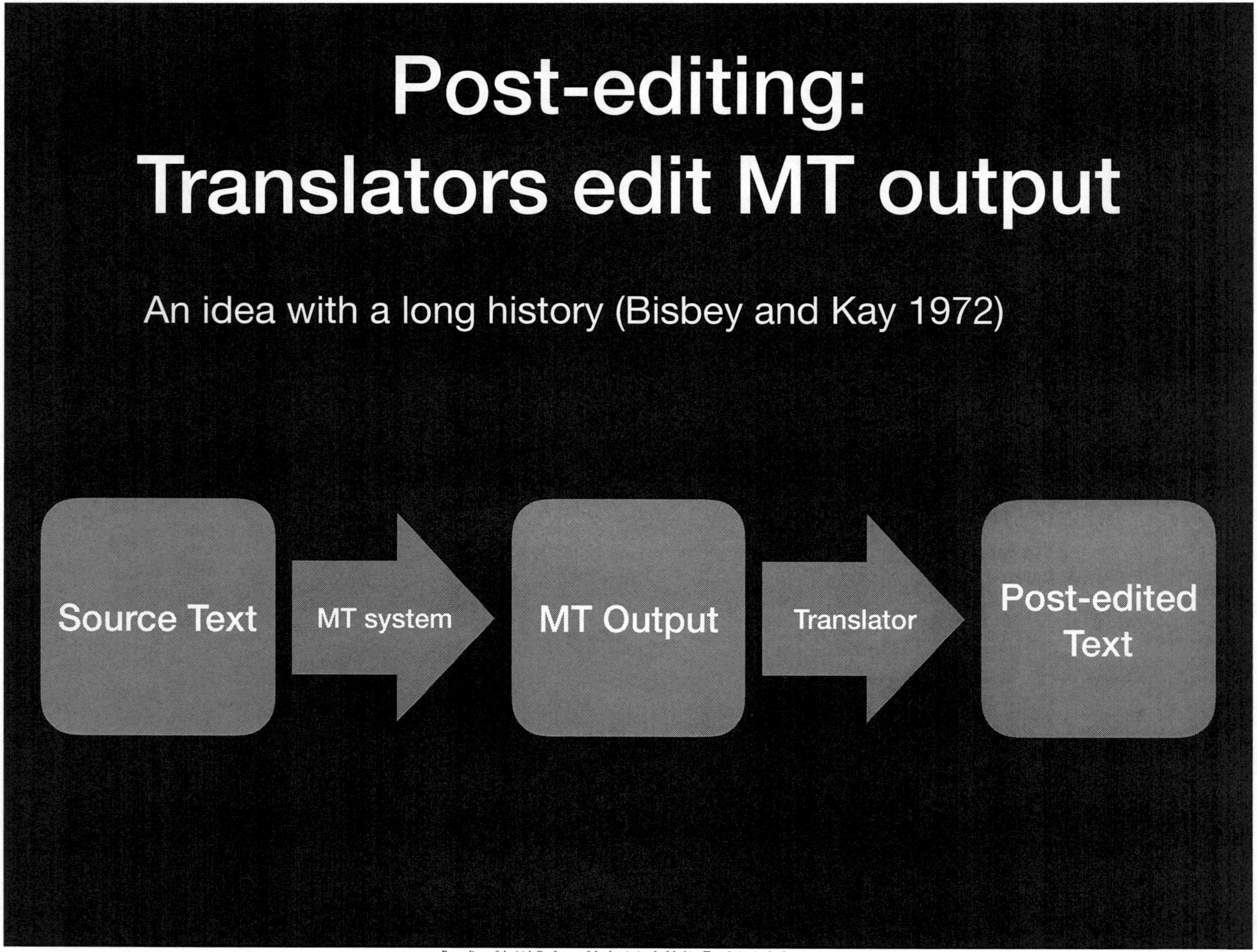

Post-editing: Translators edit MT output

An idea with a long history (Bisbey and Kay 1972)

Proceedings of the 14th Conference of the Association for Machine Translation in the Americas
October 6 – 9, 2020, Workshop on the Impact of Machine Translation

Post-editing:
Translators edit MT output

The physicist Arthur Eddington drew on Borel's

image further in The Nature of the Physical World

(1928), writing: If I let my fingers wander idly over

the keys of a typewriter it might happen that my

screed made an intelligible sentence.

Le physicien Arthur Eddington a attiré sur l'image de
Borel dans le caractère du monde physique (1928), écrit:
Si je laisse mes doigts se promener les bras croisés sur
les touches de la machine à écrire, il peut arriver que
mon chape fait une phrase intelligible.

Submit

Image Source

Green, Spence, Jeffrey Heer, and Christopher D. Manning. "The efficacy of human post-editing for language translation." *Proceedings of the SIGCHI conference on human factors in computing systems*. 2013.

Proceedings of the 14th Conference of the Association for Machine Translation in the Americas
October 6 – 9, 2020, Workshop on the Impact of Machine Translation

Post-editing:
Translators edit MT output

Pros

- Easy to implement (can use off-the-shelf MT system)

- Reduces translation time [1]

Cons

- Post-edited text is more similar to MT than unassisted translations [1]

- Translators can find post-editing frustrating [2]

[1] Green, Spence, Jeffrey Heer, and Christopher D. Manning. "The efficacy of human post-editing for language translation." *Proceedings of the SIGCHI conference on human factors in computing systems*. 2013.
[2] Gaspari, Federico, et al. "Perception vs reality: Measuring machine translation post-editing productivity." *Proceedings of the 11th Conference of the Association for Machine Translation in the Americas: Workshop on Post-Editing Technology and Practice (WPTP3)*. Vancouver: AMTA, 2014.

Proceedings of the 14th Conference of the Association for Machine Translation in the Americas
October 6 – 9, 2020, Workshop on the Impact of Machine Translation

Predictive Translation Memory

MT system suggests text predictions that complete the translation the user has already entered

If the MT suggestion is correct, user can accept it; if it isn't, user can type as normal.

MT suggestions update and improve as users type.

Proceedings of the 14th Conference of the Association for Machine Translation in the Americas
October 6 - 9, 2020, Workshop on the Impact of Machine Translation

Transtype (Foster 2000)

The Canadian International Development Agency and the Canada Mortgage and Housing Corporation will be taking part in a conference which will deal with housing for the needy .

The conference will be held in the fall of 1987 .

The Canada Mortgage and Housing Corporation is now looking into the possibility of financing further conferences and forums of this

Opération afrique 2000 qui a été lancée par moi est une exemple de la détermination du Canada pour aider les gens des régions rurales d' Afrique à surmonter la famine et à briser le cycle de pauvreté

L' a

Proceedings of the 14th Conference of the Association for Machine Translation in the Americas
October 6 – 9, 2020, Workshop on the Impact of Machine Translation

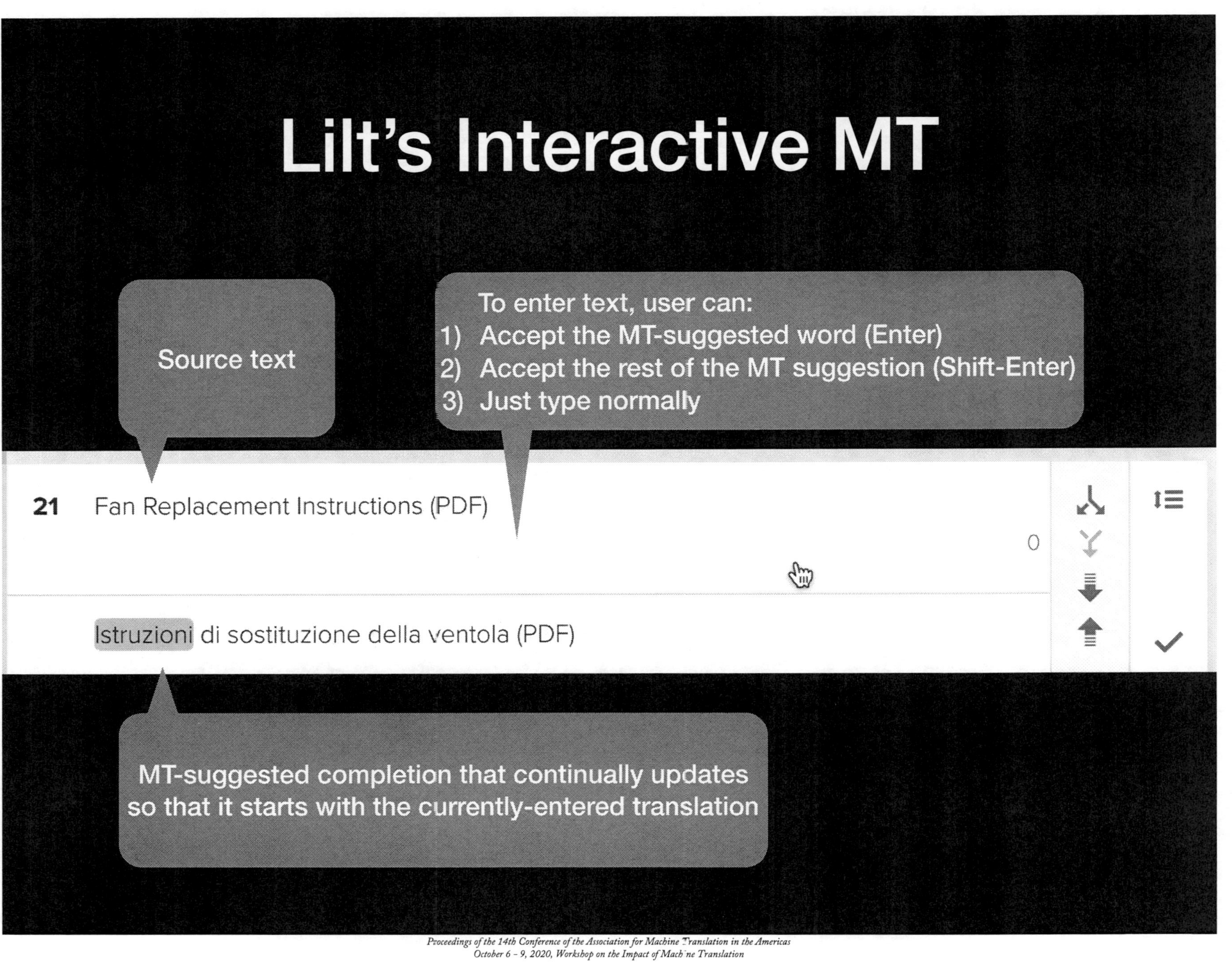

Proceedings of the 14th Conference of the Association for Machine Translation in the Americas
October 6 – 9, 2020, Workshop on the Impact of Machine Translation

Interactive MT Implementation

Prefix-constrained MT model (based on Transformer architecture). Details at lilt.com/research

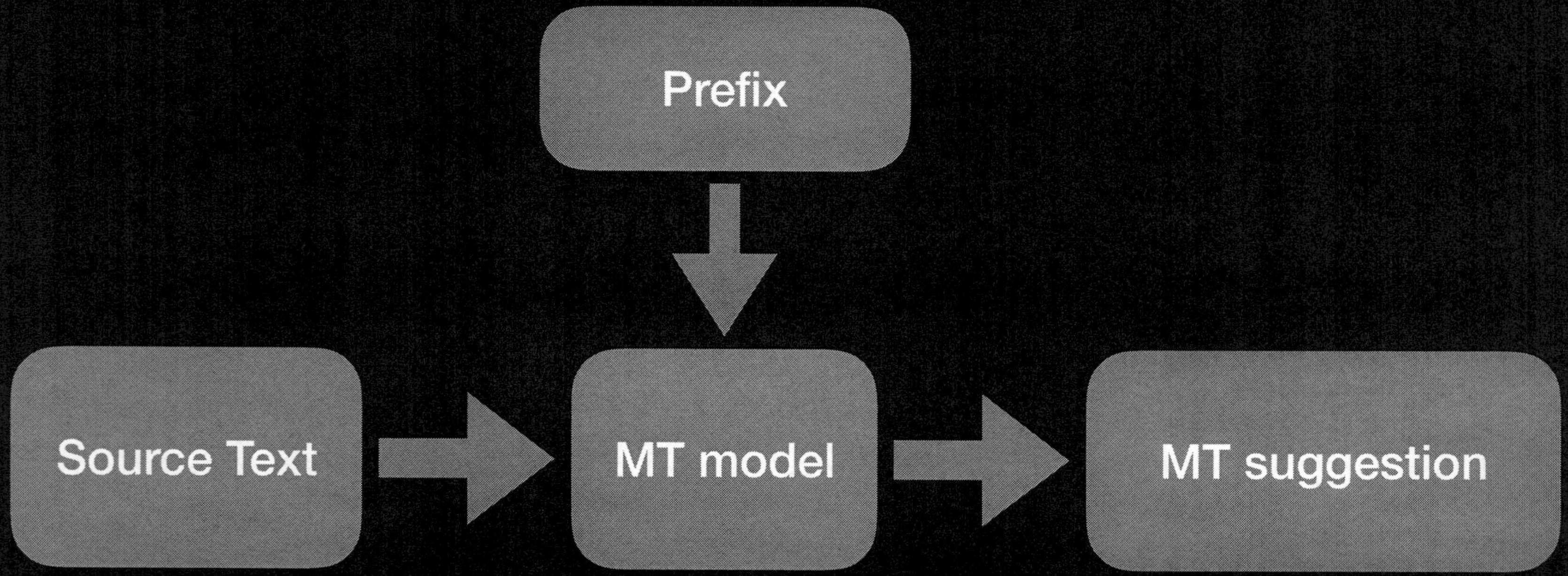

Proceedings of the 14th Conference of the Association for Machine Translation in the Americas
October 6 – 9, 2020, Workshop on the Impact of Machine Translation

Interactive MT Implementation

Prefix-constrained MT model (based on Transformer architecture). Details at lilt.com/research

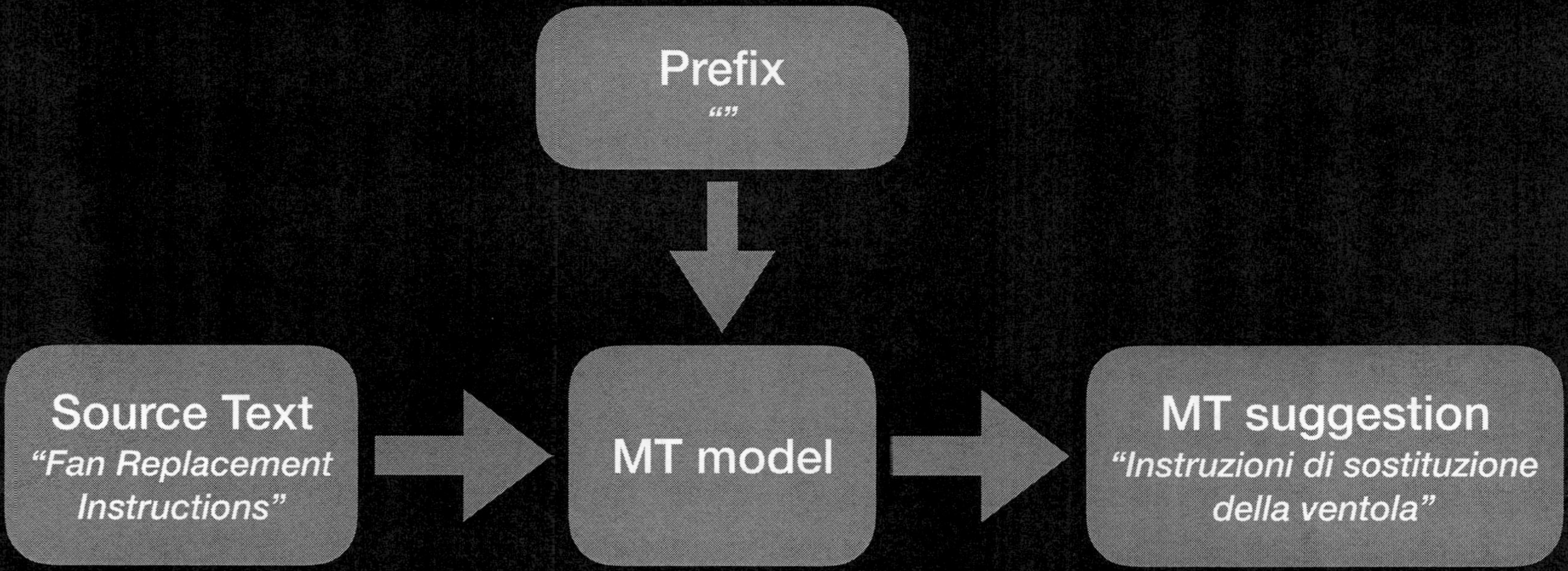

Proceedings of the 14th Conference of the Association for Machine Translation in the Americas
October 6 – 9, 2020, Workshop on the Impact of Machine Translation

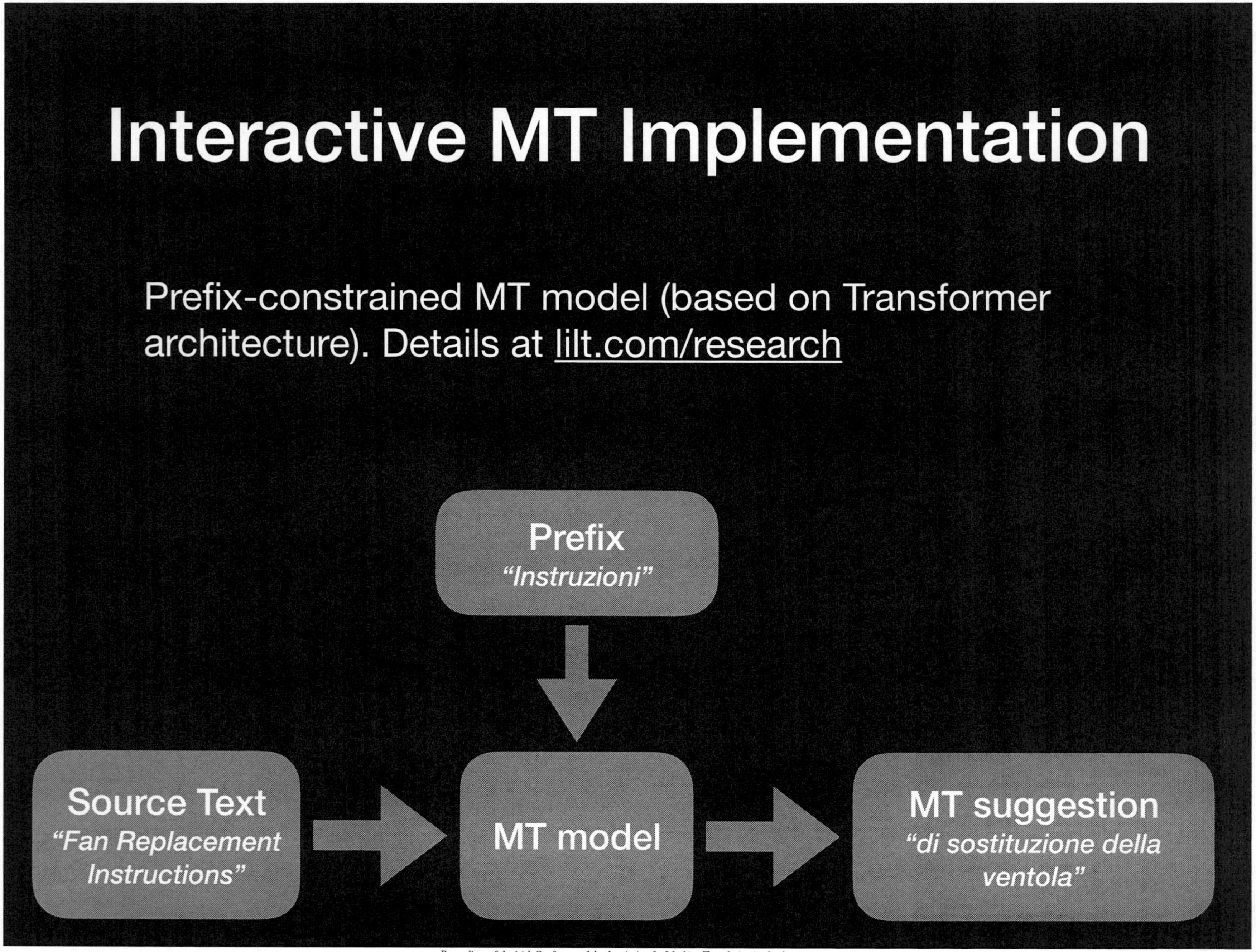

Interactive MT Implementation

Prefix-constrained MT model (based on Transformer architecture). Details at lilt.com/research

Proceedings of the 14th Conference of the Association for Machine Translation in the Americas
October 6 – 9, 2020, Workshop on the Impact of Machine Translation

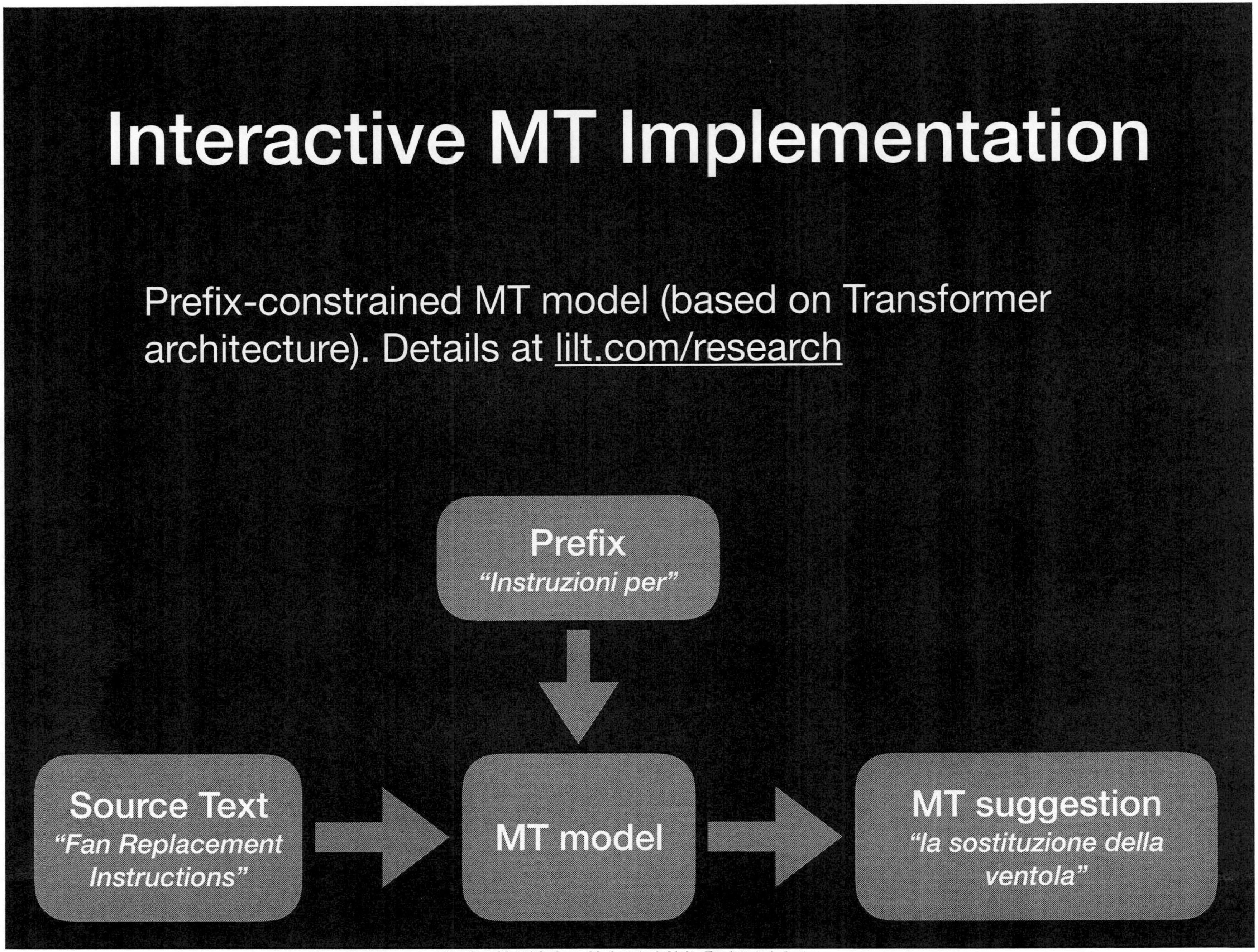
Interactive MT Implementation
Prefix-constrained MT model (based on Transformer architecture). Details at lilt.com/research
Prefix
"Instruzioni per"
Source Text
"Fan Replacement Instructions"
MT model
MT suggestion
"la sostituzione della ventola"

Proceedings of the 14th Conference of the Association for Machine Translation in the Americas
October 6 - 9, 2020, Workshop on the Impact of Machine Translation

Interactive MT Implementation

Prefix-constrained MT model (based on Transformer architecture). Details at lilt.com/research

Proceedings of the 14th Conference of the Association for Machine Translation in the Americas
October 6 – 9, 2020, Workshop on the Impact of Machine Translation

Interactive MT Implementation

Prefix-constrained MT model (based on Transformer architecture). Details at lilt.com/research

Proceedings of the 14th Conference of the Association for Machine Translation in the Americas
October 6 - 9, 2020, Workshop on the Impact of Machine Translation

Interactive MT Implementation

Prefix-constrained MT model (based on Transformer architecture). Details at lilt.com/research

Proceedings of the 14th Conference of the Association for Machine Translation in the Americas
October 6 - 9, 2020, Workshop on the Impact of Machine Translation

Interactive MT needs to be fast

New MT suggestion needs to be computed whenever the user's entered text no longer matches the MT prediction.

90% of our MT requests are computed in less than 500ms

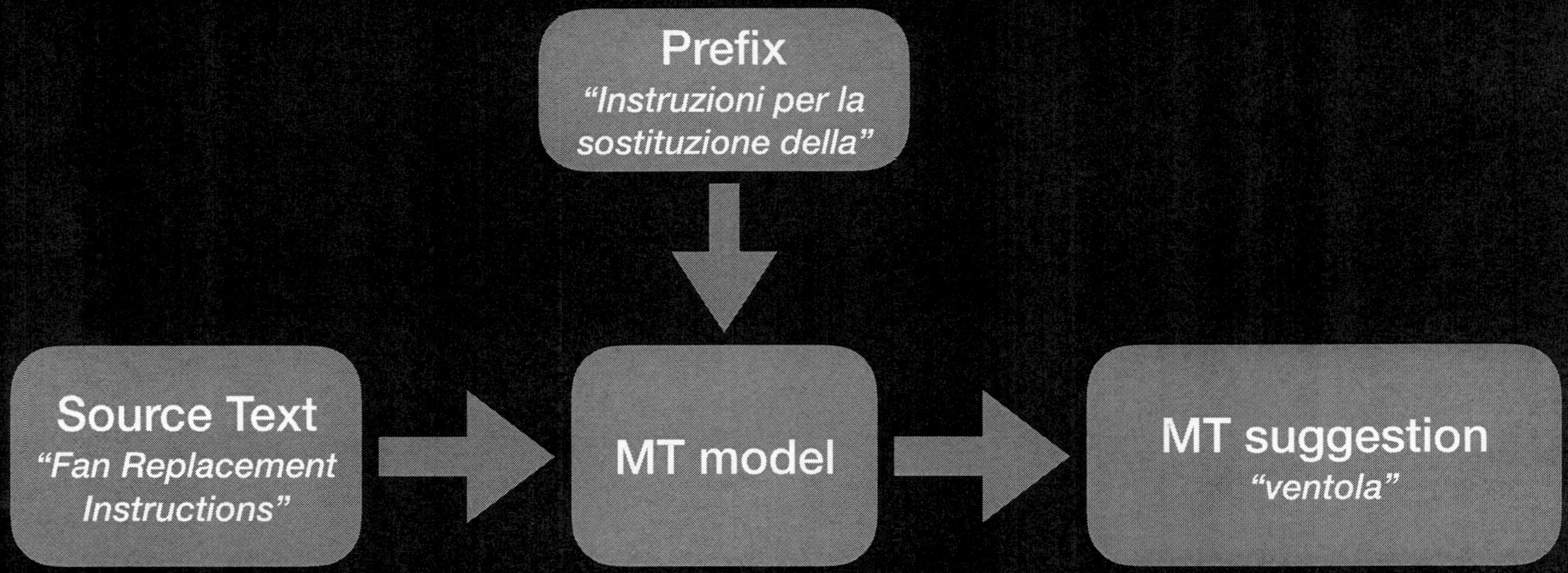

Proceedings of the 14th Conference of the Association for Machine Translation in the Americas
October 6 – 9, 2020, Workshop on the Impact of Machine Translation

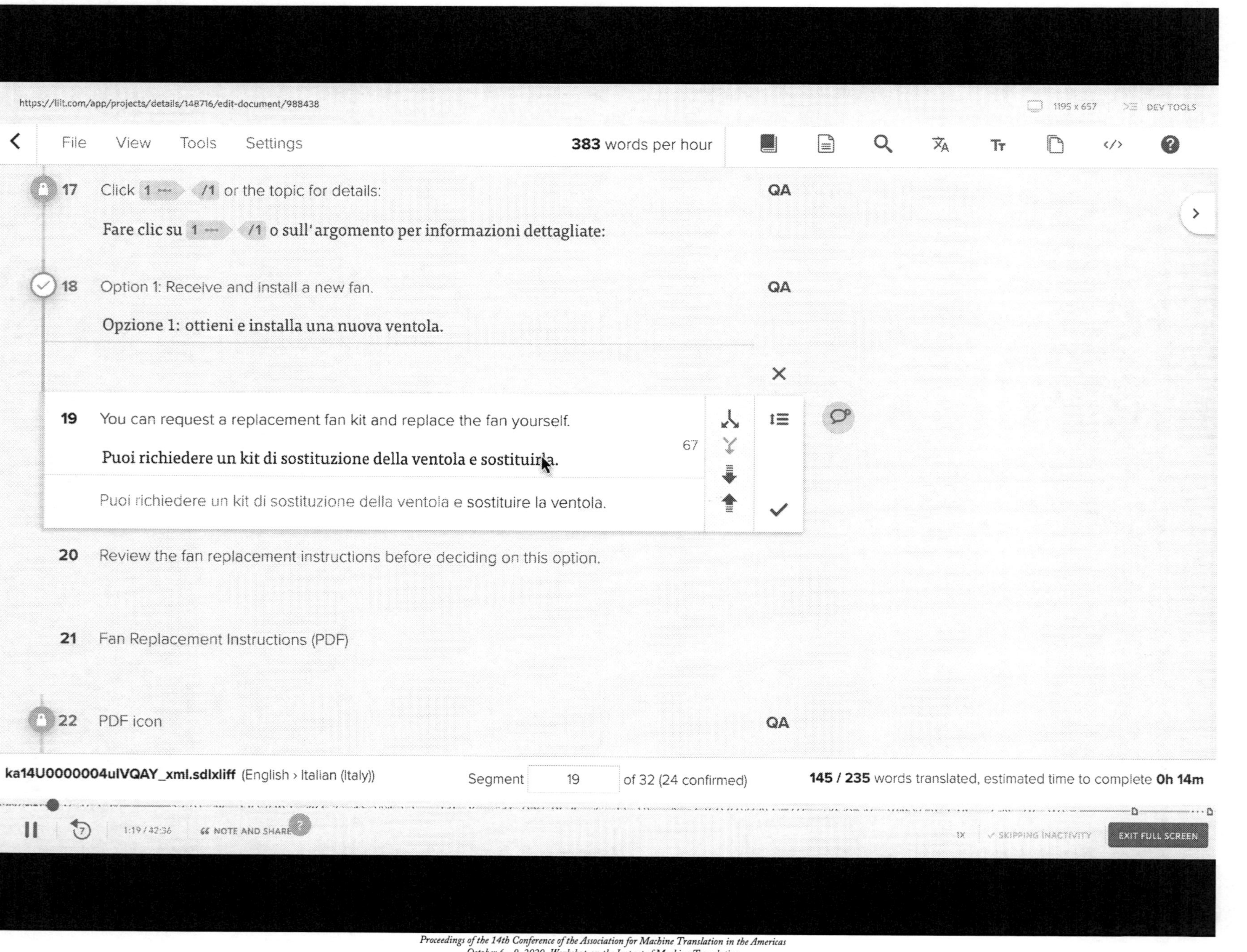

https://lilt.com/app/projects/details/148716/edit-document/988438
1195 x 657
DEV TOOLS
File   View   Tools   Settings
383 words per hour
17   Click 1 --- /1 or the topic for details:
Fare clic su 1 --- /1 o sull'argomento per informazioni dettagliate:
QA
18   Option 1: Receive and install a new fan.
Opzione 1: ottieni e installa una nuova ventola.
QA
19   You can request a replacement fan kit and replace the fan yourself.
67
Puoi richiedere un kit di sostituzione della ventola e sostituirla.
Puoi richiedere un kit di sostituzione della ventola e sostituire la ventola.
20   Review the fan replacement instructions before deciding on this option.
21   Fan Replacement Instructions (PDF)
22   PDF icon
QA
ka14U0000004ulVQAY_xml.sdlxliff (English › Italian (Italy))
Segment   19   of 32 (24 confirmed)
145 / 235 words translated, estimated time to complete 0h 14m
1:19 / 42:36   66 NOTE AND SHARE
1X   SKIPPING INACTIVITY   EXIT FULL SCREEN

How helpful is Lilt's Interactive MT?

- How often do translators use our MT suggestions?

- How often are our MT suggestions available and correct?

- How much do translators use our word-level suggestions, and how much do they post-edit?

- How do translators spend time on Lilt?

Proceedings of the 14th Conference of the Association for Machine Translation in the Americas
October 6 - 9, 2020, Workshop on the Impact of Machine Translation

How often do translators use our MT suggestions?

- Check how much text is inserted via Enter and Shift-Enter

- Data is from August to September 2020

- We consider only newly-generated* segments

*newly-generated segments = no TM matches, no segments majority copy-pasted

Proceedings of the 14th Conference of the Association for Machine Translation in the Americas
October 6 – 9, 2020, Workshop on the Impact of Machine Translation

Keys through which text is inserted

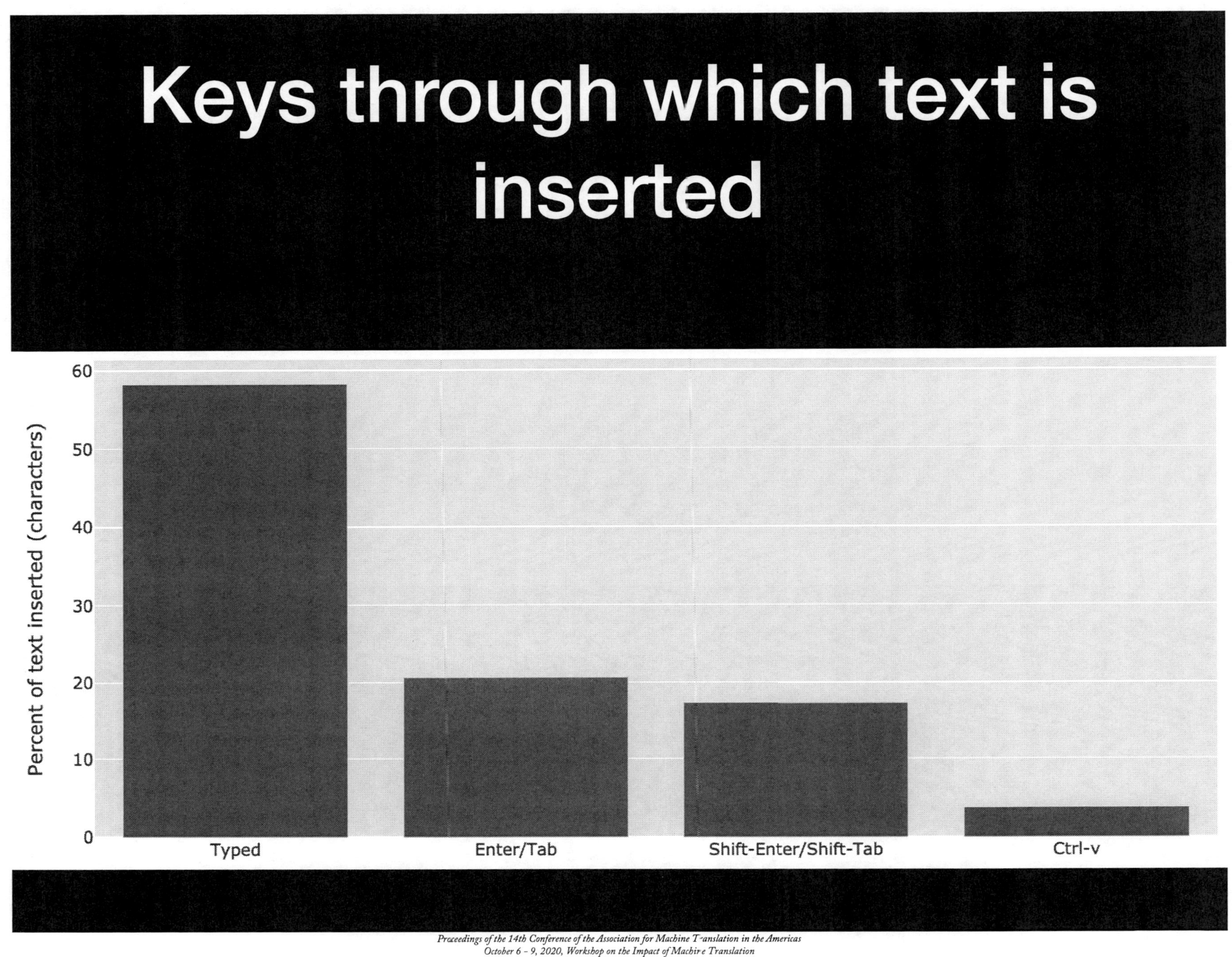

Proceedings of the 14th Conference of the Association for Machine Translation in the Americas
October 6 - 9, 2020, Workshop on the Impact of Machine Translation

Keys through which text is inserted

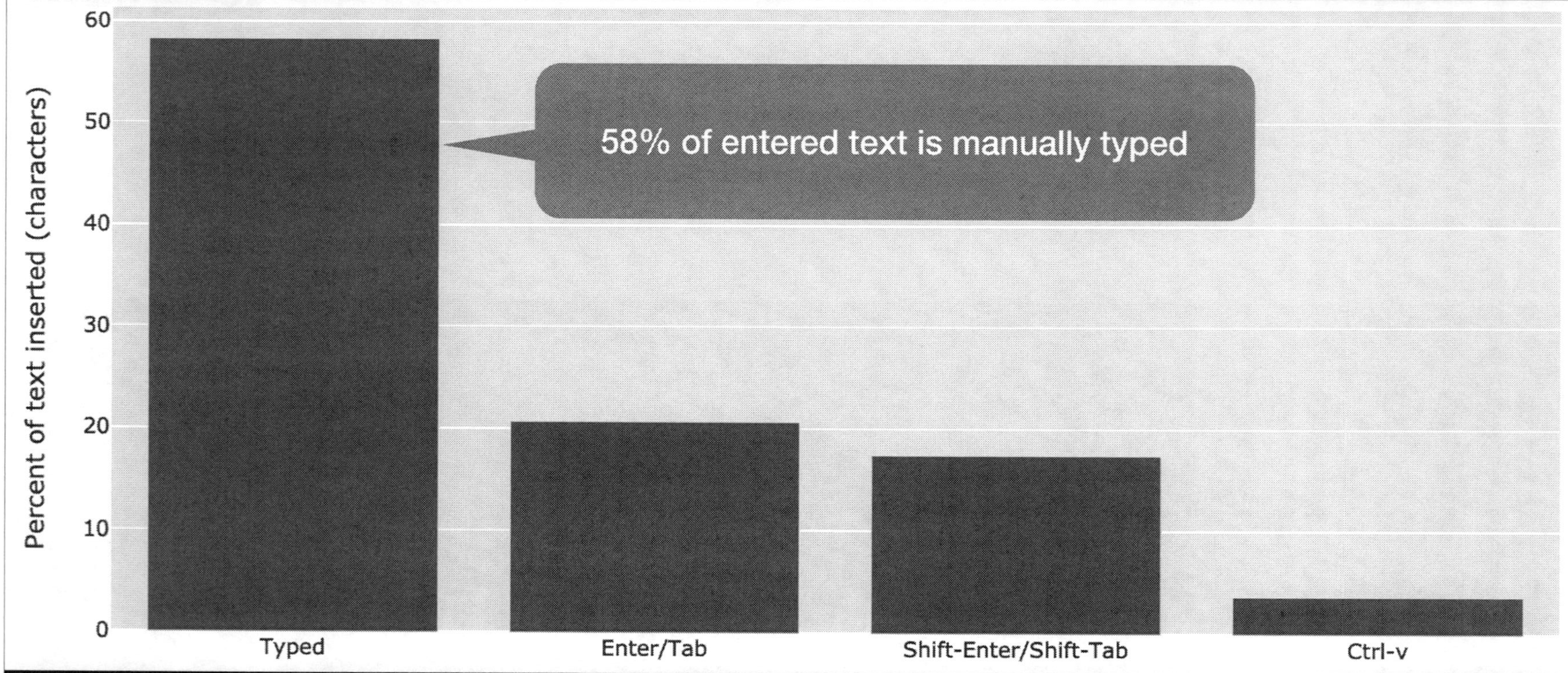

Proceedings of the 14th Conference of the Association for Machine Translation in the Americas
October 6 – 9, 2020, Workshop on the Impact of Machine Translation

Keys through which text is inserted

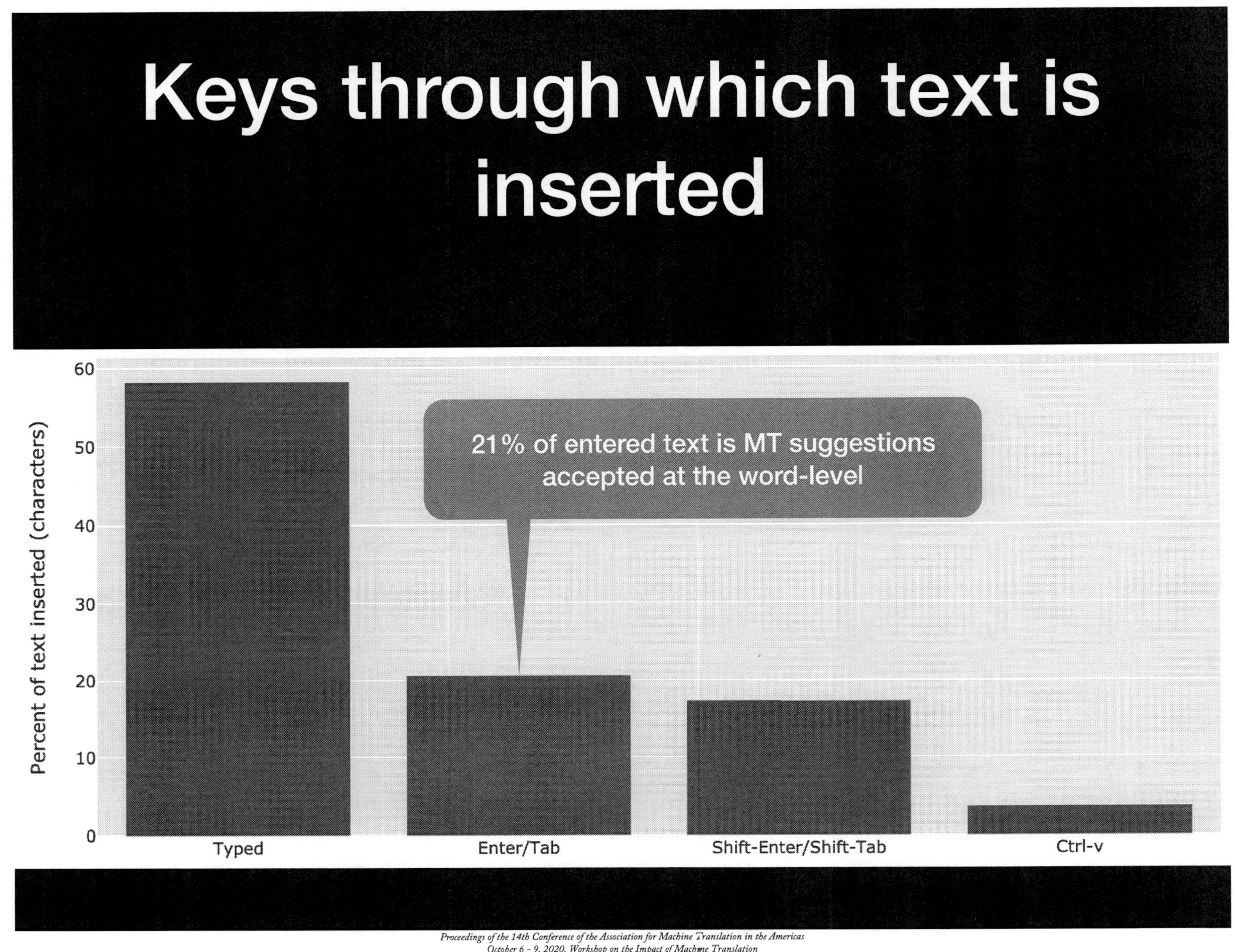

Proceedings of the 14th Conference of the Association for Machine Translation in the Americas
October 6 – 9, 2020, Workshop on the Impact of Machine Translation

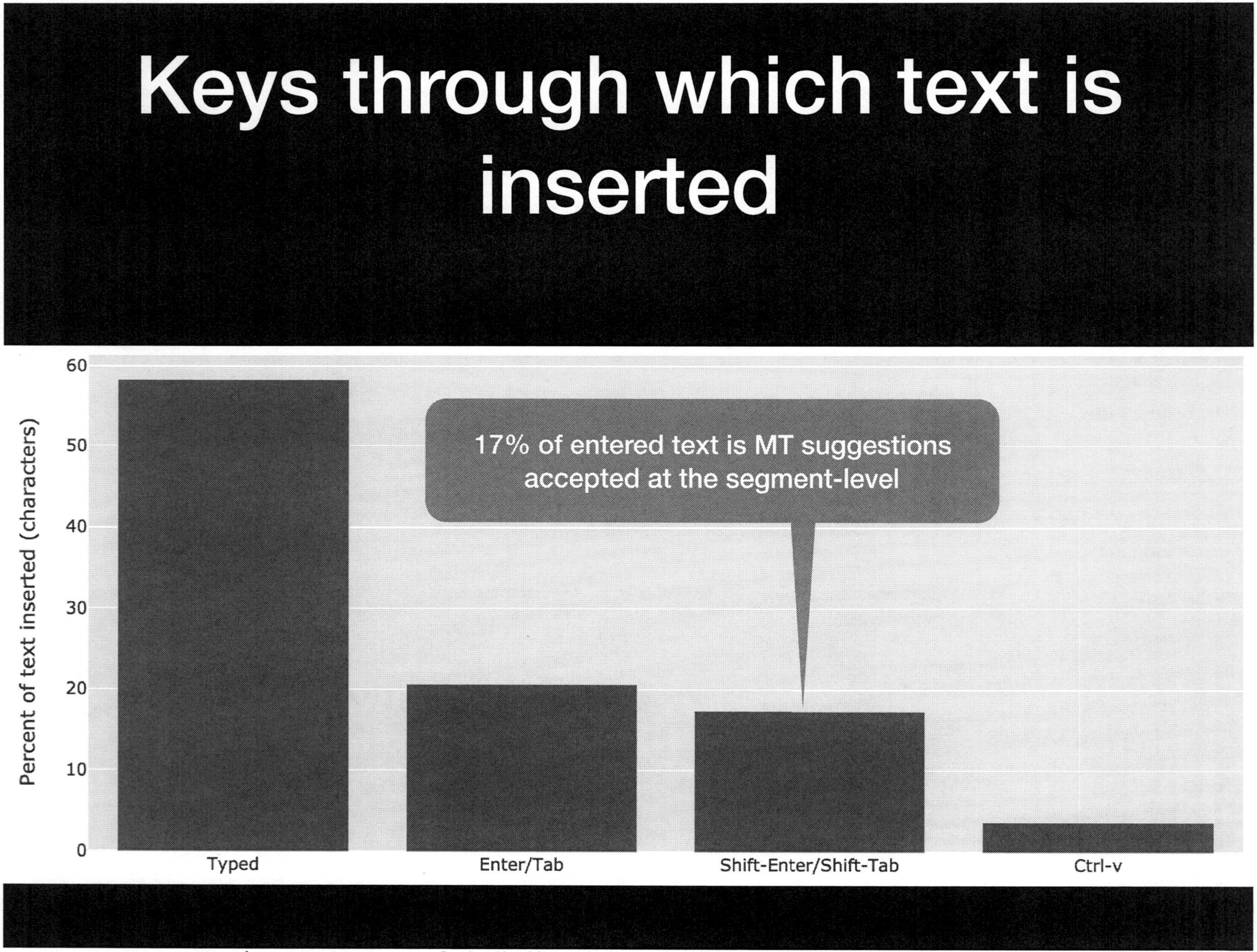

Keys through which text is inserted

Proceedings of the 14th Conference of the Association for Machine Translation in the Americas
October 6 – 9, 2020, Workshop on the Impact of Machine Translation

Why aren't translators using our MT suggestions more?

- Maybe translators aren't aware they can press Enter?

- Maybe they aren't editing at the end of the segment?

- Maybe the MT suggestion takes too long to show up?

- Maybe the MT suggestions don't match what the translator wants to type?

Proceedings of the 14th Conference of the Association for Machine Translation in the Americas
October 6 - 9, 2020, Workshop on the Impact of Machine Translation

How often are our MT suggestions available and correct?

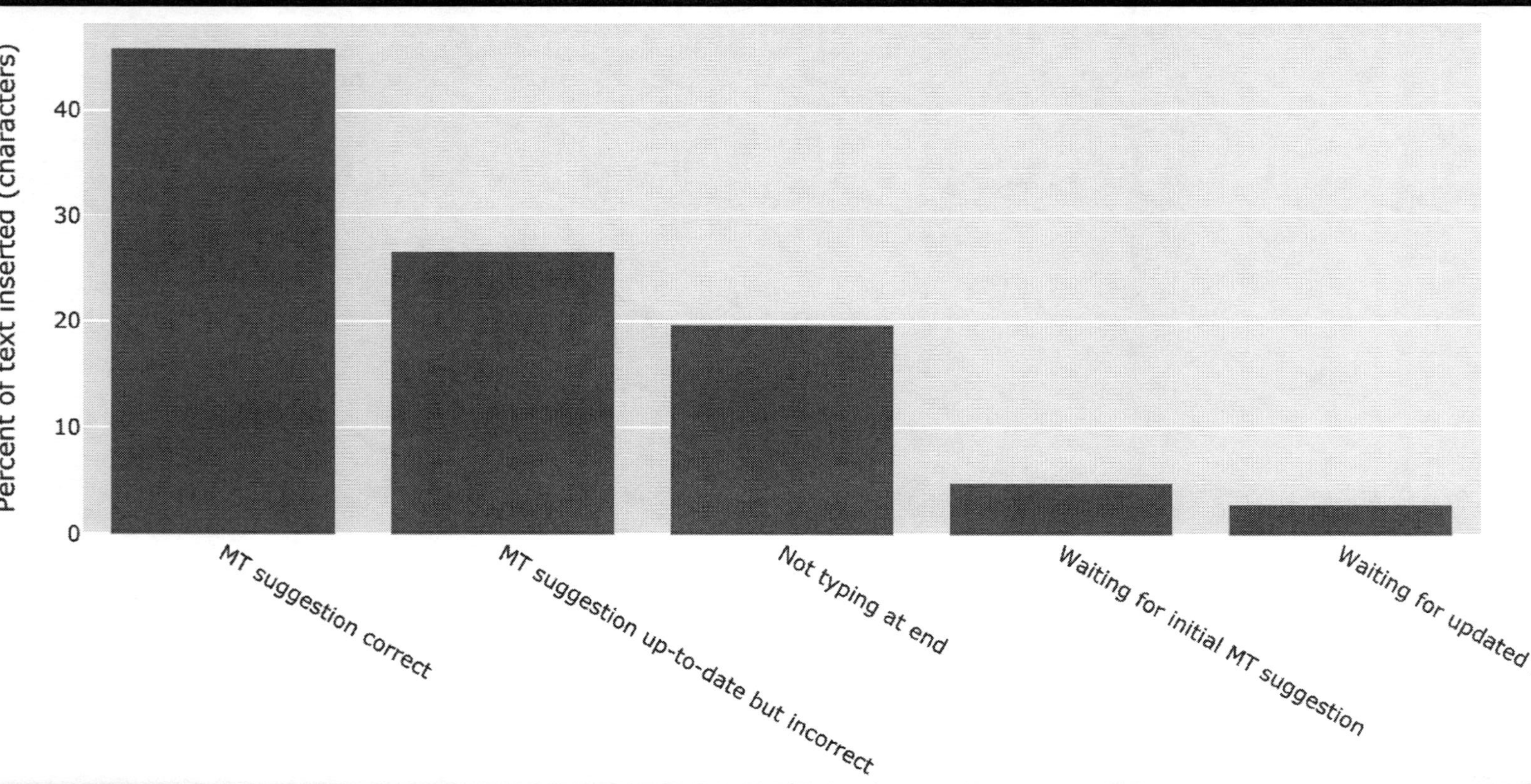

Proceedings of the 14th Conference of the Association for Machine Translation in the Americas
October 6 – 9, 2020, Workshop on the Impact of Machine Translation

How often are our MT suggestions available and correct?

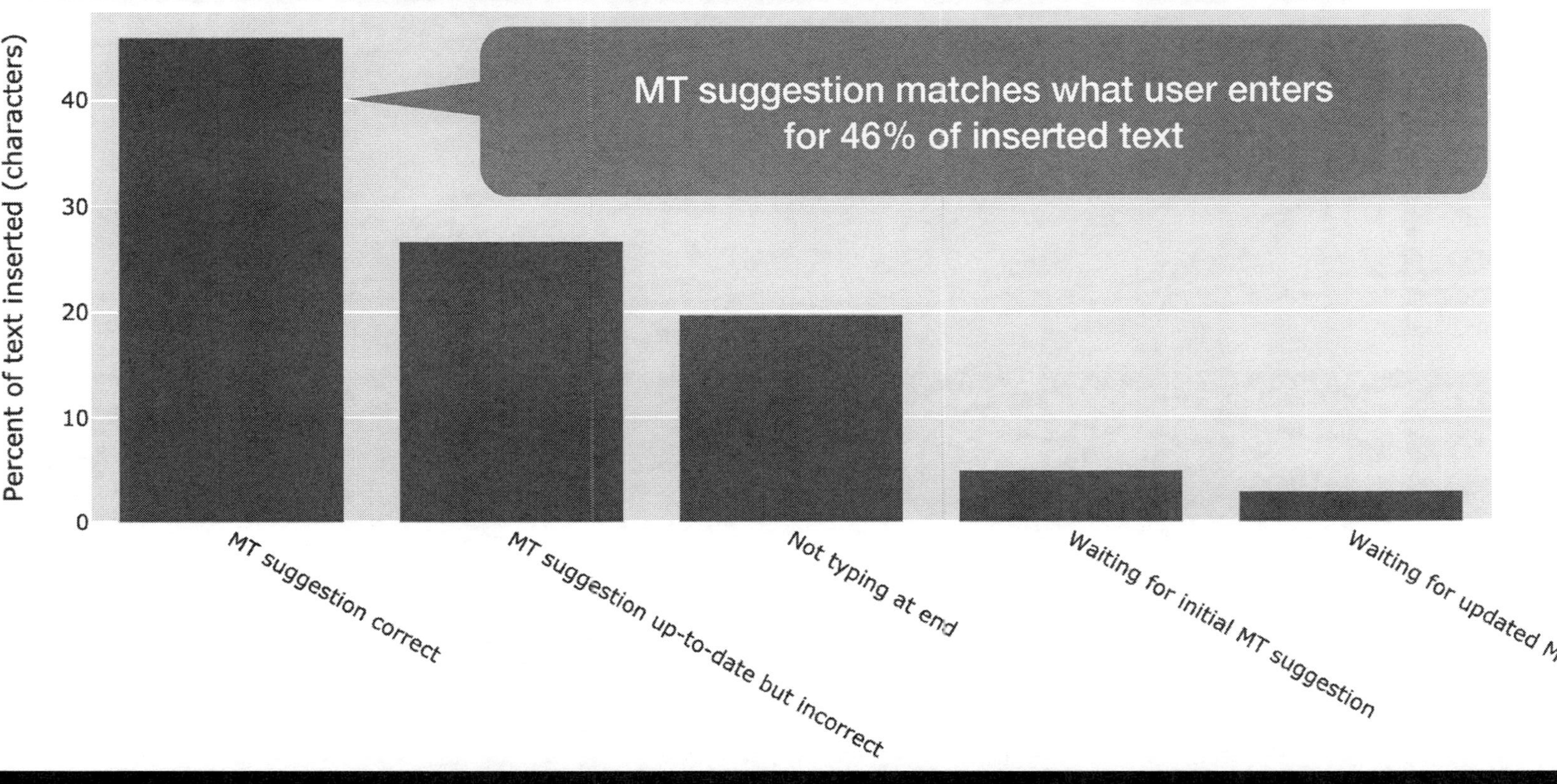

Proceedings of the 14th Conference of the Association for Machine Translation in the Americas
October 6 - 9, 2020, Workshop on the Impact of Machine Translation

How often are our MT suggestions available and correct?

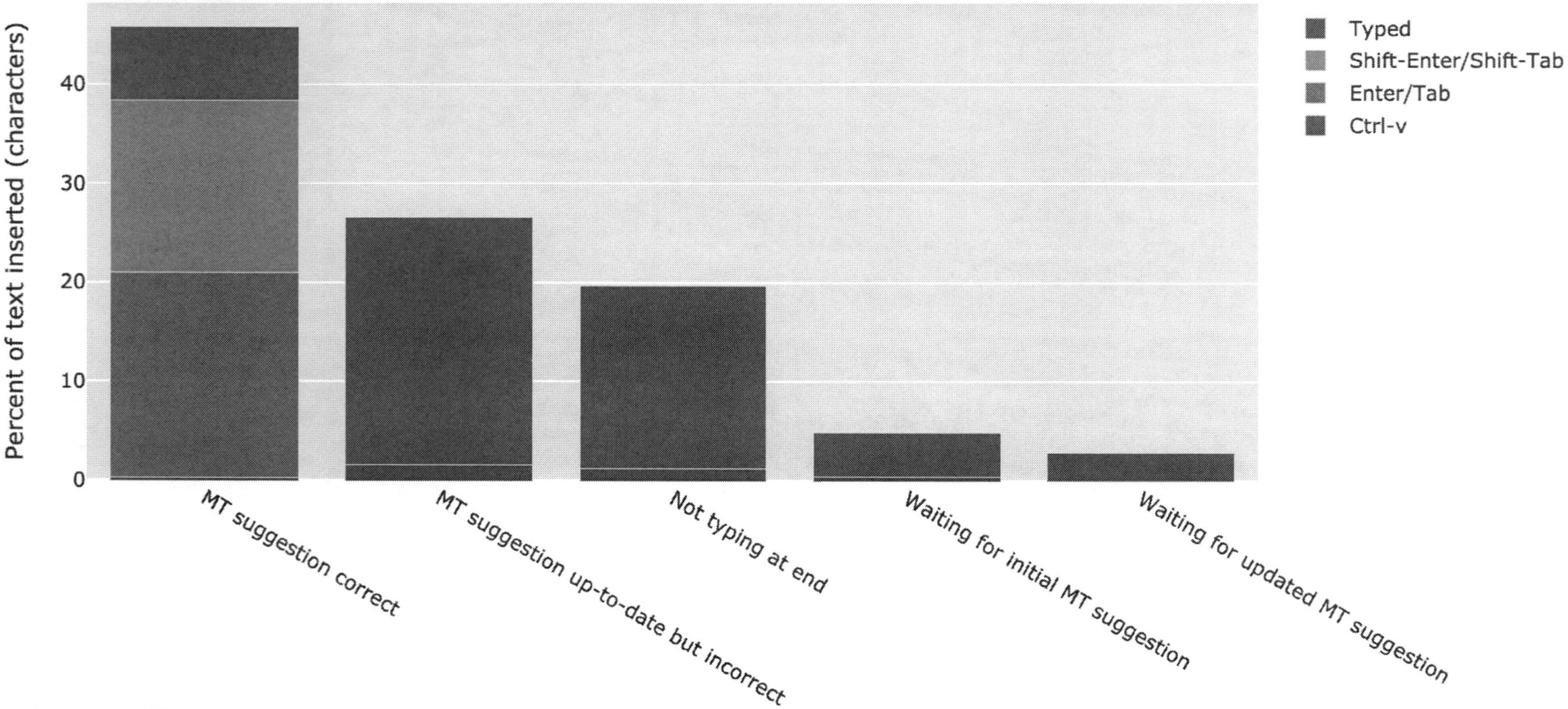

Proceedings of the 14th Conference of the Association for Machine Translation in the Americas
October 6 – 9, 2020, Workshop on the Impact of Machine Translation

How often are our MT suggestions available and correct?

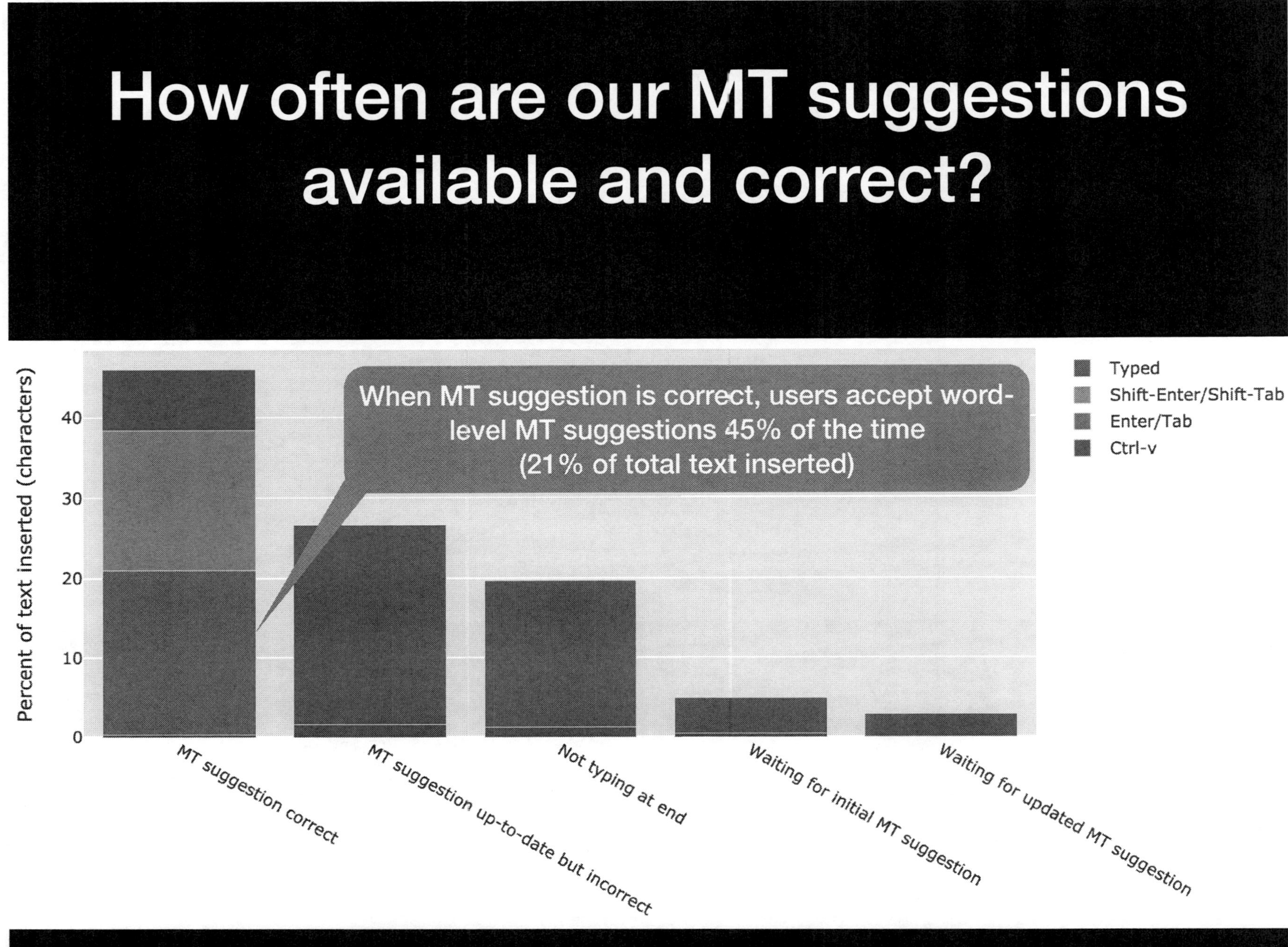

Proceedings of the 14th Conference of the Association for Machine Translation in the Americas
October 6 - 9, 2020, Workshop on the Impact of Machine Translation

How often are our MT suggestions available and correct?

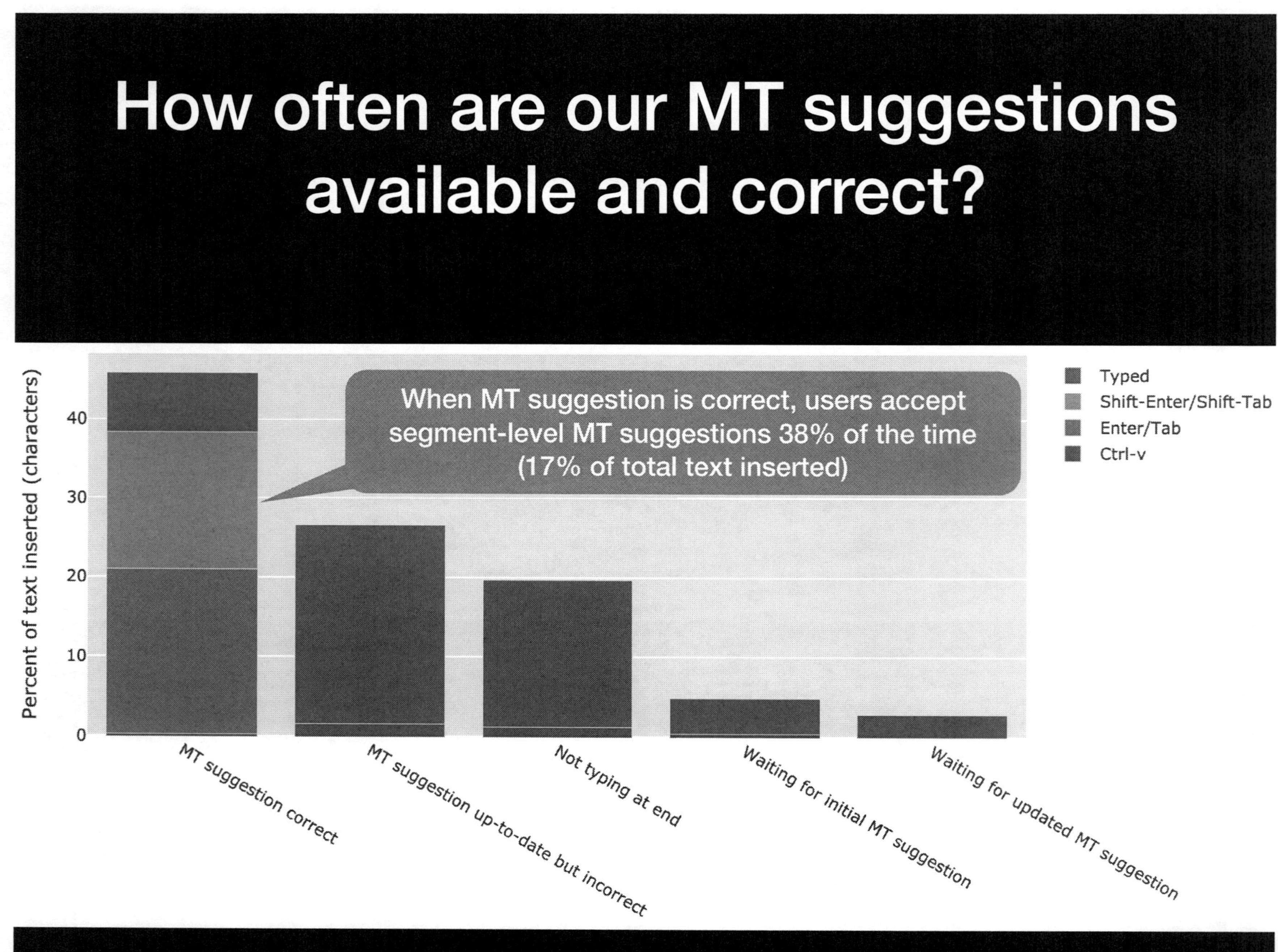

Proceedings of the 14th Conference of the Association for Machine Translation in the Americas
October 6 - 9, 2020, Workshop on the Impact of Machine Translation

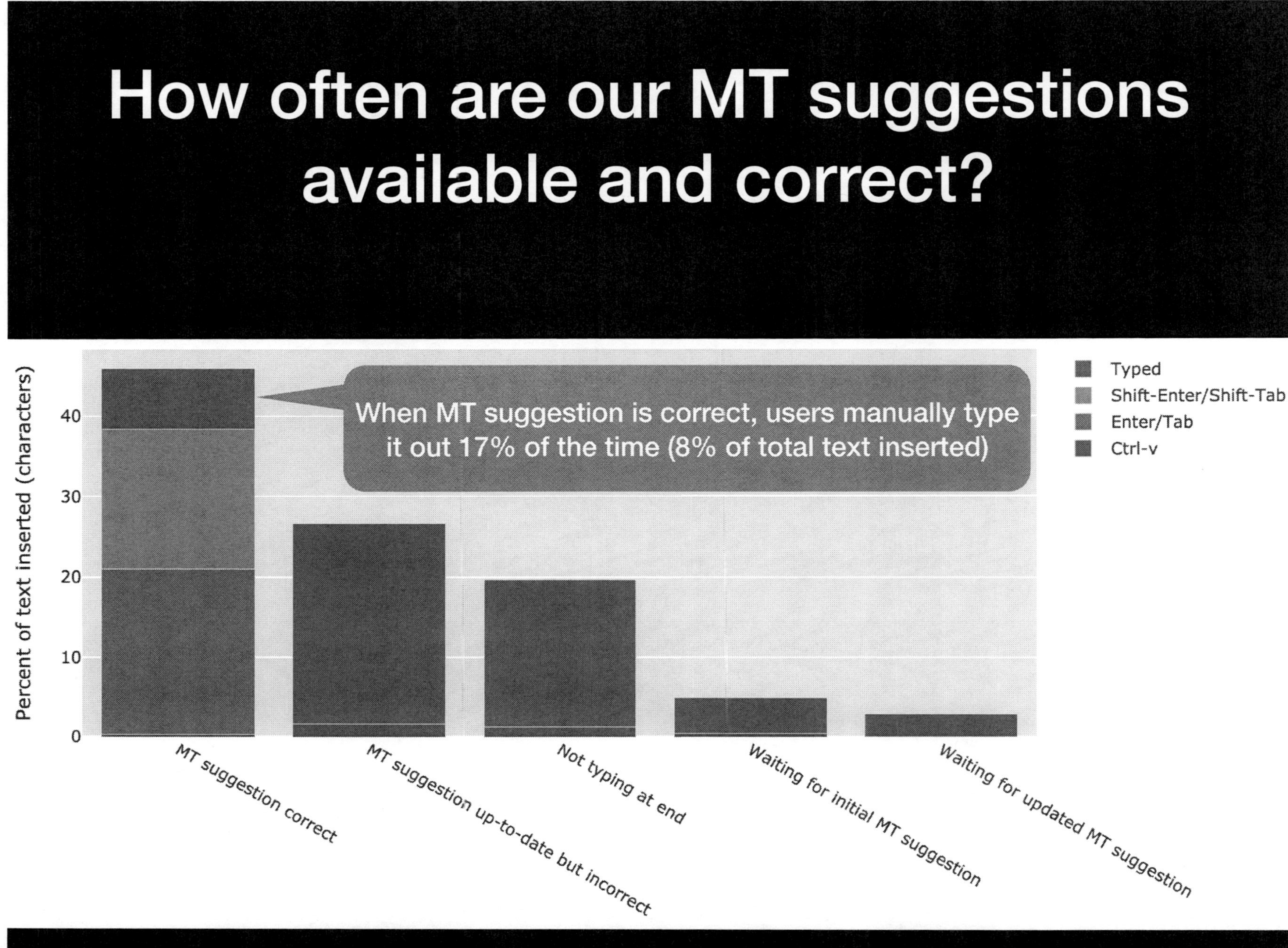

Proceedings of the 14th Conference of the Association for Machine Translation in the Americas
October 6 – 9, 2020, Workshop on the Impact of Machine Translation

How often are our MT suggestions available and correct?

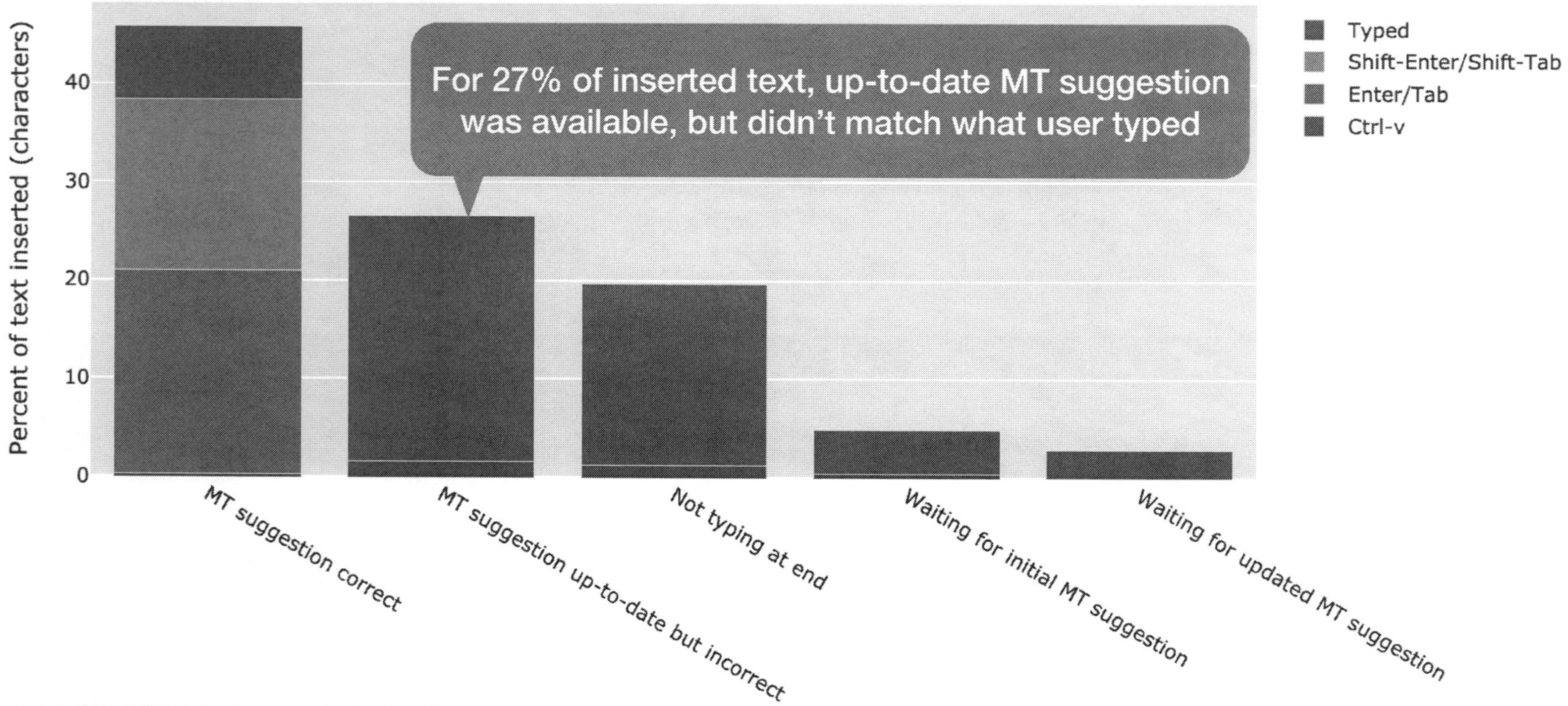

Proceedings of the 14th Conference of the Association for Machine Translation in the Americas
October 6 – 9, 2020, Workshop on the Impact of Machine Translation

How often are our MT suggestions available and correct?

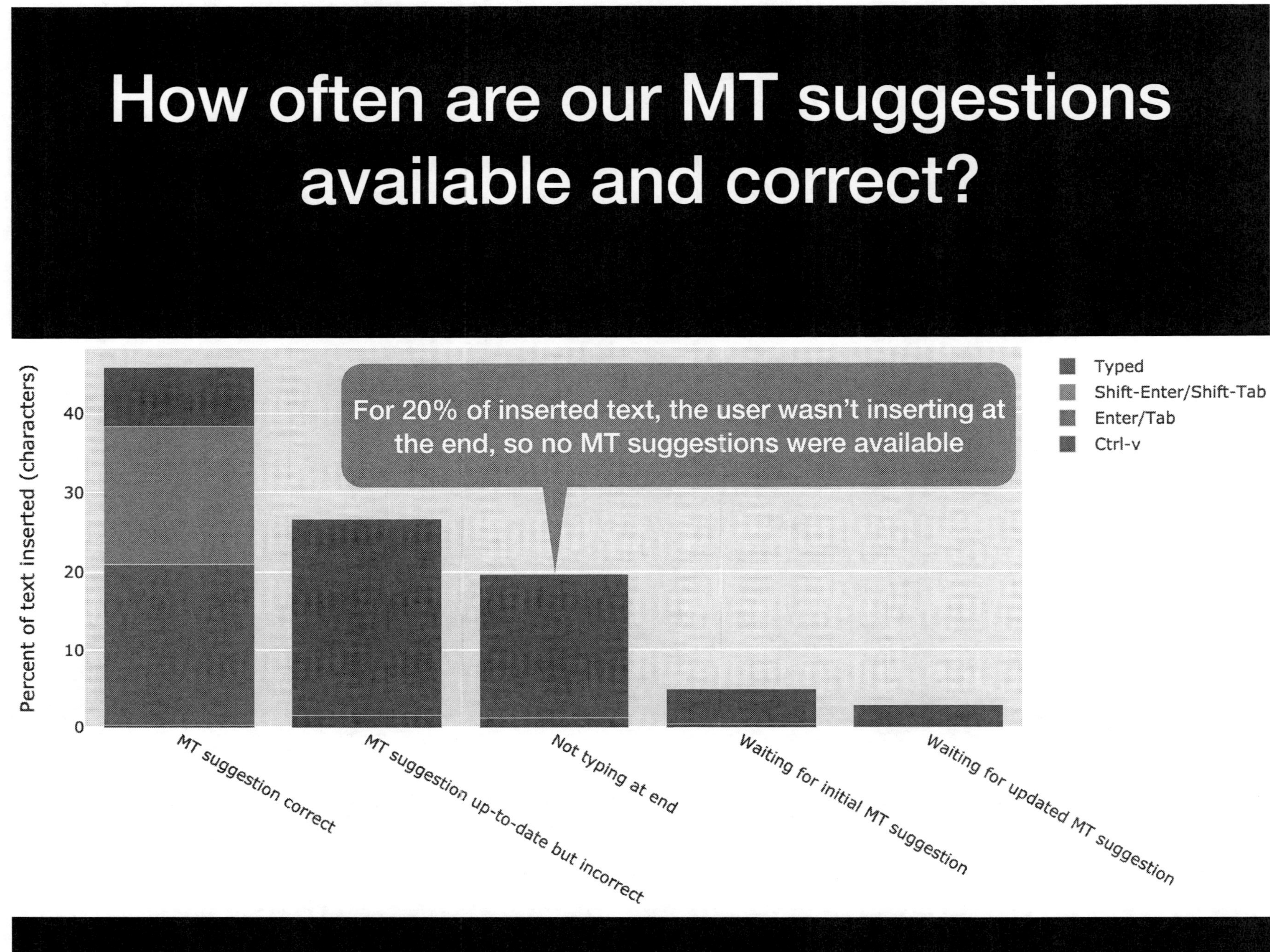

Proceedings of the 14th Conference of the Association for Machine Translation in the Americas
October 6 – 9, 2020, Workshop on the Impact of Machine Translation

How often are our MT suggestions available and correct?

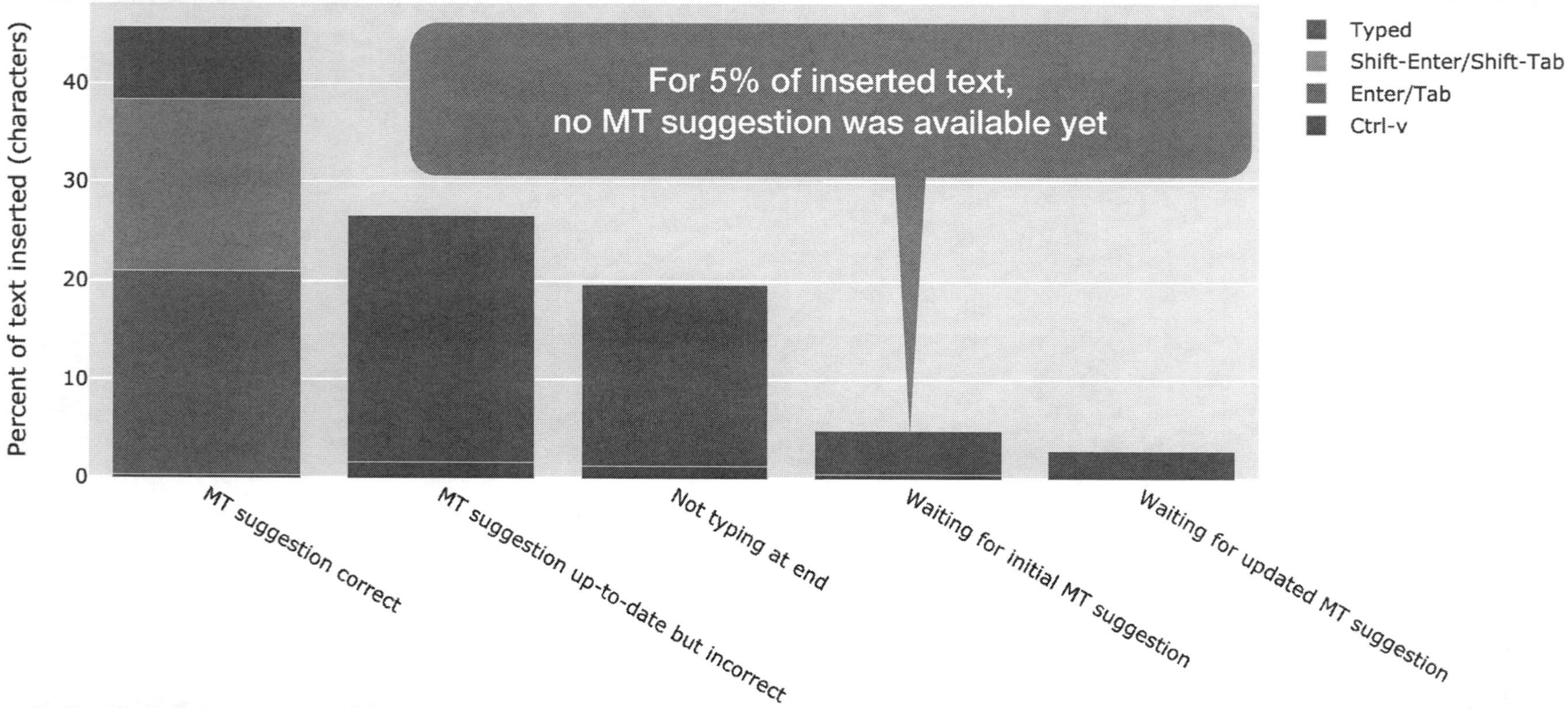

Proceedings of the 14th Conference of the Association for Machine Translation in the Americas
October 6 – 9, 2020, Workshop on the Impact of Machine Translation

How often are our MT suggestions available and correct?

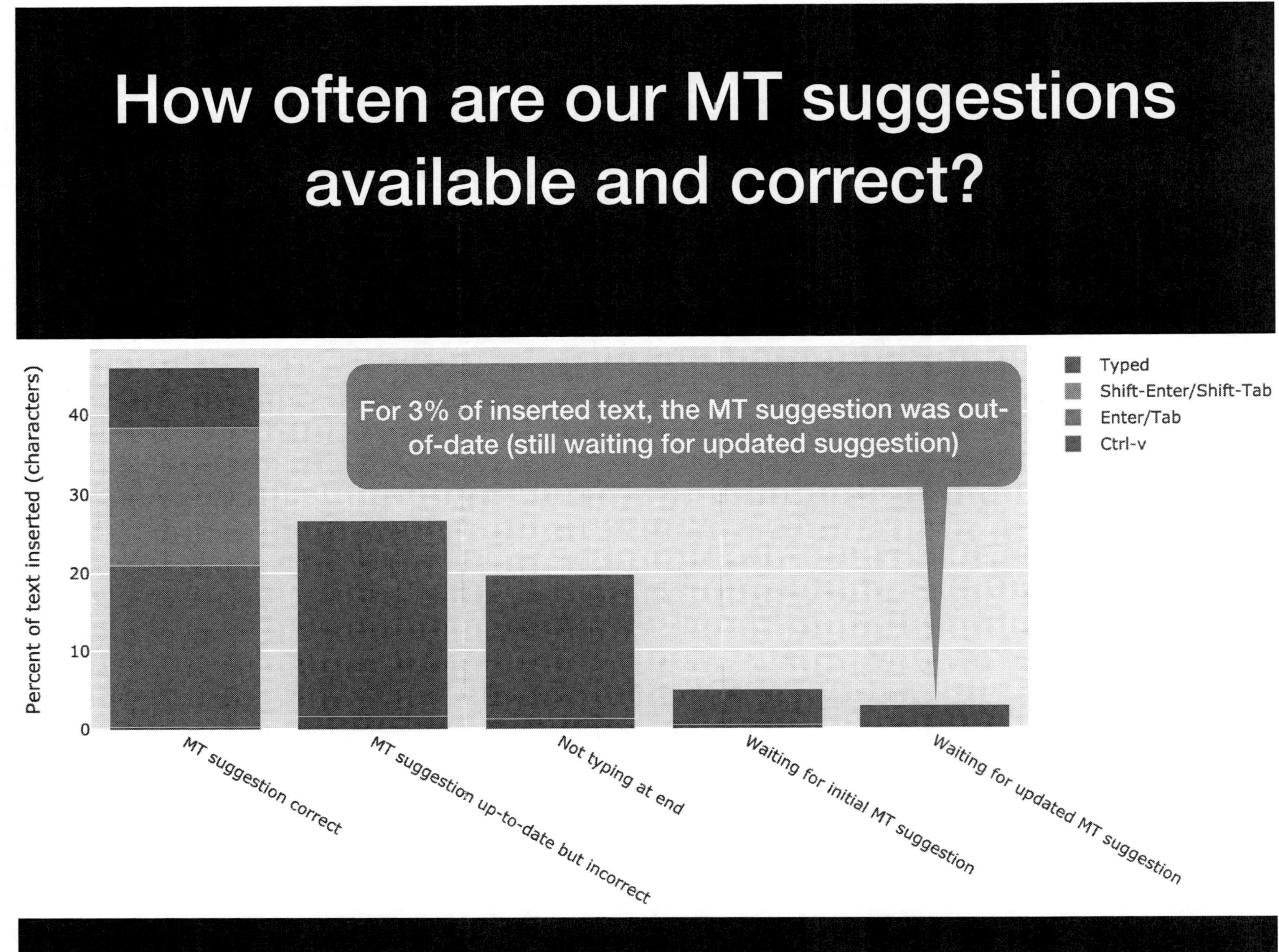

Proceedings of the 14th Conference of the Association for Machine Translation in the Americas
October 6 – 9, 2020, Workshop on the Impact of Machine Translation

Are users using Lilt interactively, or as a post-editing system?

- We see a lot of users are using Shift-Enter (accept the entire remaining MT suggestion)

- We also see a lot of users making insertions outside the end of the segment

- Are more users using Lilt in an interactive, suffix-suggestion style, or post-editing?

Proceedings of the 14th Conference of the Association for Machine Translation in the Americas
October 6 - 9, 2020, Workshop on the Impact of Machine Translation

Are users using Lilt interactively, or as a post-editing system?

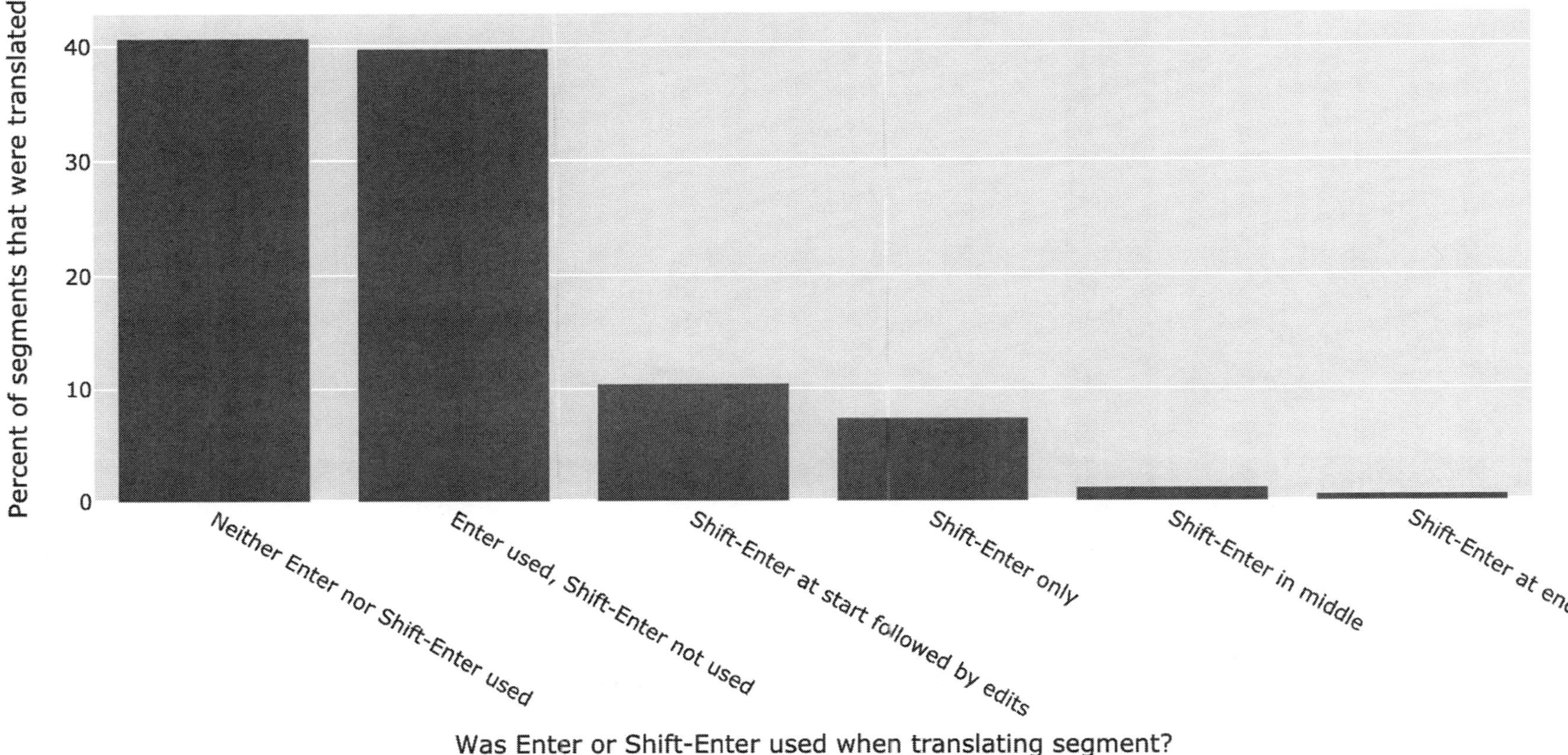

Proceedings of the 14th Conference of the Association for Machine Translation in the Americas
October 6 - 9, 2020, Workshop on the Impact of Machine Translation

Are users using Lilt interactively, or as a post-editing system?

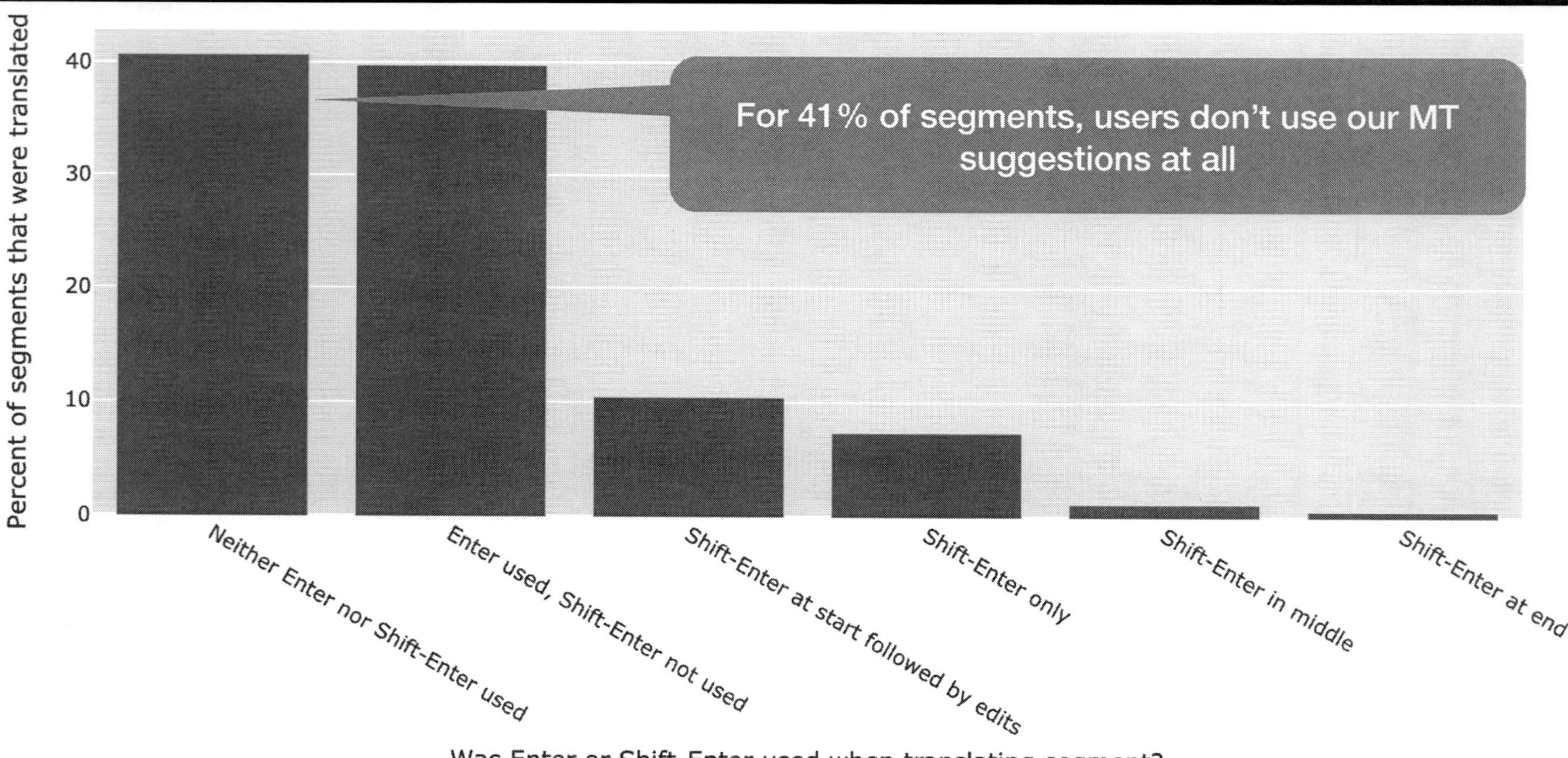

Proceedings of the 14th Conference of the Association for Machine Translation in the Americas
October 6 – 9, 2020, Workshop on the Impact of Machine Translation

Are users using Lilt interactively, or as a post-editing system?

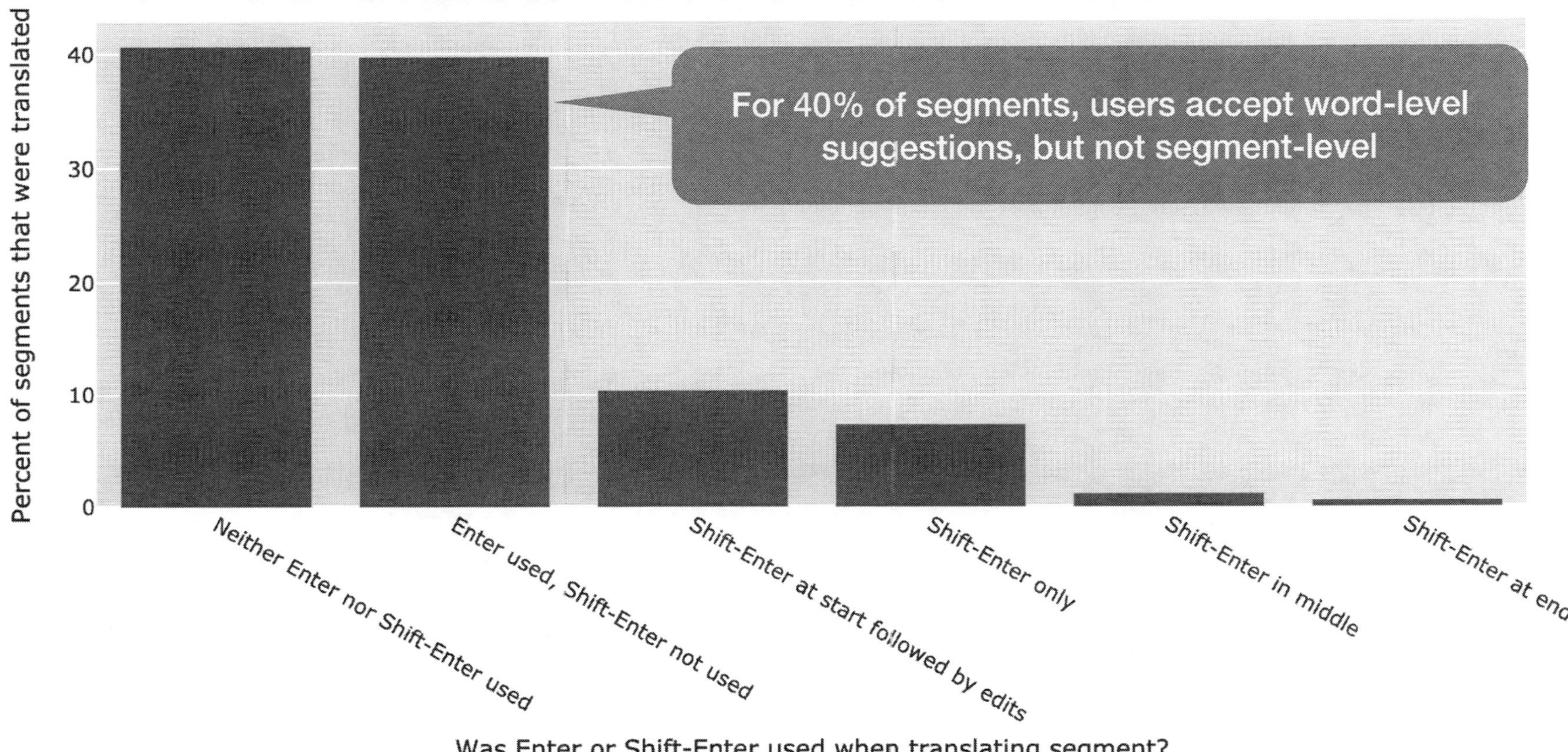

Proceedings of the 14th Conference of the Association for Machine Translation in the Americas
October 6 – 9, 2020, Workshop on the Impact of Machine Translation

Are users using Lilt interactively, or as a post-editing system?

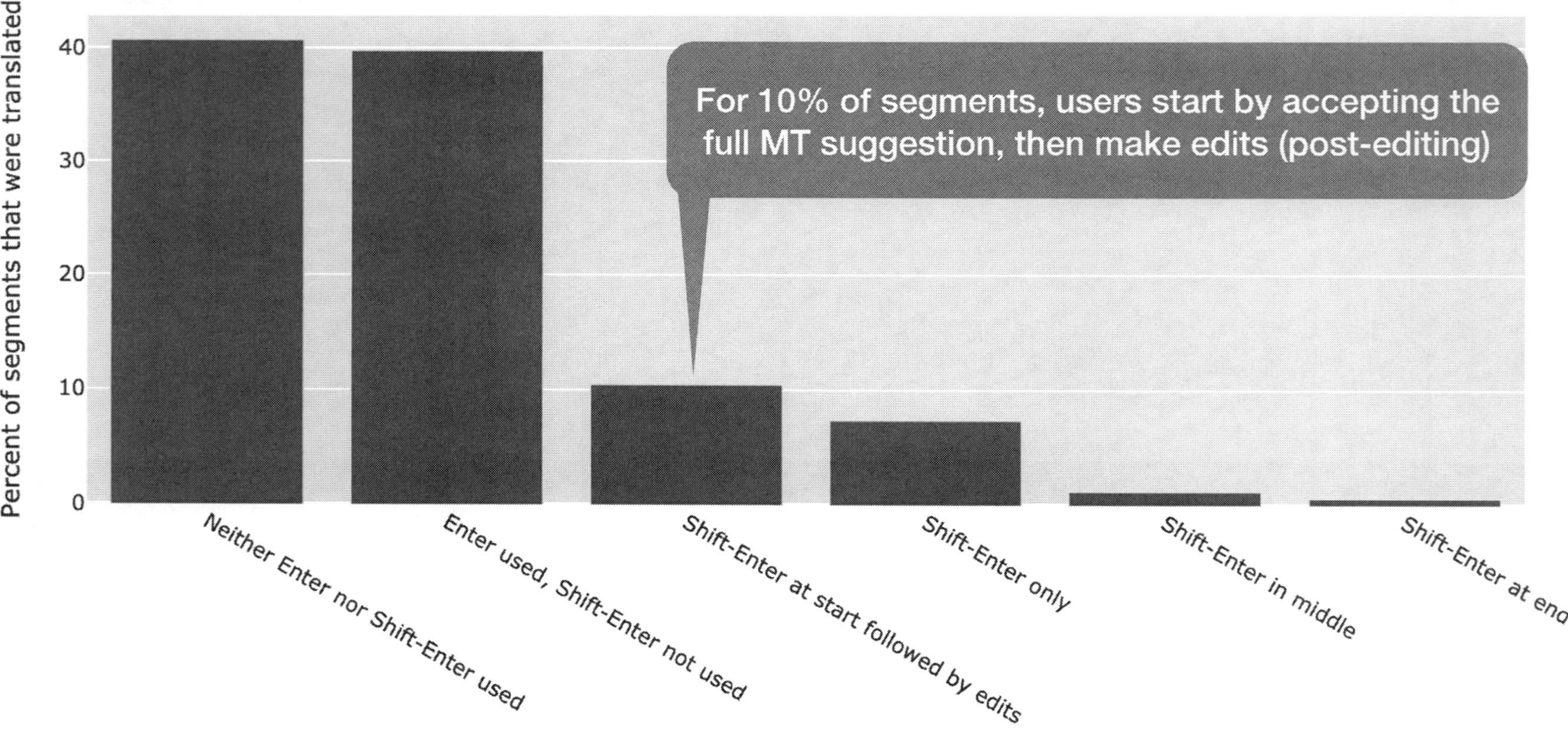

Proceedings of the 14th Conference of the Association for Machine Translation in the Americas
October 6 – 9, 2020, Workshop on the Impact of Machine Translation

Are users using Lilt interactively, or as a post-editing system?

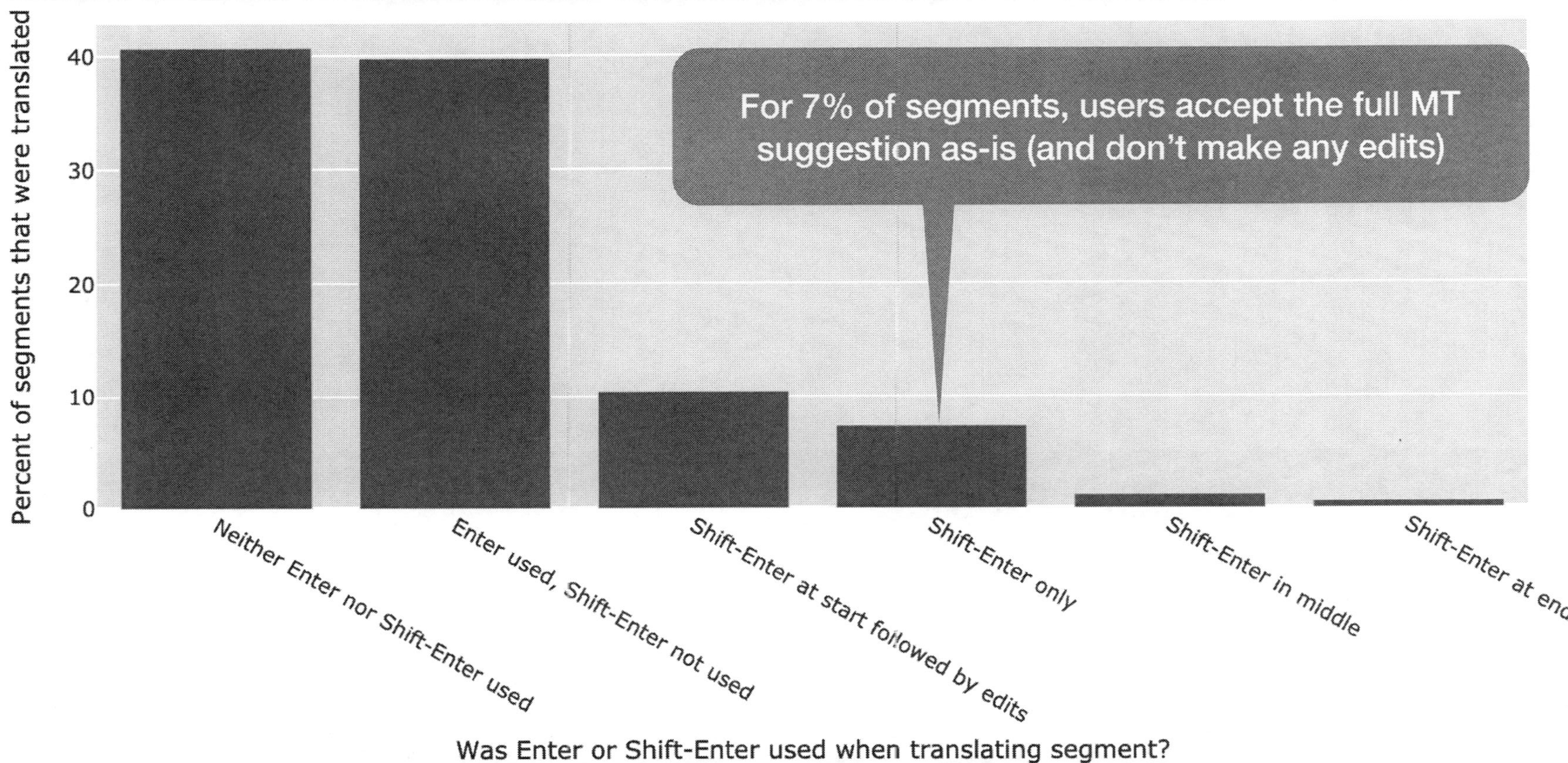

Preceedings of the 14th Conference of the Association for Machine Translation in the Americas
October 6 – 9, 2020, Workshop on the Impact of Machine Translation

Histogram of users by percent of segments they post-edit

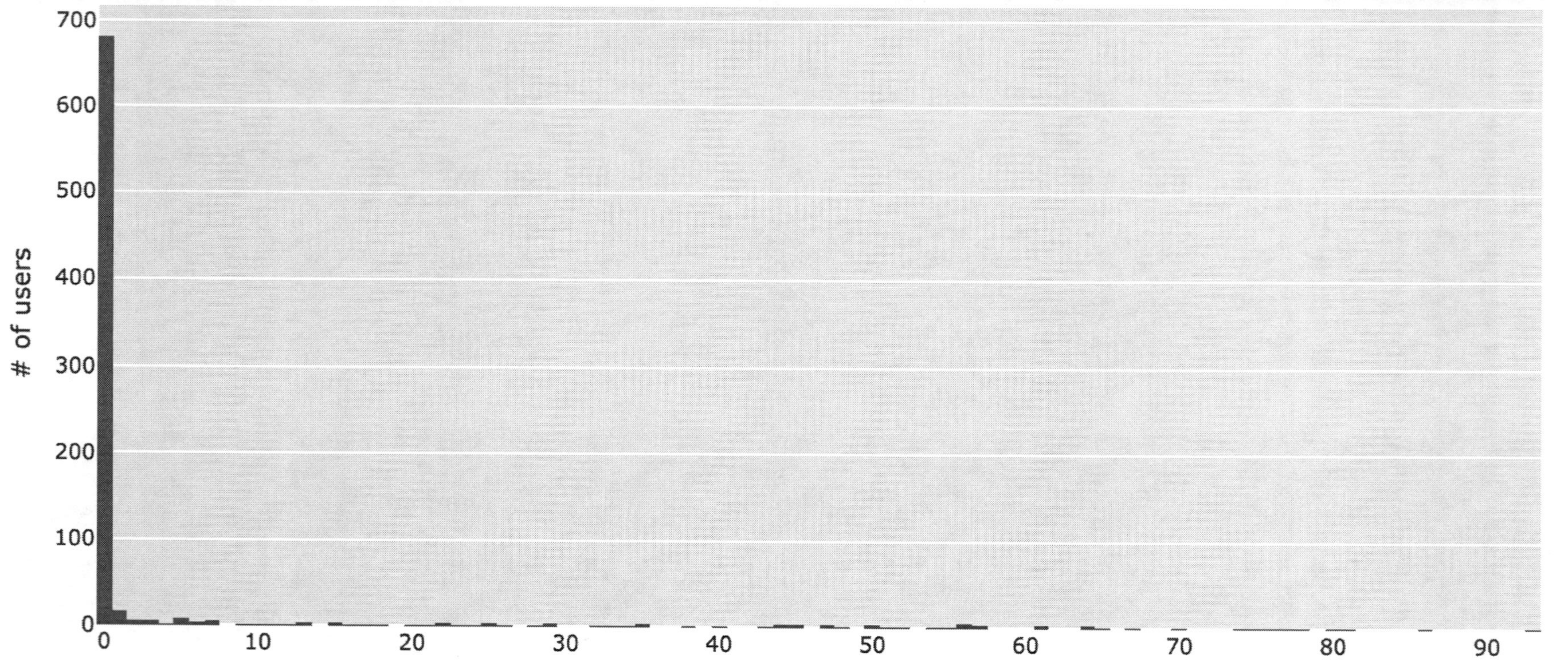

Proceedings of the 14th Conference of the Association for Machine Translation in the Americas
October 6 – 9, 2020, Workshop on the Impact of Machine Translation

Histogram of users by percent of segments they post-edit

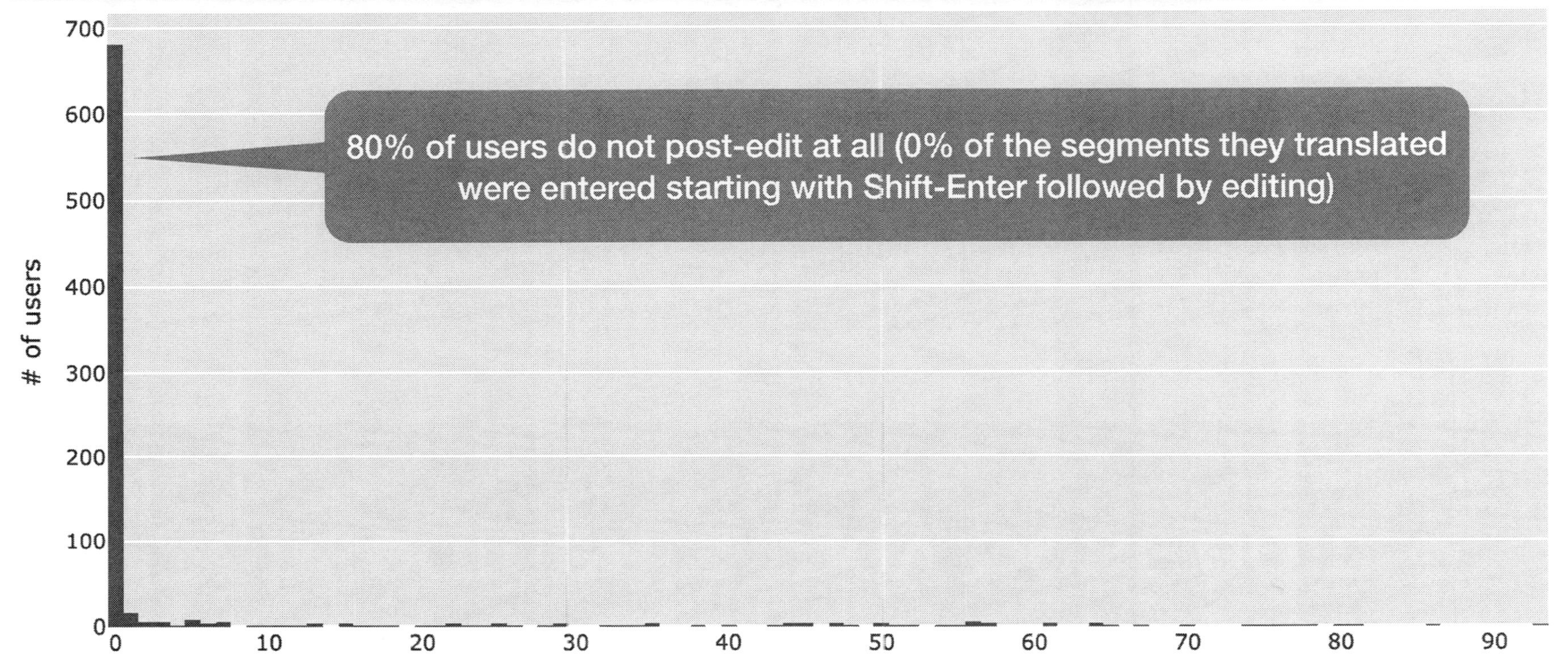

Percent of segments user translates via post-editing

Proceedings of the 14th Conference of the Association for Machine Translation in the Americas
October 6 – 9, 2020, Workshop on the Impact of Machine Translation

Histogram of users by percent of segments they post-edit

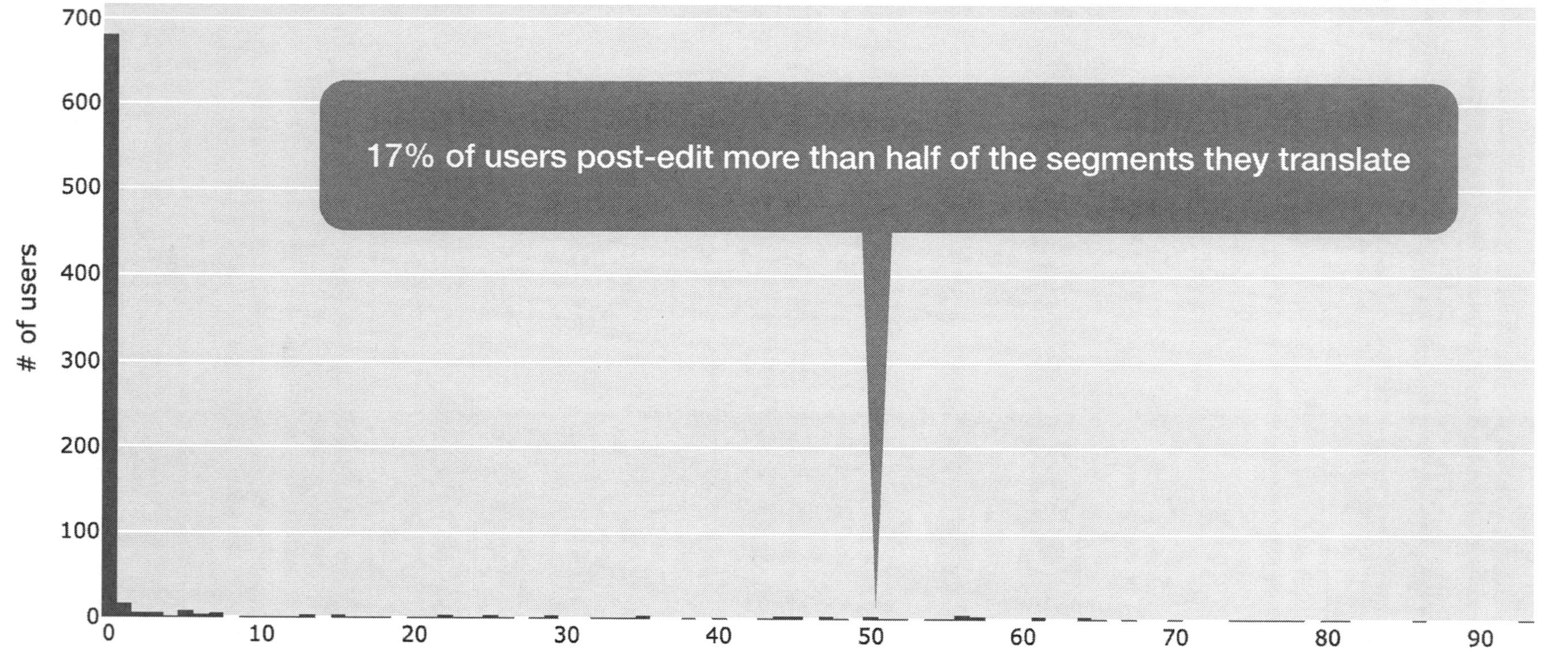

Proceedings of the 14th Conference of the Association for Machine Translation in the Americas
October 6 – 9, 2020, Workshop on the Impact of Machine Translation

How do translators spend their time on Lilt?

Our efforts have focused on helping translators type translations faster via interactive MT. Is that actually most time-consuming part?

Data based on mouse and keyboard activity while using Lilt in translation mode, permitting up to 30 seconds of idle time between events

Proceedings of the 14th Conference of the Association for Machine Translation in the Americas
October 6 – 9, 2020, Workshop on the Impact of Machine Translation

How do translators spend their time on Lilt?

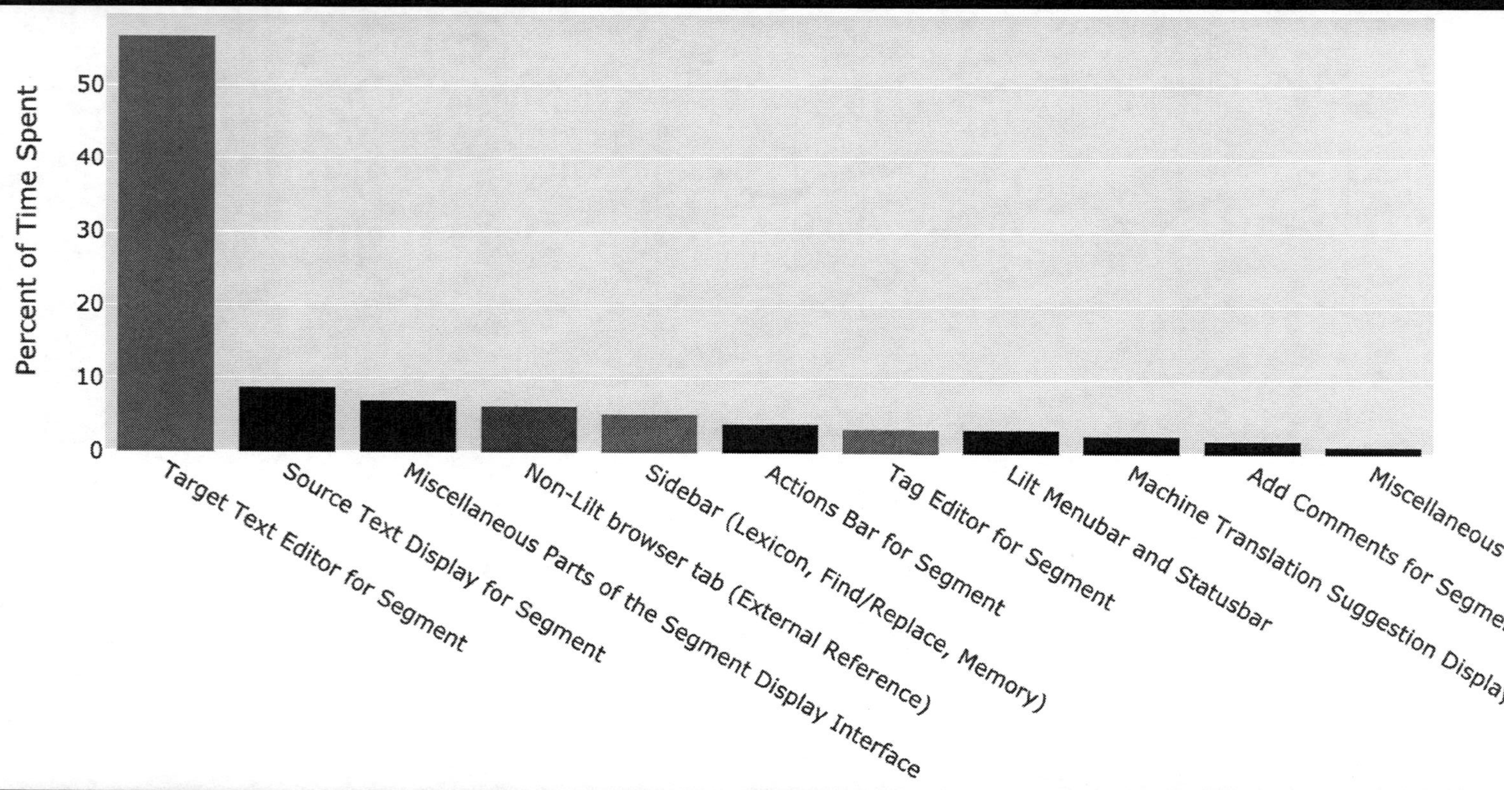

Proceedings of the 14th Conference of the Association for Machine Translation in the Americas
October 6 - 9, 2020, Workshop on the Impact of Machine Translation

How do translators spend their time on Lilt?

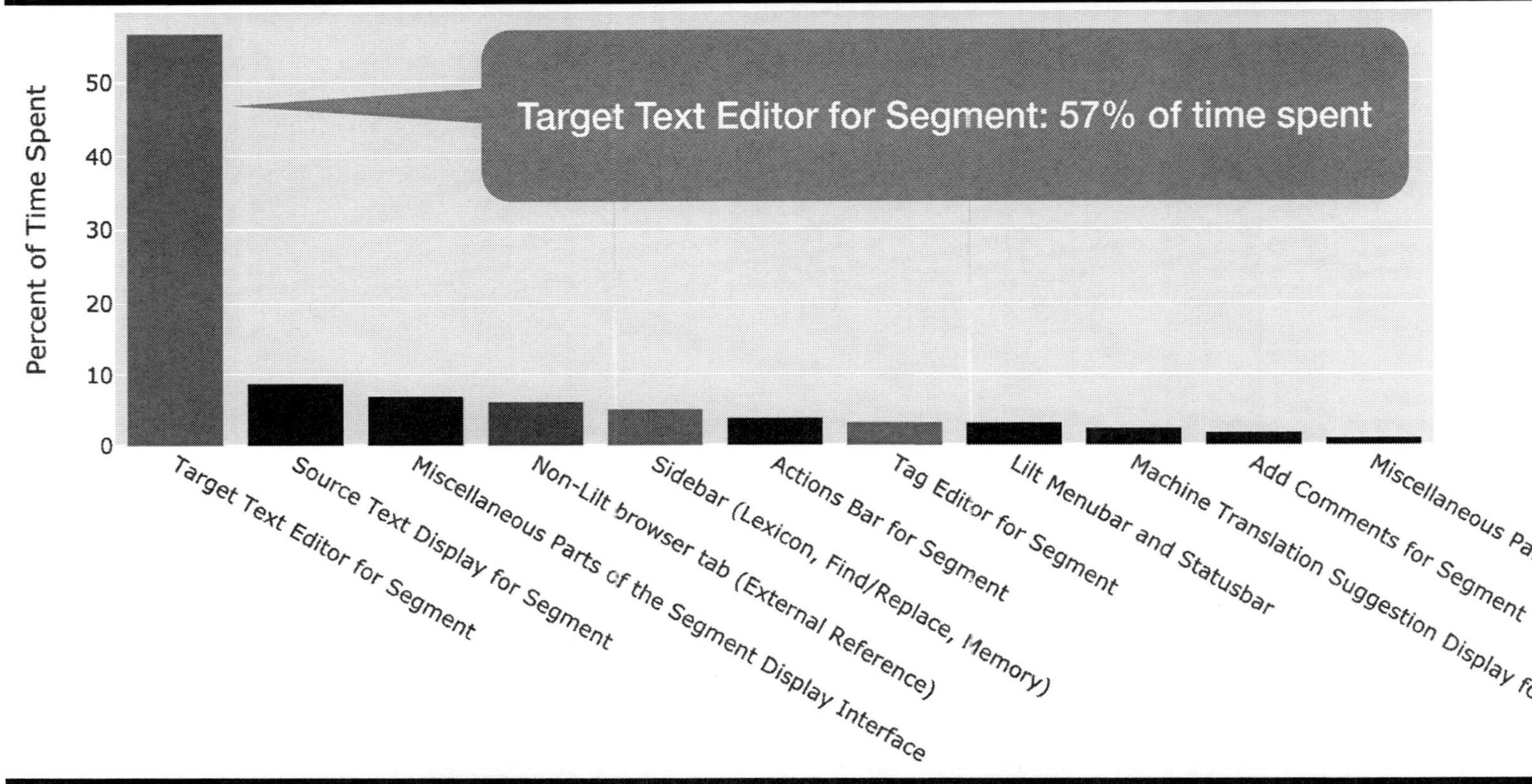

Proceedings of the 14th Conference of the Association for Machine Translation in the Americas
October 6 – 9, 2020, Workshop on the Impact of Machine Translation

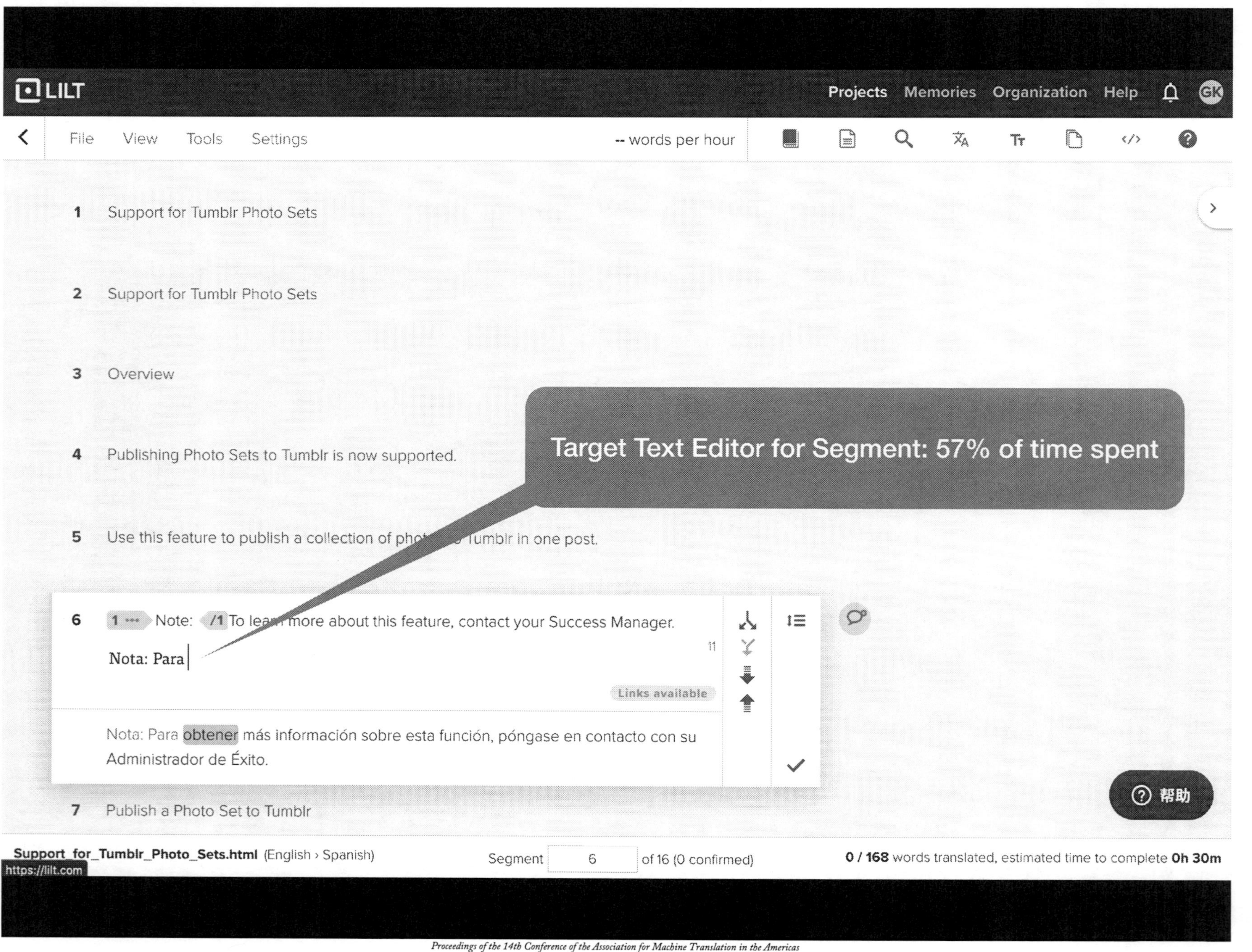
LILT
Projects   Memories   Organization   Help
File   View   Tools   Settings
-- words per hour
1   Support for Tumblr Photo Sets
2   Support for Tumblr Photo Sets
3   Overview
4   Publishing Photo Sets to Tumblr is now supported.
Target Text Editor for Segment: 57% of time spent
5   Use this feature to publish a collection of photos to Tumblr in one post.
6   1   Note: /1 To learn more about this feature, contact your Success Manager.
Nota: Para
11
Links available
Nota: Para obtener más información sobre esta función, póngase en contacto con su Administrador de Éxito.
7   Publish a Photo Set to Tumblr
Support_for_Tumblr_Photo_Sets.html (English › Spanish)
https://lilt.com
Segment   6   of 16 (0 confirmed)
0 / 168 words translated, estimated time to complete 0h 30m
? 帮助
198

How do translators spend their time on Lilt?

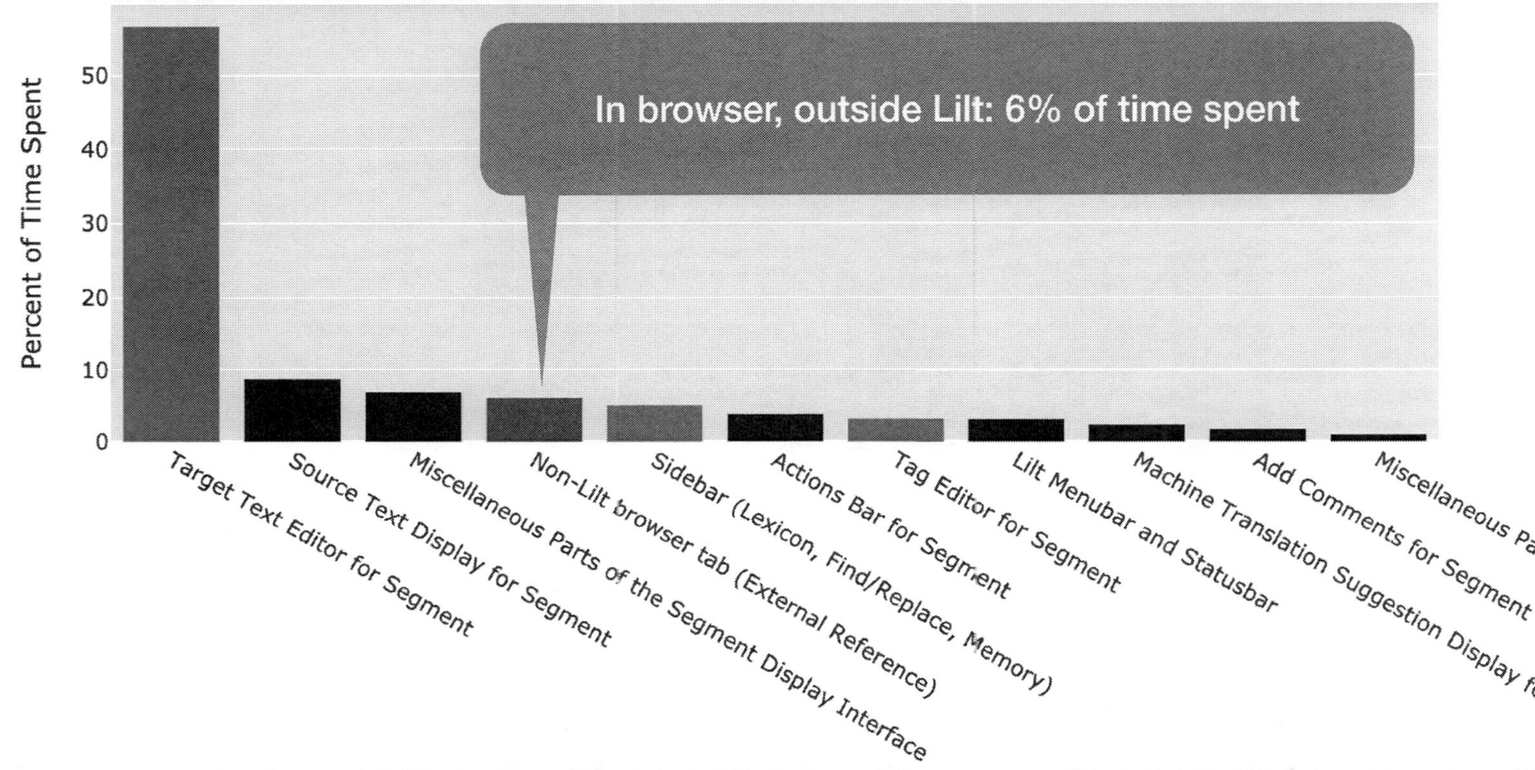

Proceedings of the 14th Conference of the Association for Machine Translation in the Americas
October 6 - 9, 2020, Workshop on the Impact of Machine Translation

How do translators spend their time on Lilt?

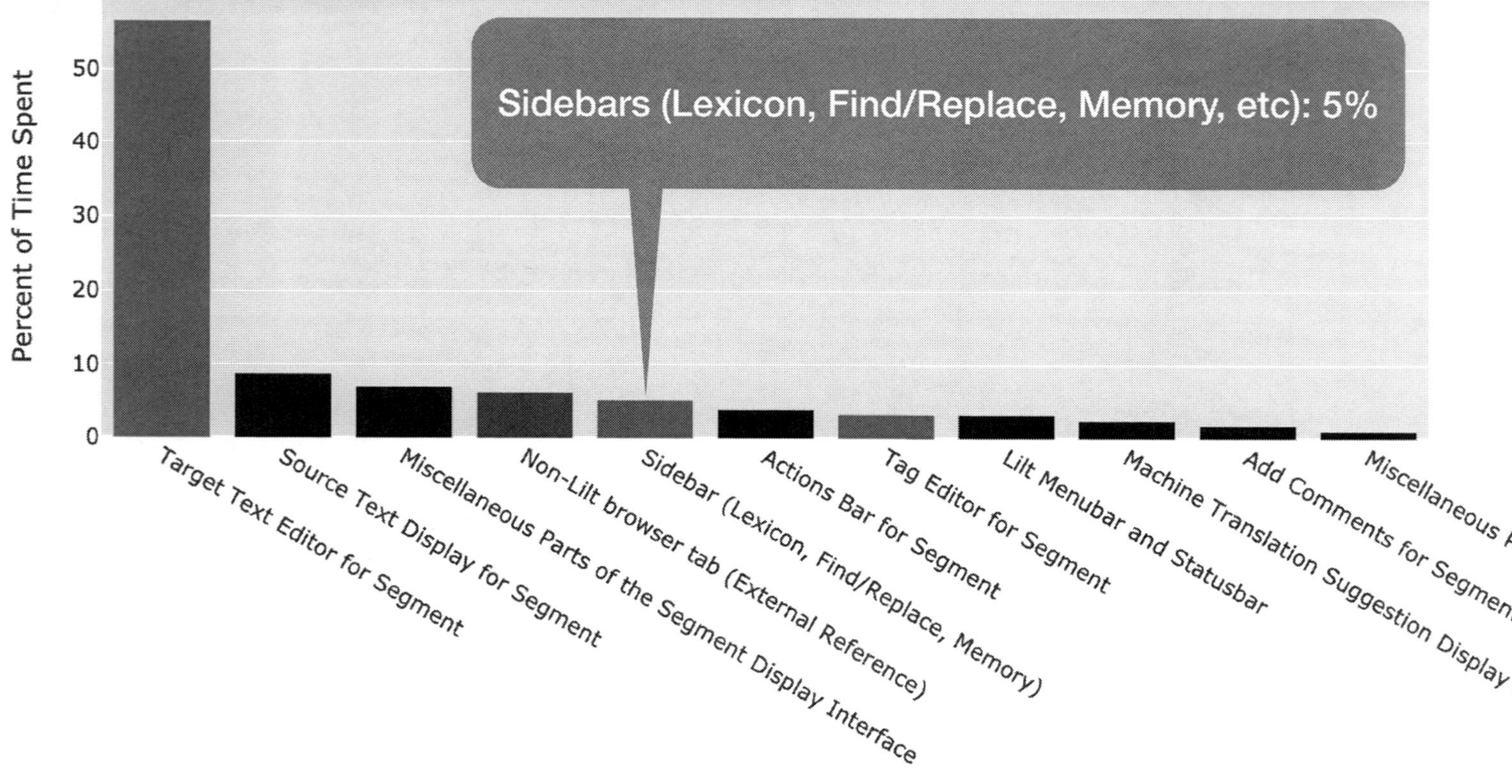

Proceedings of the 14th Conference of the Association for Machine Translation in the Americas
October 6 - 9, 2020, Workshop on the Impact of Machine Translation

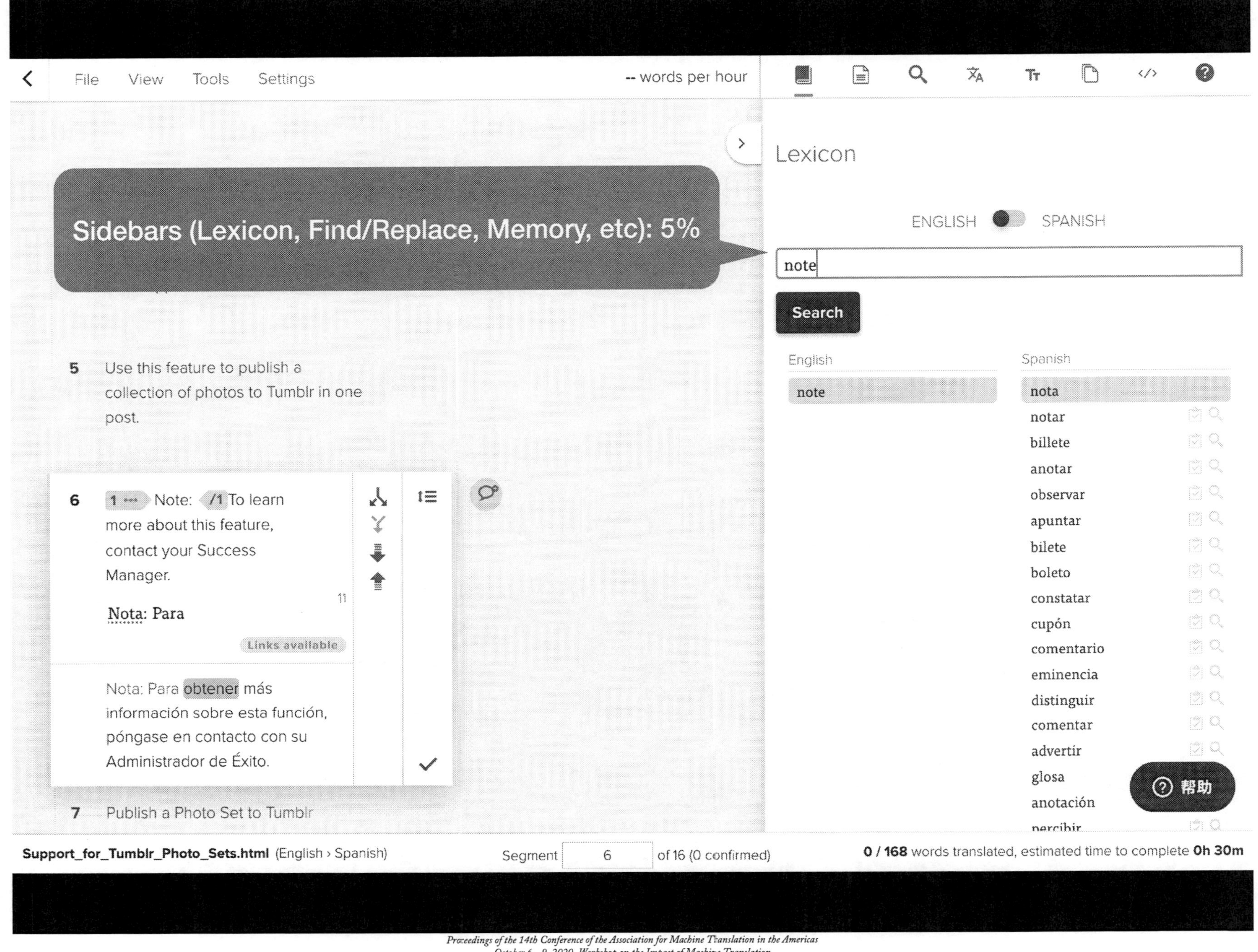

File   View   Tools   Settings
-- words per hour
Lexicon
ENGLISH ● SPANISH
note
Search
English
note
Spanish
nota
notar
billete
anotar
observar
apuntar
bilete
boleto
constatar
cupón
comentario
eminencia
distinguir
comentar
advertir
glosa
anotación
percibir
? 帮助
Sidebars (Lexicon, Find/Replace, Memory, etc): 5%
5   Use this feature to publish a
collection of photos to Tumblr in one
post.
6   1 ⋯ Note: /1 To learn
more about this feature,
contact your Success
Manager.
11
Nota: Para
Links available
Nota: Para obtener más
información sobre esta función,
póngase en contacto con su
Administrador de Éxito.
7   Publish a Photo Set to Tumblr
Support_for_Tumblr_Photo_Sets.html (English › Spanish)
Segment   6   of 16 (0 confirmed)
0 / 168 words translated, estimated time to complete 0h 30m
201

How do translators spend their time on Lilt?

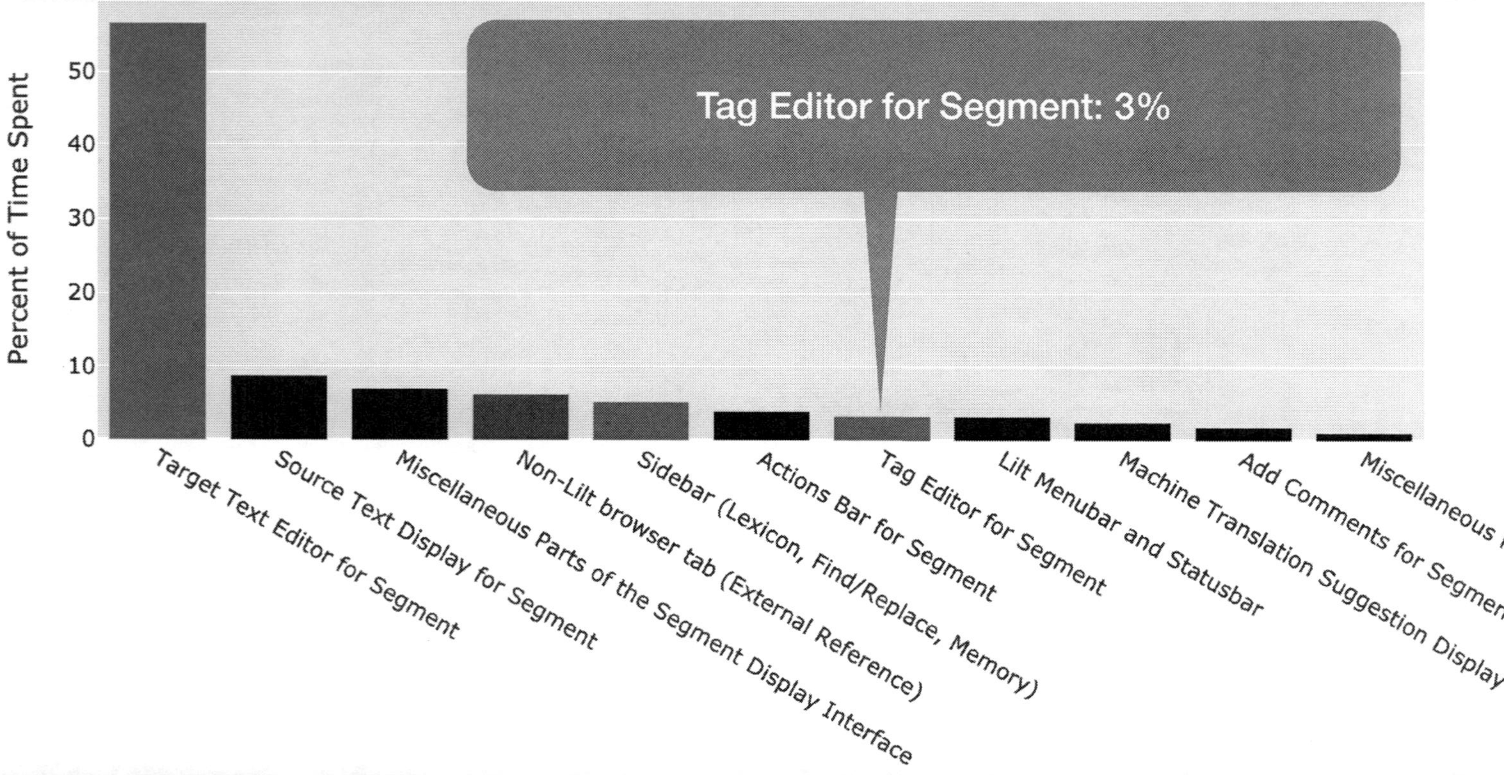

Proceedings of the 14th Conference of the Association for Machine Translation in the Americas
October 6 – 9, 2020, Workshop on the Impact of Machine Translation

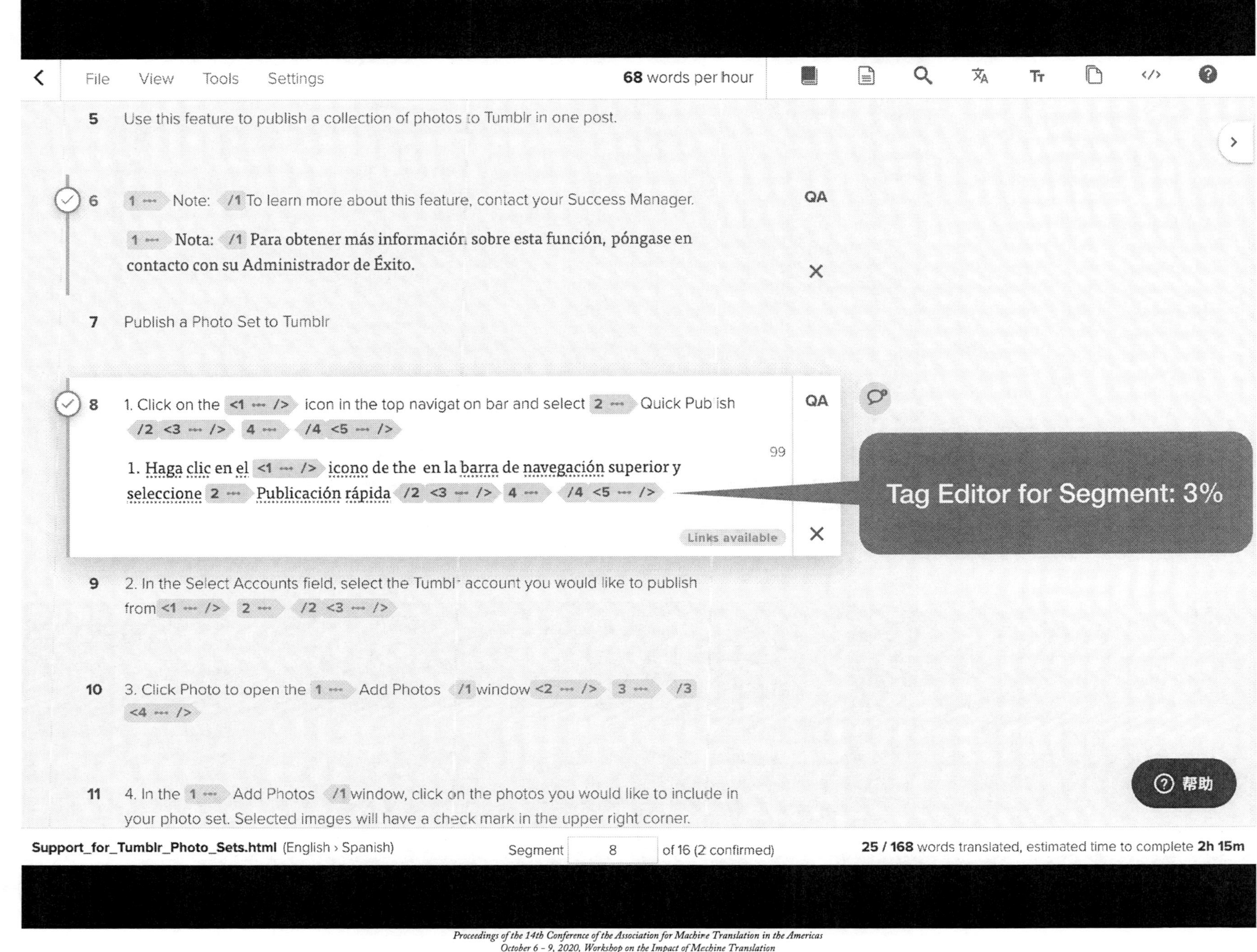

Proceedings of the 14th Conference of the Association for Machine Translation in the Americas
October 6 - 9, 2020, Workshop on the Impact of Machine Translation

Histogram of segments by the number of tags

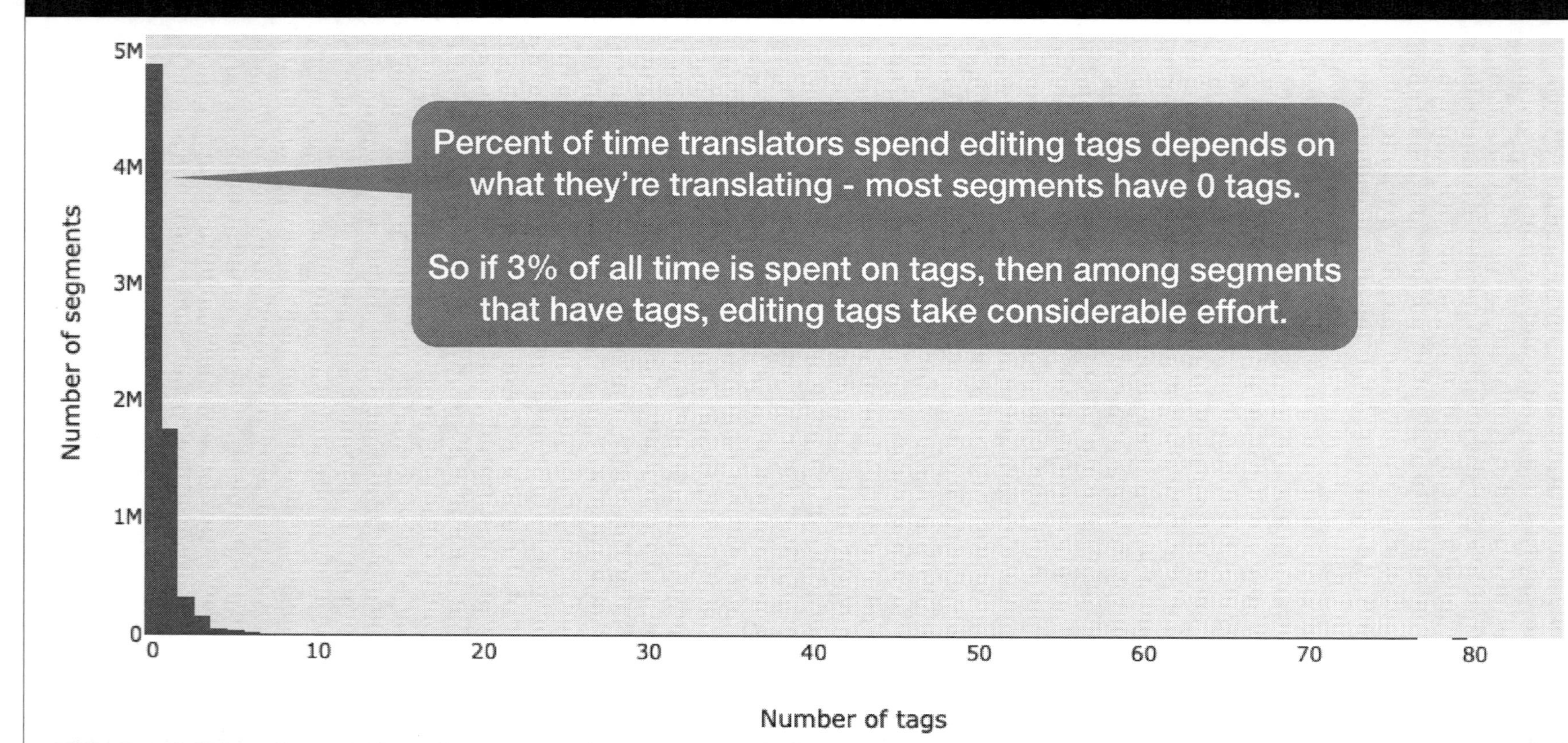

Proceedings of the 14th Conference of the Association for Machine Translation in the Americas
October 6 – 9, 2020, Workshop on the Impact of Machine Translation

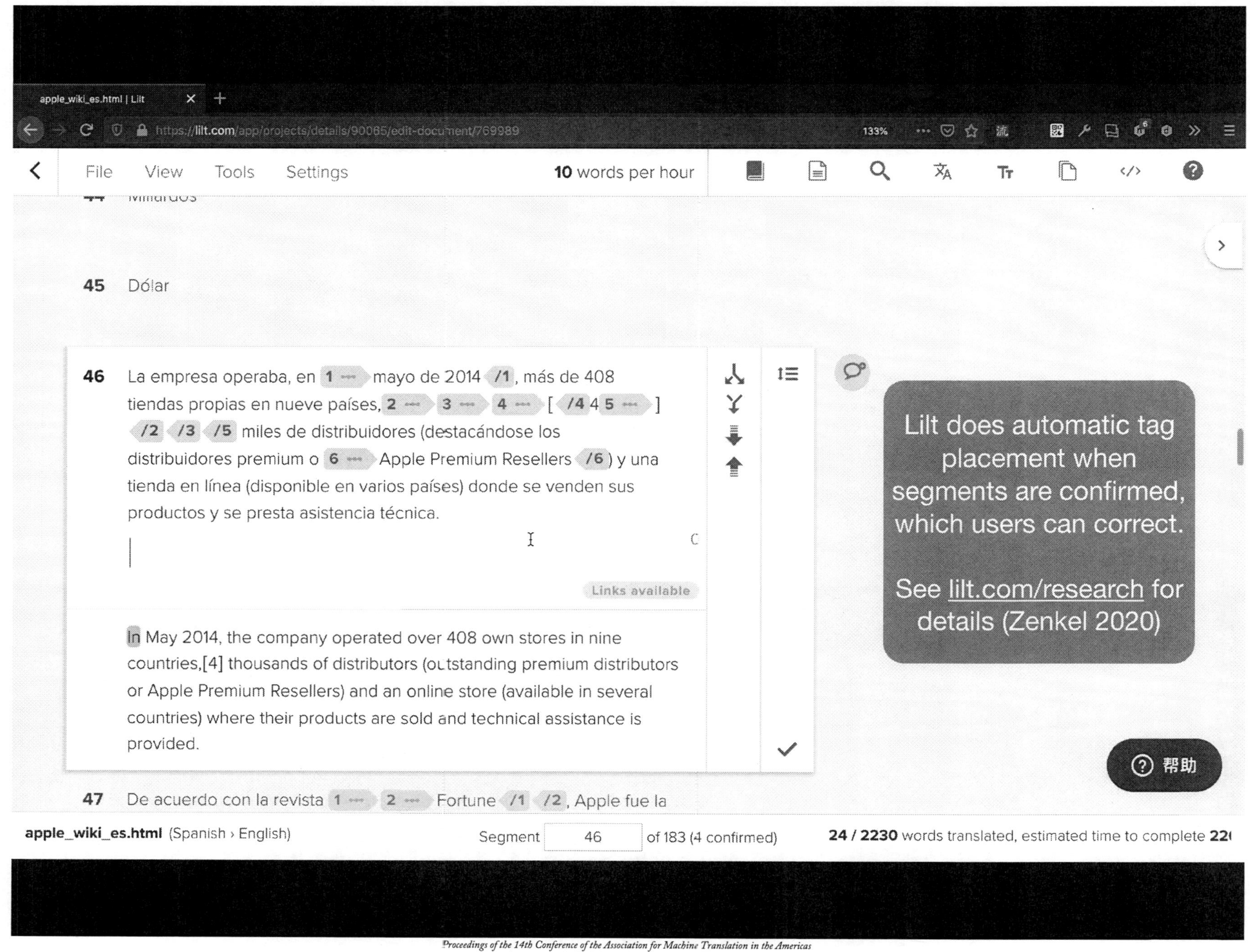

apple_wiki_es.html | Lilt
https://lilt.com/app/projects/details/90065/edit-document/769989
133%
File   View   Tools   Settings   10 words per hour
44   Millardos
45   Dólar
46   La empresa operaba, en 1 --- mayo de 2014 /1 , más de 408 tiendas propias en nueve países, 2 --- 3 --- 4 --- [/4 4 5 ---] /2 /3 /5 miles de distribuidores (destacándose los distribuidores premium o 6 --- Apple Premium Resellers /6) y una tienda en línea (disponible en varios países) donde se venden sus productos y se presta asistencia técnica.
Links available
In May 2014, the company operated over 408 own stores in nine countries,[4] thousands of distributors (outstanding premium distributors or Apple Premium Resellers) and an online store (available in several countries) where their products are sold and technical assistance is provided.
47   De acuerdo con la revista 1 --- 2 --- Fortune /1 /2 , Apple fue la
Lilt does automatic tag placement when segments are confirmed, which users can correct.
See lilt.com/research for details (Zenkel 2020)
? 帮助
apple_wiki_es.html (Spanish › English)   Segment   46   of 183 (4 confirmed)   24 / 2230 words translated, estimated time to complete 22(
205

How do translators spend their time on Lilt?

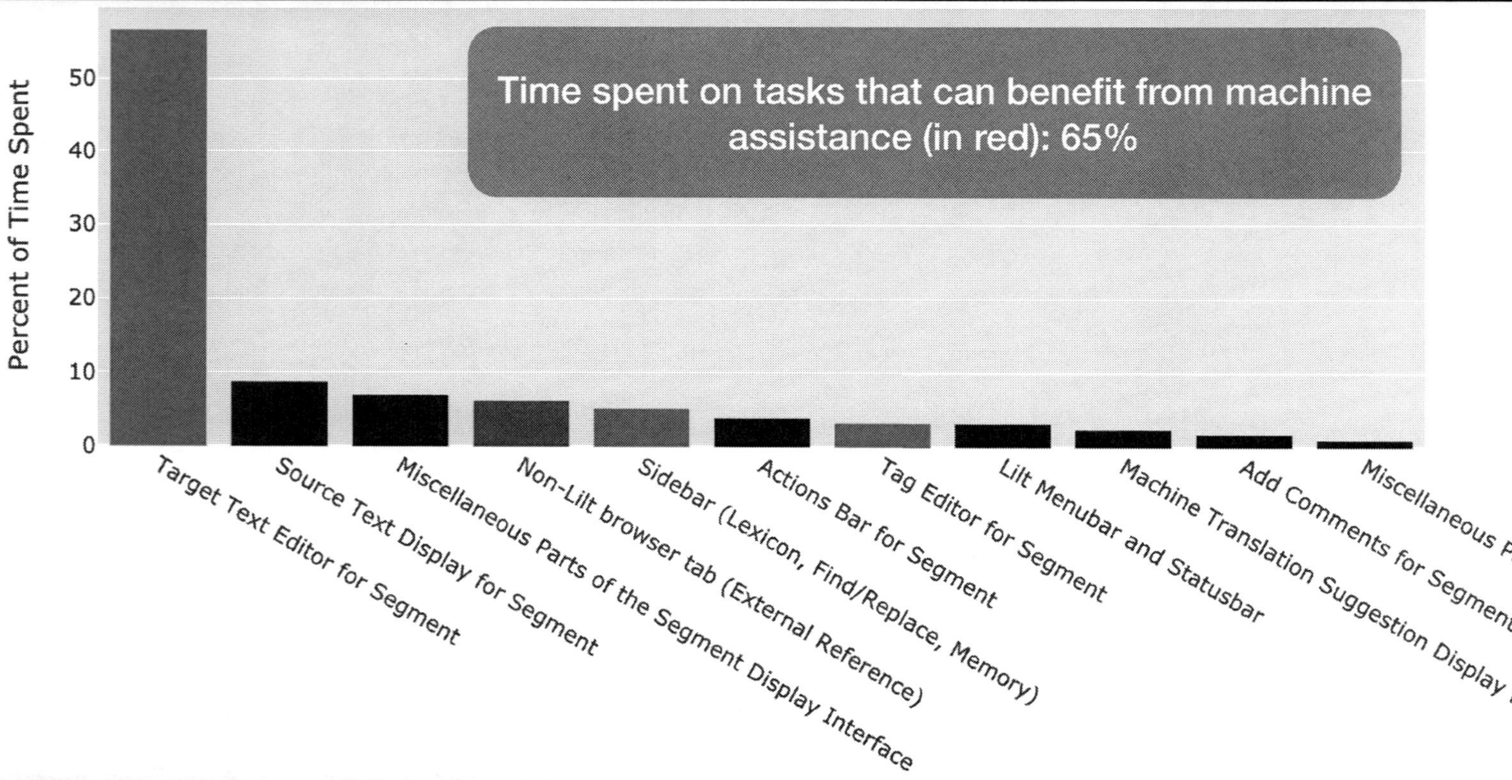

Proceedings of the 14th Conference of the Association for Machine Translation in the Americas
October 6 - 9, 2020, Workshop on the Impact of Machine Translation

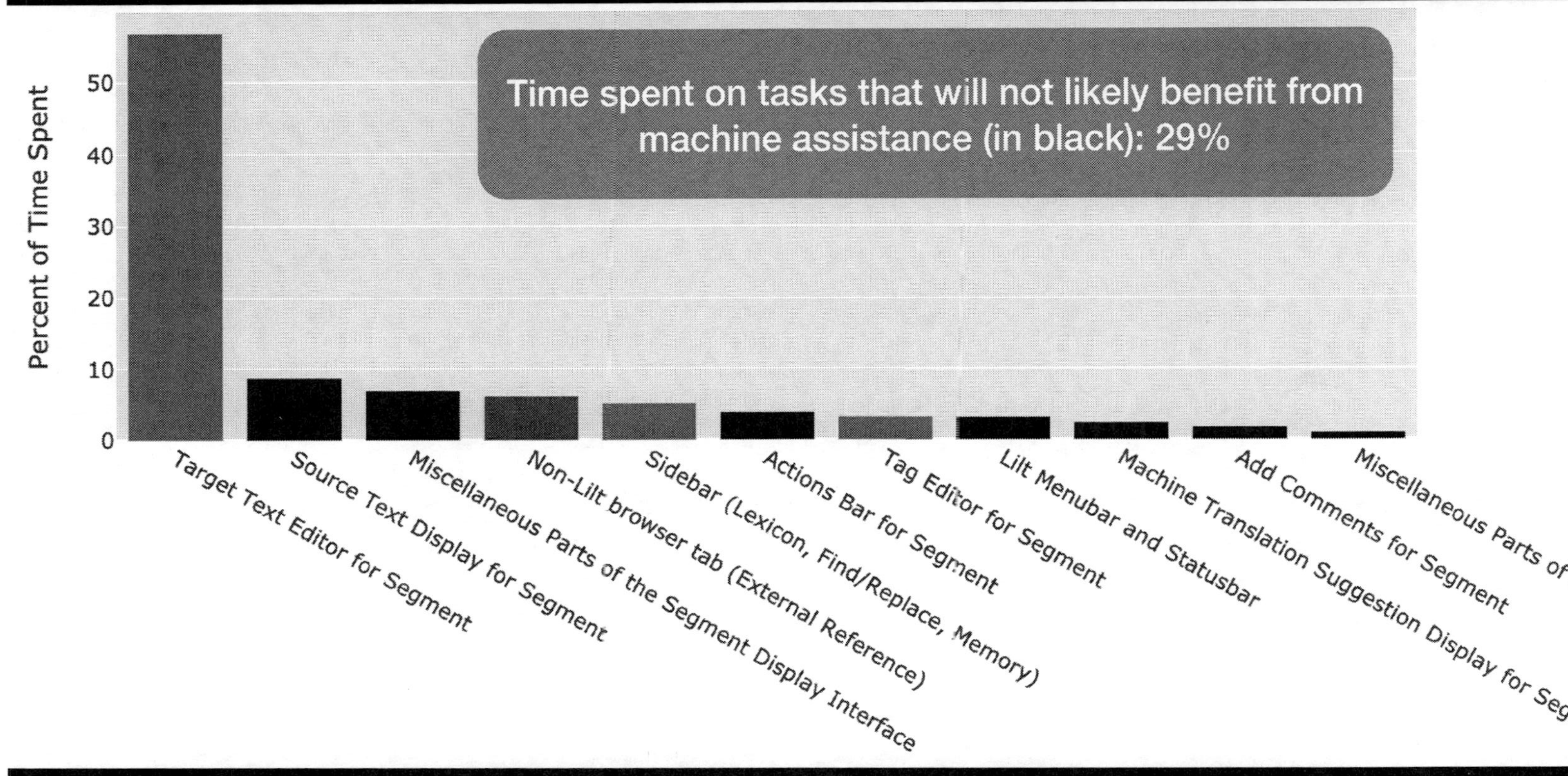

Proceedings of the 14th Conference of the Association for Machine Translation in the Americas
October 6 – 9, 2020, Workshop on the Impact of Machine Translation

Conclusion: A Study of Interactive Machine Translation Use on Lilt

- 57% of translator time is spent on actually writing the translation, which we can optimize with interactive MT.

- Our prefix-constrained interactive MT shows the correct suggestion to translators for 46% of the text they type. Of this, they use our autocompletion for 83% of the text.

- Main areas for improvement are MT quality and showing suggestions when user isn't typing at the end. Latency is very good (< 500ms).

- While Lilt is used in an interactive style 4x more than post-editing, 17% of our users primarily use it for post-editing.

Proceedings of the 14th Conference of the Association for Machine Translation in the Americas
October 6 - 9, 2020, Workshop on the Impact of Machine Translation

209

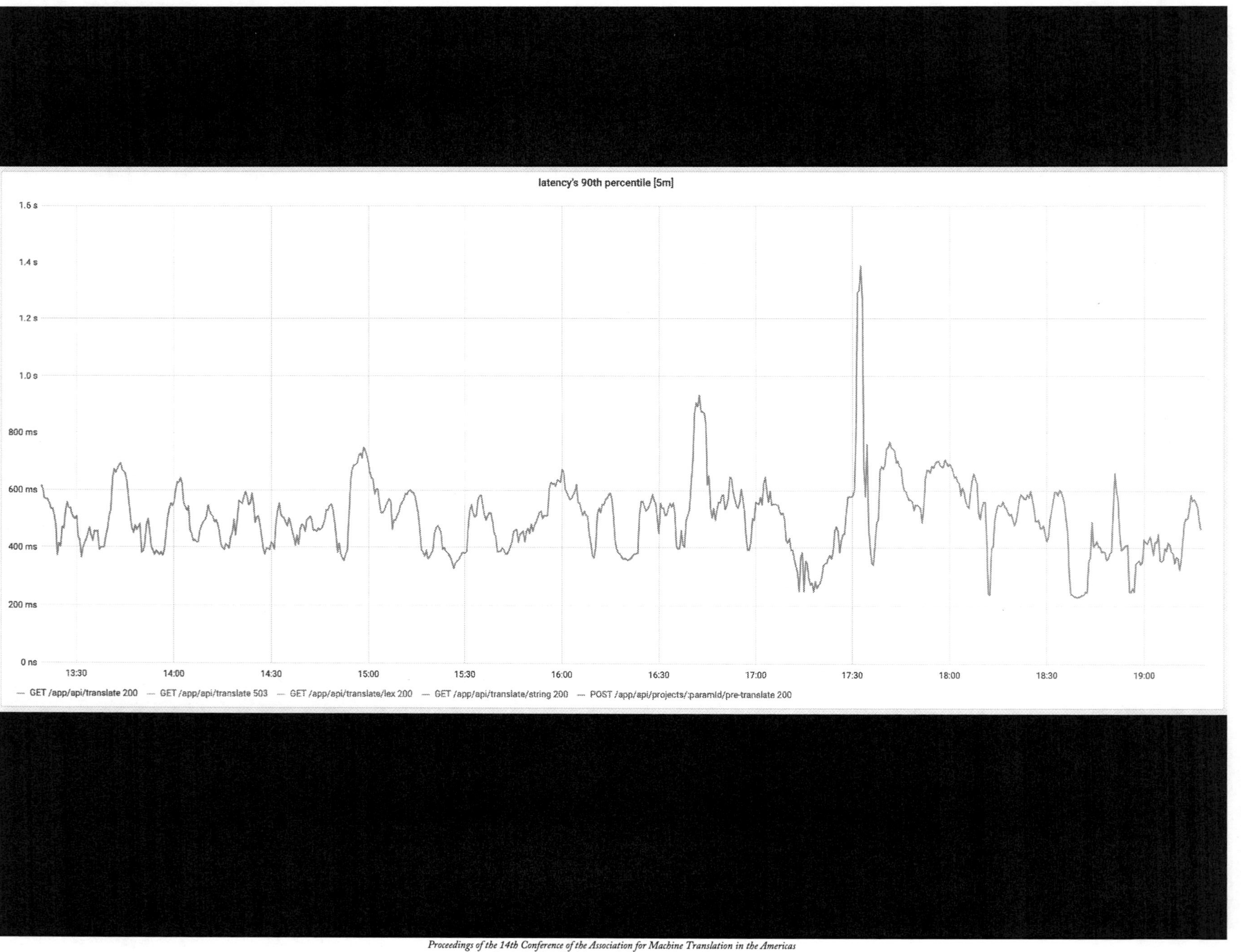

Proceedings of the 14th Conference of the Association for Machine Translation in the Americas
October 6 – 9, 2020, Workshop on the Impact of Machine Translation

Keys through which text is inserted, broken down by MT state

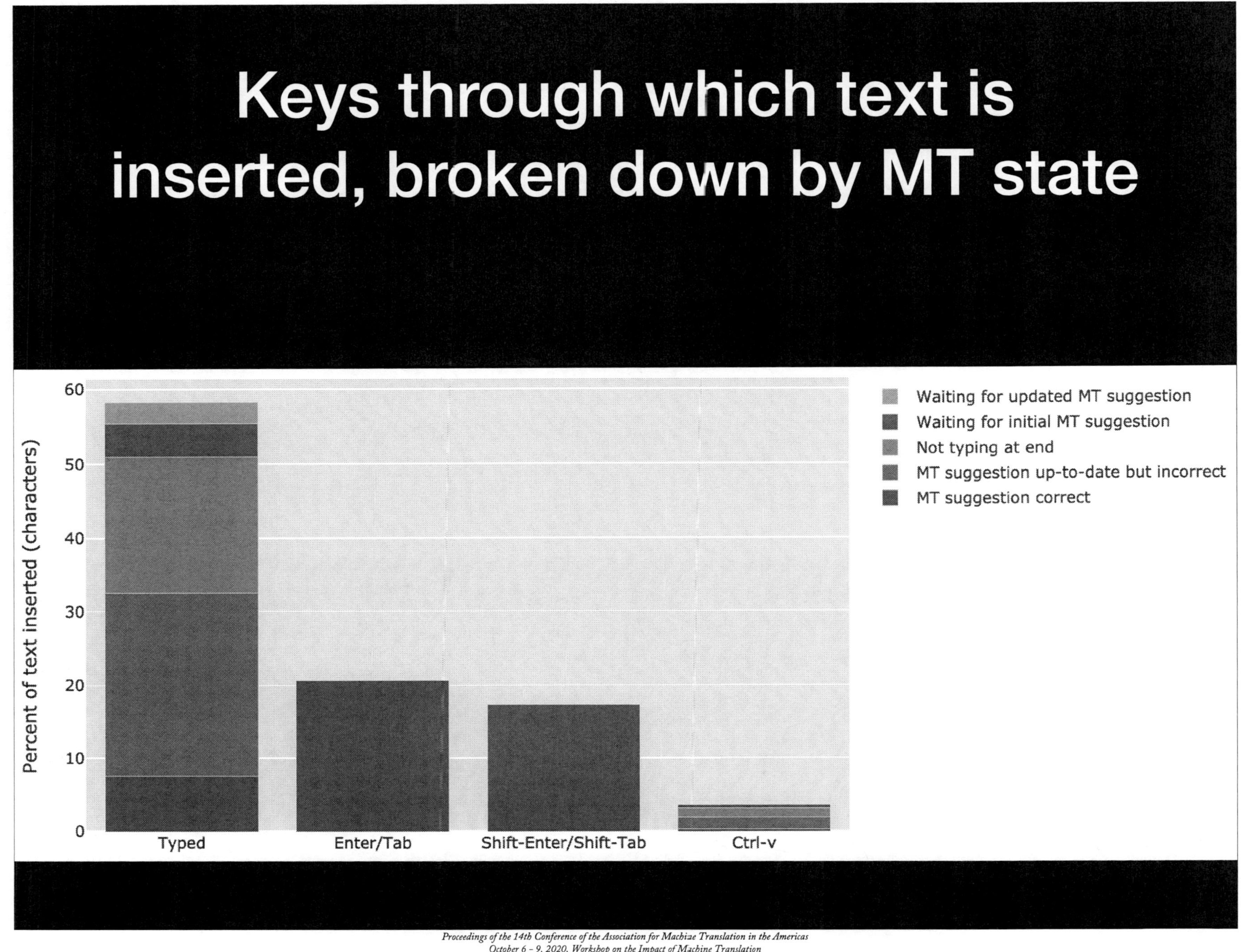

Proceedings of the 14th Conference of the Association for Machine Translation in the Americas
October 6 – 9, 2020, Workshop on the Impact of Machine Translation

Keys through which text is inserted, broken down by MT state

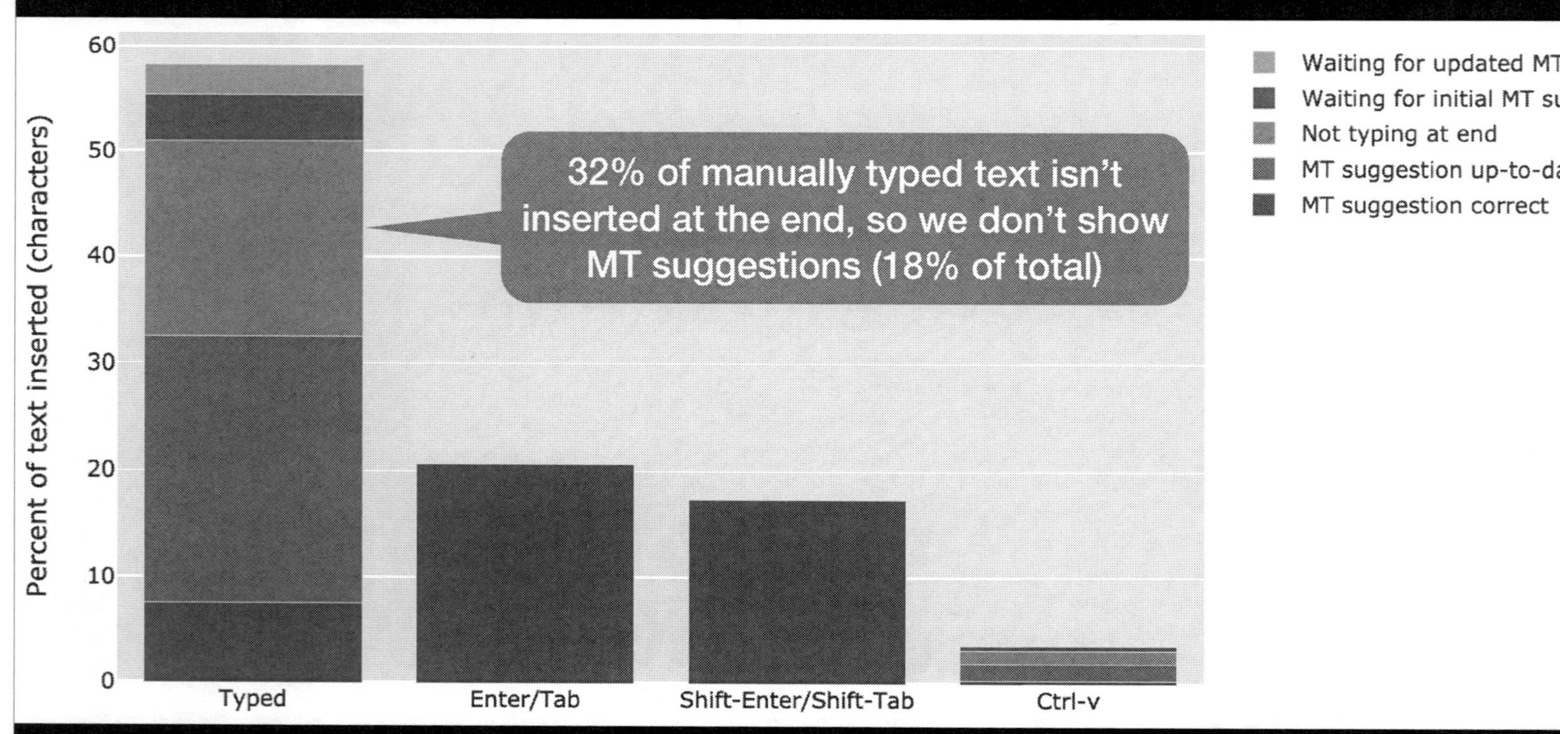

Proceedings of the 14th Conference of the Association for Machine Translation in the Americas
October 6 – 9, 2020, Workshop on the Impact of Machine Translation

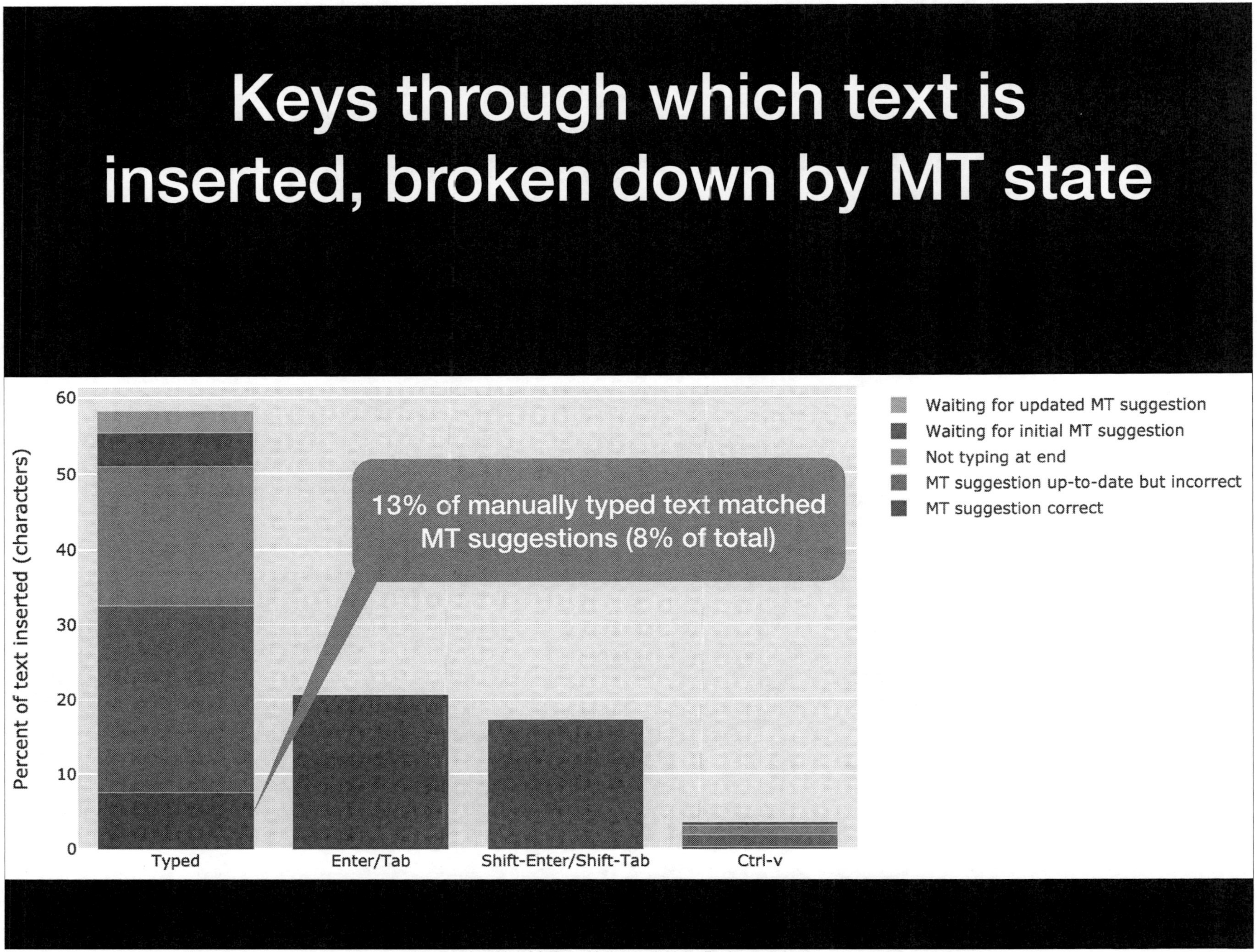

Keys through which text is inserted, broken down by MT state

Proceedings of the 14th Conference of the Association for Machine Translation in the Americas
October 6 – 9, 2020, Workshop on the Impact of Machine Translation

Keys through which text is inserted, broken down by MT state

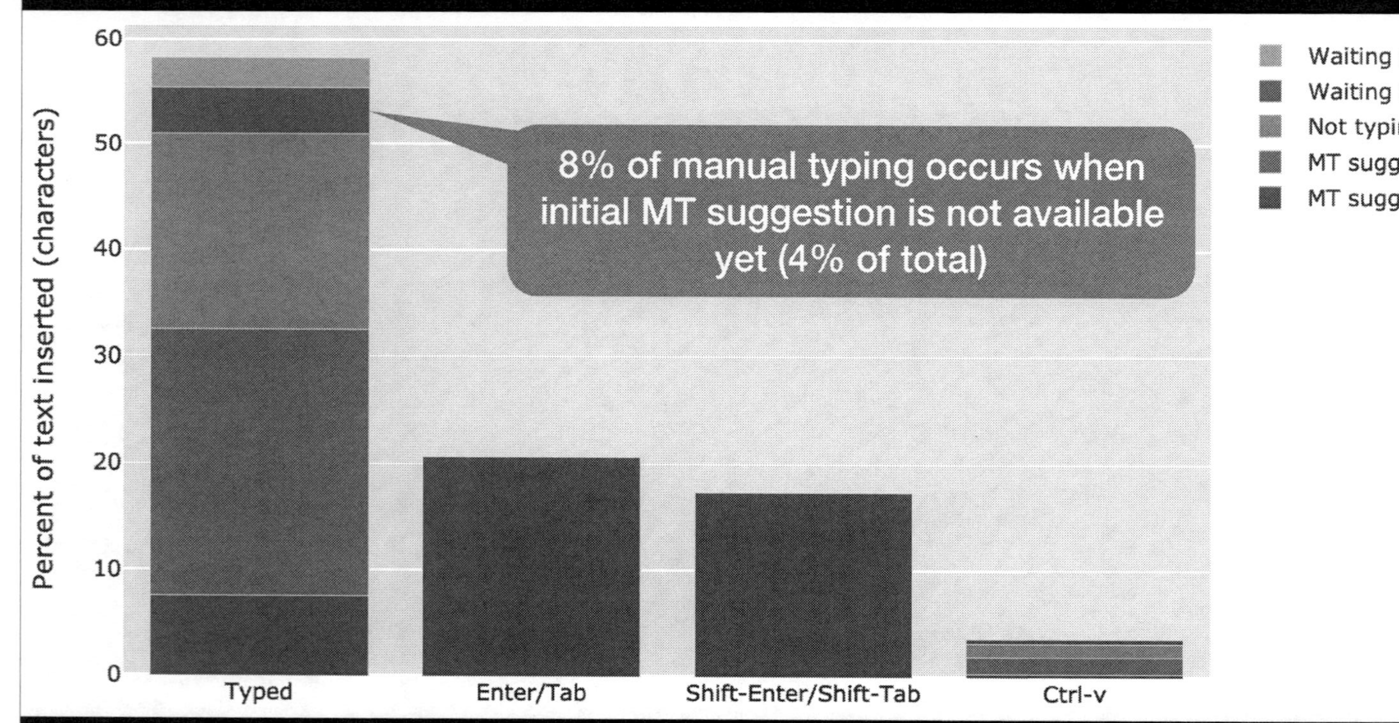

Proceedings of the 14th Conference of the Association for Machine Translation in the Americas
October 6 – 9, 2020, Workshop on the Impact of Machine Translation

Keys through which text is inserted, broken down by MT state

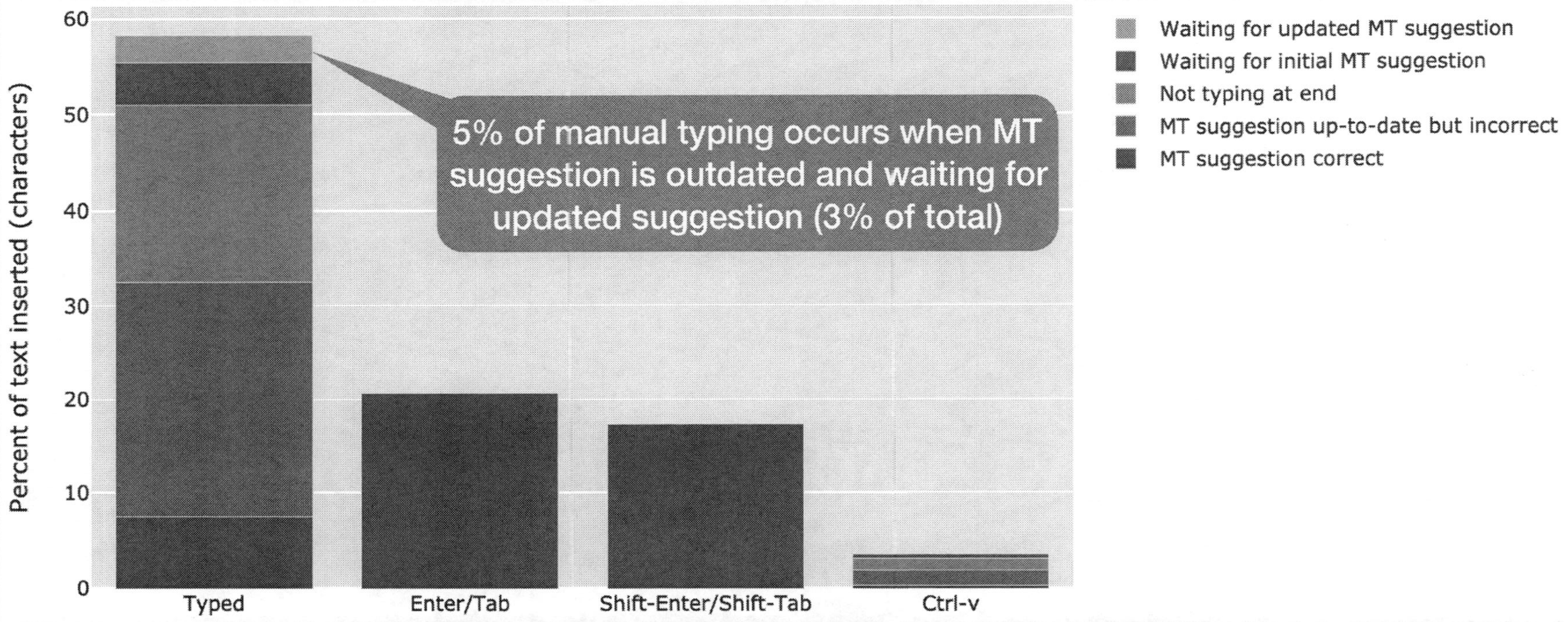

Proceedings of the 14th Conference of the Association for Machine Translation in the Americas
October 6 - 9, 2020, Workshop on the Impact of Machine Translation

Keys through which text is inserted, broken down by MT state

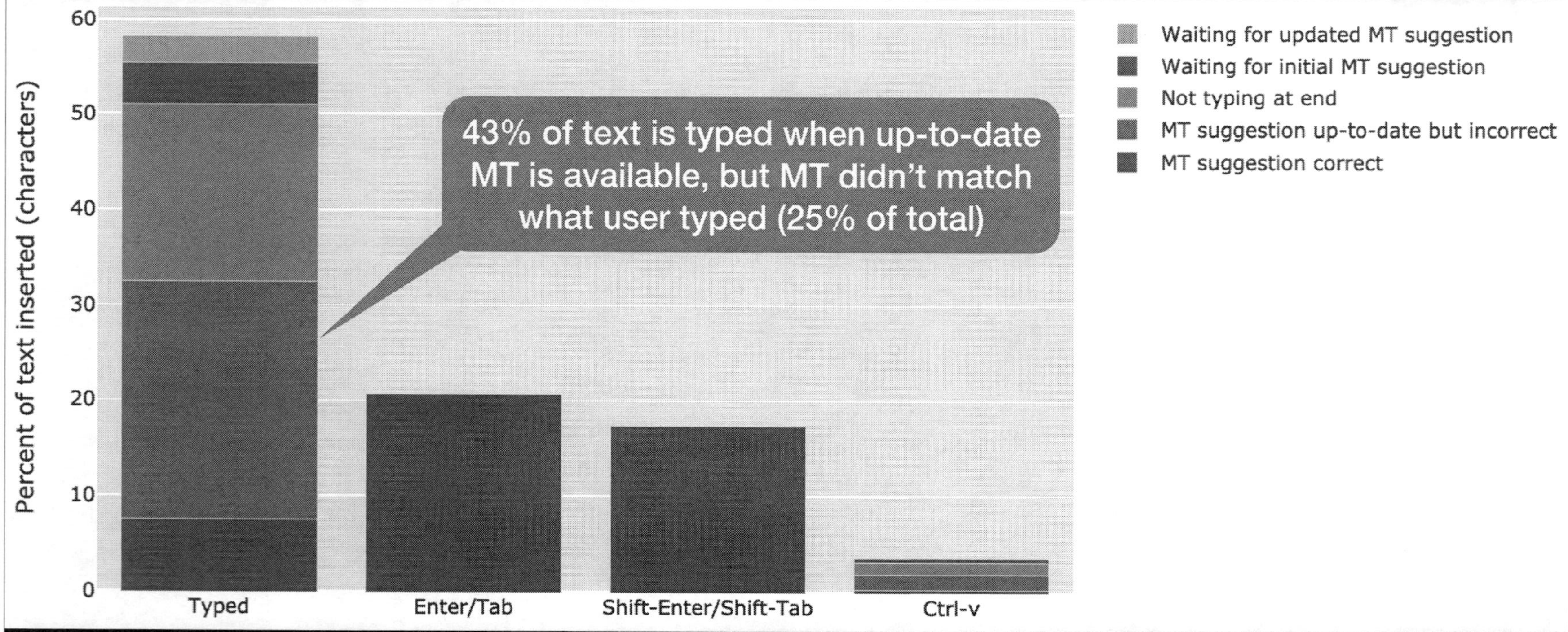

Proceedings of the 14th Conference of the Association for Machine Translation in the Americas
October 6 – 9, 2020, Workshop on the Impact of Machine Translation

Association for Computational Linguistics
209 N. Eighth Street
Stroudsburg, Pennsylvania 18360

ISBN 978-1-7138-2377-3